Reading Popular Culture in Victorian Print

Nineteenth-Century Major Lives and Letters

Series Editor: Marilyn Gaull

The nineteenth century invented major figures: gifted, productive, and influential writers and artists in English, European, and American public life who captured and expressed what Hazlitt called "The Spirit of the Age." Their achievements summarize, reflect, and shape the cultural traditions they inherited and influence the quality of life that followed. Before radio, film, and journalism deflected the energies of authors and audiences alike, literary forms such as popular verse, song lyrics, biographies, memoirs, letters, novels, reviews, essays, children's books, and drama generated a golden age of letters incomparable in Western history. *Nineteenth-Century*

Major Lives and Letters presents a series of original biographical, critical, and scholarly studies of major figures evoking their energies, achievements, and their impact on the character of this age. Projects to be included range from works on Blake to Hardy, Erasmus Darwin to Charles Darwin, Wordsworth to Yeats, Coleridge and J. S. Mill, Joanna Baillie, Jane Austen, Sir Walter Scott, Byron, Shelley, Keats to Dickens, Tennyson, George Eliot, Browning, Hopkins, Lewis Carroll, Rudyard Kipling, and their contemporaries. The series editor is Marilyn Gaull, PhD from Indiana University. She has served on the faculty at Temple University, New York University, and is now Research Professor at the Editorial Institute at Boston University. She brings to the series decades of experience as editor of books on nineteenth century literature and culture. She is the founder and editor of *The Wordsworth Circle*, author of *English Romanticism: The Human Context*, publishes editions, essays, and reviews in numerous journals and lectures internationally on British Romanticism, folklore, and narrative theory.

PUBLISHED BY PALGRAVE:

Shelley's German Afterlives, by Susanne Schmid
Romantic Literature, Race, and Colonial Encounter, by Peter J. Kitson
Coleridge, the Bible, and Religion, by Jeffrey W. Barbeau
Byron: Heritage and Legacy, edited by Cheryl A. Wilson
The Long and Winding Road from Blake to the Beatles, by Matthew Schneider
British Periodicals and Romantic Identity, by Mark Schoenfield
Women Writers and Nineteenth-Century Medievalism, by Clare Broome Saunders
British Victorian Women's Periodicals, by Kathryn Ledbetter
Romantic Diasporas, by Toby R. Benis
Romantic Literary Families, by Scott Krawczyk
Victorian Christmas in Print, by Tara Moore
Culinary Aesthetics and Practices in Nineteenth-Century American Literature, Edited by Monika Elbert and Marie Drews
Poetics en passant, by Anne Jamison
Reading Popular Culture in Victorian Print, by Alberto Gabriele

FORTHCOMING TITLES:

Romanticism and the Object, Edited by Larry H. Peer
From Song to Print, by Terence Hoagwood
Populism, Gender, and Sympathy in the Romantic Novel, by James P. Carson
Victorian Medicine and Social Reform, by Louise Penner
Byron and the Rhetoric of Italian Nationalism, by Arnold A. Schmidt
Gothic Romanticism, by Tom Duggett
Regions of Sara Coleridge's Thought, by Peter Swaab
Royal Romances, by Kristin Samuelian
The Poetry of Mary Robinson, by Daniel Robinson

Reading Popular Culture in Victorian Print

Belgravia and Sensationalism

Alberto Gabriele

palgrave
macmillan

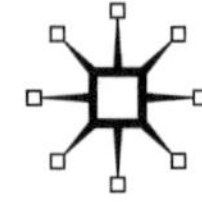

READING POPULAR CULTURE IN VICTORIAN PRINT

First published in 2009 by
PALGRAVE MACMILLAN®
in the United States—a division of St. Martin's Press LLC,
175 Fifth Avenue, New York, NY 10010.

Where this book is distributed in the UK, Europe and the rest of the world, this is by Palgrave Macmillan, a division of Macmillan Publishers Limited, registered in England, company number 785998, of Houndmills, Basingstoke, Hampshire RG21 6XS.

Palgrave Macmillan is the global academic imprint of the above companies and has companies and representatives throughout the world.

Palgrave® and Macmillan® are registered trademarks in the United States, the United Kingdom, Europe and other countries.

ISBN: 978–0–230–61521–2

Library of Congress Cataloging-in-Publication Data

Gabriele, Alberto, 1970–
Reading popular culture in Victorian print : Belgravia and sensationalism / Alberto Gabriele.
p. cm.—(Nineteenth-century major lives and letters)
Includes bibliographical references and index.
ISBN 978–0–230–61521–2 (alk. paper)
1. Belgravia. 2. English periodicals—History—19th century.
3. Popular culture—Great Britain—History—19th century.
4. Sensationalism in journalism—Great Britain—History—19th century. I. Title

PN5130.B45G33 2009
052.0942′109034.—dc22 2009011167

A catalogue record of the book is available from the British Library.

Design by Newgen Imaging Systems (P) Ltd., Chennai, India.

First edition: November 2009

10 9 8 7 6 5 4 3 2 1

Printed in the United States of America.

To my parents

Contents

List of Illustrations

Preface

Any study of the periodical press mediates between an empirical, inductive approach, based on archival research, and a more deductive one that orders archival findings into a narrative. The empirical approach may be daunting, as the historical traces are so dispersed and fragmented that they may resist narrative. A general view is often the product of an inductive approach, based on the select material included in one's discussion. In defining a preliminary methodology to approach the periodical press, I looked for a midpoint between empirical description and theoretical view, thus avoiding the multidirectional fragmentation of the many titles, issues, and editions that make the archive of Victorian periodicals. At the same time, I refrained from a purely thematic approach. In my initial study of *Belgravia* I tipped the scales of the inductive-deductive dichotomy toward the first of the two. I approached *Belgravia* by reading the whole run of the magazine published under the direction of Mary Elizabeth Braddon (1866–76). My starting interest was the fiction published in it, but reading the novel installments alongside every other item in the magazine made immediately apparent that the material history of serialized editions places fiction not only within the context of the single magazine issue but in the context of the whole run of the magazine. The textual unity that I first put under the lens of a close textual reading, thus, is the whole history of the magazine. Patterns, echoes, and cross-references create an internal web that is, I believe, the foundation for an empirical and inductive analysis that every title in the canon of Victorian periodicals would benefit from.

After having assessed the history of the whole magazine, while at the same time allowing the process of interpretation to take notice of these patterns and retain these repetitions in my memory, I pursued a path that is more invisible and harder to chart than traditional textual analysis. I chose to follow two intertwined research paths: first, I studied the discursive formations that circulate in the magazine and in the surrounding culture at large. Second, I focused on the status of the reader of periodical fiction in order to trace the changes in the history of reading that a perusal of the periodical text within the sensorium of urban modernity implies. Since the experience of reading a periodical title allows several approaches guided by the reader's interest, memory, and combinatory associations, I shifted focus from the diachronic level of the history of one magazine, that I cover in the first chapter, to a study of the synchronic level represented by the reader's response to the magazine issue in the midst of the many visual and intellectual stimuli coming from different areas of contemporaneous culture. Reading at the time was not limited to the periodical issue; the suggestions coming from periodical fiction were intertwined with larger theoretical reflections, with other forms of entertainment, with all sorts of visual and intellectual suggestions that circulated the many and at times conflicting discursive formations that constituted Victorian ideology.

Discursive formations, as the work of Michel Foucault has defined them, have a pervasive reach that impinges on a whole culture: they inform media of all sorts, shape everyday life, generate social practices as well as being generated by them. Discursive formations form a mosaic made of a plurality of contrasting voices; no genre of cultural production is representative of one particular discursive formation only. The fact that discursive formations are not easily traceable to a single origin or visible within a defined pattern makes it difficult to chart them; these formations, which are textual only if textuality is to be read as a broad metaphorical concept, resist any inscription in a philologist's *stemma codicum* (chart of manuscript tradition). Discursive formations cannot feature in a map of the linear transmigration of any text or idea within specific cultural centers, which was the goal of traditional philological studies. The level of interpolation is so high, the inscription of multiple meanings so layered, the disciplinary contingencies so numerous that in order to entertain a cohesive view of print culture the methodology of historical philology that structured literary and historical studies for centuries needs to be redefined.

Nineteenth-century modernity presents a wide array of stimuli and formations that cannot be traced to a clear, definite, univocal origin but must rather be seen as intertwined in the broader cultural fabric of the age. Nineteenth-century modernity, moreover, multiplies the forms of communication: new forms of dissemination circulate discursive formations through media of all sorts that compete with the surrounding urban landscape for the reader's attention. The sensorium of nineteenth-century urban culture constructs a new form of reading through fragmentation that places the reader under the bombardment of disparate stimuli, as the figure of the urban flâneur can attest. The occasions for perceiving and reading signs increase, involving both men and women, in the public as well as in the private sphere, through advertisements and magazine issues, popular entertainment and illustrations. Does this mean that experiencing the complexity of industrial modernity inevitably hinders any theoretical view of the whole culture, any synthesis of the scattered cultural products experienced daily? I believe that a theoretical view of the whole culture is still possible, not only through the scholar's demarcation of one's field and the methodological need to construct a historical narrative. The presence of a discourse of unity, in fact, can be documented in the very material, psychological, and intellectual life of late Victorian culture. I traced, therefore, this discourse of unity alongside the more obvious representations of the fragmentation of the urban sensorium. I found that the polarity fragmentation/unity was a very productive epistemological model present in many cultural fields that I explored. Instead of imagining a structured lineage of a select tradition extrapolated from the complex network of cultural products, as a thematic approach would entail, I traced a system of less visible relations among coexisting cultural products. I noticed the presence of a recurrent modality of organization that reappears in each aspect of culture considered: the psychology of reading, the perception of the public sphere, art criticism, periodical literature, advertising, and pre-cinema. I identified a recurrent polarity between the experience of fragmentation and the perception of unity through intellectual mediation that crosses each of these cultural fields, affecting perception as well theory, technology innovation as well as everyday life. A polarity opposing fragmentation and order, multiplicity and unity is both an experiential given and a more subtle mode of functioning in nineteenth-century culture at large.

I have already underlined how the massive industrial production of cultural products in high as well as popular culture complicates any drawing of a map of cultural tradition. The sheer proliferation of commodities made possible by industrial production, which is a visible phenomenon, is not limited to the availability of these commodities for sale. The same principle of multiplication introduced by industrial production reemerges in other social and cultural spheres. The increase of possibilities—in the production, marketing, and consumption of commodities—becomes a cultural force that invisibly ties to its incessant possibilities other cultural and social fields. The same principle of multiplicity affects psychological patterns of perception; an increasingly stimulated sensorium characterizes the new form of aesthetic perception made possible by industrial modernity. Multiplying the number of products implies also augmenting the agents involved in the economic production of commodities. The changes that high industrialization brought impacted the traditional nuclear economy of the household-workshop of old by multiplying the stages and the agents involved in the system of production. The generative power of this principle of multiplicity present in industrial societies is endless. New agents in the economic field will seek recognition in the public sphere and an active agency in the existing structures of power. Each of these cultural formations—psychological perception, market economy, political identity—are far from being directed only by the dominant economic cultural movement that shapes them. Each cultural formation—aesthetic perception, market economy, political identity—develops a subsidiary existence within disciplines and practices that have been articulated over the "long" nineteenth century in increasingly more specialized and complex ways. In becoming more specialized, each cultural formation often looses any direct link with the other cultural formations, thus appearing as a field of its own. Confronted with the parallel workings of so many social and cultural formations, scholarship has tended to specialize and compartmentalize its scope. A broader perspective is still possible, however, if the goal of one's research is the link that ties these formations, which with time has become more invisible. I identified this link between different cultural fields in the presence of common structuring patterns that appear in each of them. My chapters, thus, explore this common link connecting advertising as well as fiction, journalistic prose as well as political theory, practices of visual entertainment and theories of culture.

The pattern that I recognized, the dichotomy multiplicity/unity, entails a move away from the myriad of stimuli of factual and intellectual nature that constitute the culture of modernity. This going past the fragmented nature of the experience of modernity is a form of transcending materiality in an attempt to encompass it by inscribing its vagaries in a general synthesis. This pattern, which is also a recurrent discursive formation and a mode of knowledge, attains the status of what I want to call a paradigm in nineteenth-century culture. Multiplicity is entertained not simply in a purely empirical manner but as a preliminary step that aims to inscribe its parts in a wider unity, in a wider structural order. The appeal of commodities appears to the urban dweller through a diverse range of distinct and overwhelming stimuli targeting any individual perception. The same sensational overkill of unrelated products can be read into a wider theoretical network, the system of capitalist production, as the Marxist narrative attempts to do. Some sensation novels by Mary Elizabeth Braddon interpret the same motley and multidirectional spectacle of commodity capitalism through a plot that creates a cohesive narrative out of the many existences, commodities, means of transportation, and of communication that urban modernity made possible. Moving from fragmentation to a larger unity applies not only to economic theory and novelistic narrative. This move from diversity to unity structures also the public sphere in its traditional forms of political representation: new social groups demanding recognition find a voice in a political system that reproduces and sustains its overall unity past the fragmentation of its social body. When I suggest that the discursive practices of modernity defined by the dichotomy of fragmentation/unity become paradigmatic, I mean that each reflects the whole system from any site in the cultural map. Giorgio Agamben defines "paradigm" in his work *Signatura Rerum*[1] as that which represents analogy between individual things that point to a general system. In doing so, Agamben recasts a similar epistemological concern that animated the use in Walter Benjamin of the notion of the monad that I have used in this sense throughout this study. In the roughly seventy years of the Victorian age that heralded the practices of mass culture still shaping ours, this double register of perception and knowledge structures many attempts to know and represent contemporary culture: the scattered productions of material culture and the all-encompassing view that preserves unity and cohesion go together.[2]

The chapters of *Reading Popular Culture in Victorian Print*, therefore, are excavations of apparently distinct fields of Victorian popular culture such as the periodical press, art criticism, political theory, popular fiction, advertising, commodity culture, pre-cinema, and silent film. Together with the empirical attention to the workings of each system of meaning and representation, however, I placed an equally empirical focus on a frequent recourse in many of them to a general abstract theory that encompasses materiality and fragmentation by superseding it. Pointing to a larger unity is not only an epistemological move from multiplicity to unity in order to manage different singularities; unity past fragmentation is also a practice of identity formation, of aesthetic and economic value, as well as of contemporary forms of popular entertainment. The "we" of a public political voice supersedes the diversities it wishes to represent; classicist art appreciation accords importance to works of art privileging transcendental insights at the expense of ephemeral multidirectional impressions; the language of advertising trumpets its democratizing effect by creating a new, democratic, and united community of equal buyers; the ideological formation of the nation unites and policies the many political forces active in society by projecting its principle of unity on colonial expansion. The process of creating unity was not only an ideological projection, since material culture, for instance, pre-cinematic entertainment and, to some degree, print culture also contributed to making familiar to the average viewer the process of going past fragmentation by creating a cohesive and fictional narrative of unity past the fragmented sensations of perception.

However defined by a synaesthetic experience, urban modernity preserves very recognizable traces of a totalizing construction that gives meaning to all singularities through specific logic and intellectual strategies: synecdochic abstractions, narrative development, and complex ideological formations such as gender and the nation. The title of the magazine edited by Mary Elizabeth Braddon, *Belgravia*, named after a part of London, refers by synecdoche to the ideological referent of the upper-class neighborhood of its title, which provides the invisible unity of the whole magazine, in ironic contrast to what Mary Elizabeth Braddon herself in a most probably self-deprecatorily humorous letter to her mentor envisioned as a popular magazine targeting a Brixton audience.[3] Narrative developments of most sensation novels, despite the disturbing revelations punctuating the plot-driven development of the stories, reinstate traditional morality, as has been observed in the works of Nancy Armstrong, D.A. Miller, Ann Cvetkovich, and many others with reference to the Victorian novel at large. These emotional shocks contained in the plots that question preconceived notions of propriety have a paradoxical effect on the reader of monthly installments of a novel: on one hand the conflicts are intensified by the publication in a monthly magazine, for the reader must wait until the following month for some form of resolution of these conflicts; on the other hand, the same conflicts are defused by the content of the magazine, which reinstates a kind of unity under the brand-name of the Belgravia neighborhood. Advertising sheets, which were present to the Victorian reader but rarely preserved until this day, likewise, seem a chaotic jumble of messages when viewed superficially. A hidden ideological formation, however, links them, like the insisted availability of luxurious items, to "all," or the presupposed cultural superiority of the nation. Ideological formations such as the nation or policed gender, therefore, provide an imaginary element of cohesion to the multidirectional forces that animate industrial societies. Discursive formations intertwine two distinct planes of observation and inquiry—the empirical and the abstract—by binding them in a reciprocal relation.[4] The following chapters, besides excavating distinct fields of Victorian culture like reading practices, art criticism, political theory, advertising, and pre-cinema, illustrate how this binary discursive formation of fragmentation/unity established its paradigmatic status in structuring, at times imperceptibly, the same fields of nineteenth-century culture that are usually approached separately as distinct disciplinary areas. I want to highlight the similarities in the functioning of cultural formations, not the occasional points of contact between them.

By the end of the century this dual mode of perceiving and interpreting reality past fragmentation became entrenched in the emerging technique of the cinematograph. The cinematograph, by no means an invention to be relegated to the end of the century, as a vast literature in the field has established, coalesced in one patented form of popular entertainment a psychological perception that unites separate frames in a rapid sequence to provide the illusion of movement and narrative consistency.[5] The double mode of perceiving and representing reality as both fragmented and consequential is not an acquisition that the modern observer obtained only with the cinematograph. Perceiving reality through and beyond fragmentation affected many aspects of Victorian daily life: print culture, serialized fiction, precinematic entertainment, and commodity culture all share the same double vision, both material and intellectual, fragmentary and cogent. Victorian print culture at large, therefore, somewhat proleptically anticipates the aesthetic, narrative, and ideological structures that the twentieth-century film industry made natural for the modern(ist) viewer. Film histories have often privileged the use and development of the photographic image in relation to the attempts to capture and reproduce movement through a new medium. Studies on the early productions of the film industry, moreover, have rarely linked the development of a uniquely filmic style to the widely common psychological processes that print culture demanded of its readers. If history of art—and of culture at large—is, as Walter Benjamin reminds us, a "history of perception," nineteenth-century material culture, as the work of Jonathan Crary has underlined, is important in any narrative of the forms of representation that defined not only nineteenth-century epistemology but modernist aesthetics. Throughout the "long nineteenth century" countless forms of perception trained the senses of the urban masses of readers that were immersed in the urban sensorium and adapted to specific psychological processes of reading. Print culture at large, therefore, offered both an unprecedented exposure to centrifugal forces and a subtle way, through a "montage effect," to create cogent narratives and recurrent binding symbols out of the scattered stimuli that everyday life bombarded viewers with. Nineteenth-century mass culture managed the multidirectional fragmentation of industrial production through forms of syntheses that derived from traditional discourses of unity and order. In this sense, a study of the nineteenth-century periodical press can anticipate some trends identified by Theodor Adorno in his study of post–World War II popular culture.

Reading Popular Culture in Victorian Print, after opening with a diachronic study of the ten-year run of the magazine, adopts a synchronic perspective in the study of the reader's response to print culture. The shift in focus from text to reader's response allows to chart the practices of vision and perception that magazine reading instated, first and foremost the puzzling effect of *montage*, the juxtaposition of different elements of print culture appearing at close intervals to the eye of the reader. Considering *Belgravia* or any other magazine in a history of visual culture allows to retrace the hidden threads that link print culture, the culture of the "everyday," and the technologies of vision shaping perception and representation throughout the nineteenth and the twentieth centuries. Avant-garde directors in the 1920s and their critics saw a direct connection between print magazines and certain genres of silent film, like Vertov's realistic "Cine-Eye" documentaries.[6] At a time, the 1920s, when the poetics of silent film was still being elaborated, the periodical press appeared as a technology of reading and narrating the world, which, like film, made use of cuts in the editing of different materials; the periodical press can be seen, therefore, as an important precursor of the narrative technology that silent film and cinema at large made dominant for countless readers. The industrial production of periodicals targeted a wide audience who adapted its psychological faculties to process a new form of telling stories through cuts, detours, delays in the progress of the plot, juxtapositions, dialectical grafting of other visual and textual narratives onto the main text. The new technology of film was by no means a new, easily readable cultural production. The periodical press offers a paradigmatic system of organizing perception and understanding that proleptically suggests the forms of perception and understanding upon which the twentieth-century technology of film relies. The study of the "everyday" in relation to early cinema is an area that the volume *Cinema and the Invention of Modern Life* began charting.[7] The impact of the periodical press in establishing new patterns of perception is my contribution to this history.

How can this approach to the history of the press in terms of perception and *montage* effects change or help refine the reception of periodical literature? One of the ways to answer this question is by focusing on the lingering effect of the emotions stirred by a sensation novel read in monthly installments. These emotions inevitably become a component of the reader's memory that interacts with other visual and intellectual stimuli from the magazine issue or the surrounding culture. Does reading past the novelistic installment create a new synaesthetic text that manages, transforms, or neutralizes the emotions stirred by sensational narratives through the other elements contained in a magazine issue? The case of *Belgravia* is important in a study of mass culture across the conventional nineteenth/twentieth-century divide because it was the first magazine of the 1860s—Ellen Wood's *Argosy* closely following in its path—to capitalize on the craze for sensation novels and to theorize on the sensational in history and culture. This self-conscious assessment of the culture of modernity in terms of "shocks" created by "the sensational" is important because the magazine's treatment of sensationalism in such a broad cultural context inevitably opens up questions about its impact. Does the appearance in monthly periodical form of narratives—like sensation novels—that undermine social order increase their destabilizing factor since the progress of the narrative was halted for a month? Or, rather, is sensationalism the master trope of modernity inasmuch as its shocking and at times violent revelations serve the purpose of upsetting the readers in order to better manipulate their reactions toward a more calming synthesis? An idyllic closure of a novel that reinstates the dominant values of the time after the vagaries of the plot serves this purpose, being strategically placed at the end of the novel. In the periodical press, however, it is the rest of the magazine to which the shaken and aroused reader is redirected and manipulated into accepting the structures of order that the fiction challenges. Can Victorian sensationalism, therefore, provide a model for the many meanings and uses of sensationalized and violent shocks in pre– and post–World War II systems of government, from the violence of fascist Italy in the late teens, or the many countries that adopted it, to the "shock economics" discussed by Naomi Klein in our contemporary context? This book examines some recurrent patterns present in mass culture and reflects on their political implications. Despite the apparent open-ended and dialogical nature of the periodical form, I want to point to the structures of order and social control that emerge through an intramediatic and intradisciplinary study of the periodical *Belgravia* and of sensationalism from the 1860s to the 1880s and into the twentieth-century film industry. The apparently hidden presence of these cues is interesting precisely because a cursory look does not reveal them, thus leading into thinking of the periodical press as open exchange of equally tenable views confronting one another on the page.[8]

The methodological approach that I followed in my study of *Belgravia* reconsiders the three constitutive elements of the hermeneutic circle: the text, the author, and, most importantly, the reader. The *author-function* in a periodical title evolves from being the sole individuality responsible for a work to an abstract category modulating different voices and thus identifying with the whole cultural fabric of a specific age. The idea of *textuality* changes, too, along the intertextual and intramediatic lines I outlined earlier. The idea of the *reader* inevitably shifts, too. The reception of the ideas covered in any magazine crosses the consciousness of each individual reader while at the same time creating different reactions and different degrees of allegiance: a quiet espousing of the ideas presented or a critical one, a partial agreement implemented by other sources available at the time or an indifferent, but nonetheless not less political, cursory view. The increased readership of periodical publications and the wide availability of all sorts of print products creates any number of possible combinations of these reactions. The periodical press, therefore, does circulate discursive formations, but the innumerable individual responses to each issue, as well as the equally fragmented stimuli that may have originated in other print products or in Victorian urban culture at large, makes a charting of the impact of these normative practices among any group of readers a difficult one. Any combination of discursive formations in relation to one identity of readers is always subject to further processes of juxtaposition through exposure to more discursive formations. The sensorium of modern life entails for each reader an experience of combinatory sensations that I refer to with the loose metaphor of intertextuality. This broadly termed intertextuality encompasses text, image, everyday practices, and social formations in endless combinatory possibilities. The article may be read next to an advertisement, a novel installment may be either read within the macrotext of the magazine in question, or may resonate within readers as they moved to another title on the same day or were exposed to several other discursive formations structuring their everyday life. The multiplicity of factors that makes possible the infinite combinatory possibilities of reading the periodical press in the context of urban modernity presents a methodological *caveat* against any certain reconstruction of the reception of the periodical press. While identifying any given discursive formation may be done within a descriptive analysis, as I did with the discourses of unity, the response of any reader may be more aleatory to ascertain. This *caveat* that asks us to factor in an aleatory component in any reading of popular culture may apply to historical works on the periodical press, too. The sheer number of references and the combinatory possibilities in presenting the sources of one's study makes each discussion subject to more combinatory analyses and possibilities not entertained in any given historical narrative. This is why I decided to take the discussion of the periodical press at the closest range, by reading at first only the macrotext of the whole magazine. My study chooses, therefore, a thoroughly monographical approach, which is not the most dominant methodology in the field, and then opens up to the multiple possibility of an intertextual dialogue between the traceable discursive formations found in the periodical text and the analogous discursive or social formations in Victorian culture.

* * *

In the Appendix at the end of this volume I include a bibliographical description of the *Belgravia* magazine during the ten years in which Mary Elizabeth Braddon "conducted" the publication, that is, from November 1866 to February 1876, the latter being the last issue before format and content changed drastically with the purchase of the magazine by Chatto and Windus. While an index to the fiction published in *Belgravia* has appeared, this bibliography allows us to trace the contribution of all named poets, journalists, and writers that were part of Braddon's circle. Just by browsing through it many initials will be easily recognized, allowing us to identify the work of the more assiduous contributors. Several of the names listed will be old acquaintances for many. The bibliography will thus resonate with many readers who have devoted time to the study of the vast field of the Victorian periodical press. It is my intention—and hope—that this research tool may provide more examples to support or implement the historical narratives that have been—or will be—written.

London, August 2008

NOTES

1. Giorgio Agamben, *Signatura Rerum*, p. 19.
2. Whether a more theoretical view of culture pointing to a lost unity has a religious implication, as Giorgio Agamben seems to suggest by referring to signatura as a perceptible trace pointing to divine unity is a question that needs to be addressed in a separate study, focusing on the open question of secularization in modern intellectual practices.
3. Scholars who have written on the magazine have often assumed that the words used by Braddon described her intended audience quite literally, when in fact reading the whole run of the magazine suggests that target audience of the magazine was expected to be reading Latin and French verse, relate to personal chronicles of Oxbridge life, or go on bric-a-brac hunting sprees all over the Mediterranean basin. The magazine run reveals also an insisted interest, particularly after the experiment of the French Commune (1871), in the military, many of whose high officials lived in Belgravia, and in the manufacturing of guns. This coverage of upper-class life does not seem to contradict Braddon's claim but rather some of her interpreters writing in our times: seeking the "Brixton shillings" in marketing the magazine may imply the Victorian pretense to elevate the unruly working classes by imposing what was considered, despite the shocking revelations of the sensational novel, the model behavior of the affluent classes. Mark Tuner in "*Saint Paul's Magazine and the Project of Masculinity*" (p. 233) makes a passing and accurate reference to *Belgravia*'s market niche as a "middle- and lower-middle class periodical inviting readers to buy into the notion of 'society.'" I think one needs to envision two distinct audiences: one is the audience that the articles address as an audience of peers; the other audience, which is much more difficult to gauge, is the audience that identified with the content of *Belgravia* only by projecting into the future a dream of social mobility.
4. This double plane can be found in the experiential narrative of urban modernity provided by William Wordsworth in book 7 of *The Prelude* (1805). See Alberto Gabriele, "Visions of the City of London: Mechanical Eye and Poetic Transcendence in Wordsworth's *Prelude*-book 7."
5. See the work of Charles Musser, *The Emergence of Cinema* and Jonathan Crary's *Techniques of the Observer*. For a comprehensive study of pre-cinematic technology of vision, see also Laurent Mannoni, *The Great Art of Light and Shadow. Archeology of the Cinema* and the exhibition catalogue *Light and Movement*.
6. "O Kino-Pravde" (1923) in *Lines of Resistance: Dziga Vertov and the Twenties*, quoted in Matthew S. Witkovsky's *Foto* (2007), p. 36.

7. *Cinema and the Invention of Modern* Life. Eds. Vanessa Schwartz and Leo Charney.
8. Kate Jackson summarizes this prevalent view when she describes the "uniquely interactive, open and self-referential form of the periodical text" that "functions as social discourse rather than as direct social statement" ("George Newnes and the 'loyal Tid-Bitites': Editorial Identity and Textual Interaction in *Tid Bits*," in *Nineteenth-Century Media and the Construction of Identities*, p. 19). I think that social discourses, as dispersed as they may be, do not for this reason lose their normative force. Despite their apparent invisibility they are binding ideological forces.

Acknowledgments

Any scholarly publication emerges from a long and to some extent collaborative gestation period. I want to start by thanking, in alphabetical order, the professors I had for nurturing my interest in the subject: Ann Cvetkovich, Michail Iampolski, Antonia Lant, Sergio Perosa, Mary Poovey, Bruce Clunies-Ross, Richard Sieburth, and Jeffrey Spear. All the others with whom I have engaged in a dialogue from afar are listed in my bibliography. The Institute for International Education, which administers the Fulbright fellowships, has been instrumental in sponsoring my first two years of graduate school. Richard Sieburth has supervised my (indeed not irreversible!) transition from classical and medieval philology to nineteenth-century studies and twentieth-century theory. He has suggested wonderfully apt titles in the early stages of any research project I was interested in and has introduced me to scholars in my field who have had quite an impact in the development of this project. Jeffrey Spear has been my advisor over the last stages of my doctoral program and into the years "on the market"; he has been very supportive and has always provided good advice at a time when, as a foreigner, I most needed it. I want to thank him also for practicing the art of *conversazione*. Mary Poovey has been a crucial inspiration through her own research and has provided bibliographical advice for some parts of chapters two and three. A fellowship from the Institute for the History of the Production of Knowledge in 2002–2003 allowed me to take time off teaching in order to focus on the fields of research that I was beginning to explore. Reading the books in the library at the Institute helped me draw a link between the workings of ideology and everyday life. Ann Cvetkovich, during the seminar I took with her, has provided her students with an invaluable starting point that is often overlooked, that is, a detailed bibliography of the history of the most interesting scholarship in the field of Victorian studies. That list has been my guiding star in my research; it has shaped my methodology and introduced me to a group of scholars in the field that I look at with great admiration. I want to thank Ann Cvetkovich also for being the *engagée* intellectual that she is: in the classroom, in her writing, and in the social aspects of a scholarly life. Anne Marie Thiesse has welcomed me both in New York and at the École Normale Superieur in Paris with warm kindness, and has always suggested interesting readings. Dominique Kalifa's weekly conferences at the Sorbonne have been a great model for building intellectual communities that are fair, up-to-date, and very productive. Walter Miller has read the first drafts of chapters one–four dating back to 2003–2005. I want to thank him for his feedback.

I would like, next, to thank the staff of the many libraries I visited: the British Library in London, and Colindale, the Edinburgh National Library, the University of London and the University of Reading Libraries, the Bibliothèque Nationale of France and the Bibliothèque Richelieu in Paris, Fales Collection at New York University's Bobst Library, the Edweard Muybridge Museum at Kingston-upon-Thames, the Museo del Pre-Cinema Collezione Minici Zotti in Padua, the Museo del Cinema in Turin, and St. Deiniol's Library. Marvin Taylor must be acknowledged for his kind hospitality during my visits to the Fales Library. I met with equal kindness from Donata Pesenti Campagnoni in Turin and Laura Minici Zotti in Padua. Laura Minici Zotti promptly made available her magic lantern slides that otherwise may have been hard to view in other museums and at more jealous private collectors' houses. I want to mention again the British Library in London for the overall excellent policies implemented for scholarly research in its premises. A Penfield fellowship for the summer of 2003, for which I wish to thank Tim Reiss, covered some of the expenses associated with my stay in London to conduct research there. The British Library and the Random House Group kindly granted me permission to quote from their collections. For the references to the Chatto and Windus archive I wish to thank Jean Rose and Jo Watt from Random House Ltd. The collection Minici Zotti and Fales Library generously donated permission to use some images from their collections, the others in the book are from my own archive. St Deiniol's Library awarded me with a fellowship to complete the manuscript of the book. I want to thank Rachel Gilmour for letting me know of this opportunity and the whole staff at Howarden for their warm hospitality.

Besides the universities and the libraries I attended I should also credit the curators of many museums and cultural institutions, in New York and elsewhere, for allowing me to engage with a longer and more complex history of culture than the segment that a specialized publication like this one can chart.

The mobilization of graduate students that resulted in the first labor contract brokered by the United Auto Workers of America needs to be remembered as it has greatly improved the conditions of living for graduate students, before being crushed during the Bush presidency. While forming not exactly a cosmopolitan community, the activists involved have nonetheless shown a care for the larger social and political implications of university research and college teaching that are rare to find.

The conferences of the Research Society for the Victorian Periodicals, as well as the ones organized by the Nineteenth-Century Studies Association and the Interdisciplinary Nineteenth-Century Studies have offered occasion for informal and encouraging exchanges with many scholars. I wish to thank Linda Peterson, Laurel Brake, Anne Humpherys, Linda Hughes, Patrick Leary, Kate Flint, Mary Jane Rochelson, and Regina Hewitt. I want to thank the two amazing readers at *The European Romantic Review* who first read my article on Wordsworth and pre-cinema. The acute and stimulating comments from Anonymous Reader No. 1 have been one of the most—if not the most—rewarding and inspiring feedback I have so far received. Marilyn Gaull at Palgrave has believed in the quality of the research conducted for this publication and has seen the potential of this book from the very beginning. Her very direct and clear guidelines have been quite helpful in the publication process.

My parents have supported my studies throughout my career and have been savvy interlocutors at many stages. Their many-faceted love has been an enormous source of energy and the backbone of both my intellectual and personal adult life. I want to dedicate this book to them and also to my late grandmother Teresa. Paolo and Serena provided invaluable help when I happened to be away from my printer and scanner. Last but not least, I wish to acknowledge the dear ones that I have shared my life with, in several countries. You know who you are.

Introduction

The Cultural Trope of Sensationalism

> *Rather than asking, "What is the attitude of a work* to *the relations of production of its time?" I would ask, "What is its position* in *them?" This question directly concerns the function the work has within the literary relations of production of its time. It is connected, in other words, directly with the literary* technique *of works.*
>
> —Walter Benjamin, *The Author as Producer,* Address at the Institute for the Study of Fascism, Paris, April 27, 1934

The word "sensational" appears several times in the monthly periodical magazine *Belgravia* in the period between 1867 and 1876 when it was "conducted" by the popular author of sensation novels Mary Elizabeth Braddon. In an article on furs, published in 1871, "sensational" refers to a most precious and new kind of fur coat available in stores. In another one, describing the unraveling of the mysteries of a modern factory, the term underlines the excitement for the discovery of the secret behind the production process. India ale is advertised as "sensational" in the November 1872 issue, while in the historical novel *Bound to John Company* serialized in the magazine the term anticipates the tortures the young protagonist may be subject to in eighteenth-century India, during the British war effort of 1756–63. The semantic field of this word encompasses, therefore, several aspects of modern culture: the thrill created by the overflow of new commodities such as fur and ale, the introduction of new knowledge about the hidden workings of industrialization, and the history of the British expansion in India. In these three instances, however, the term "sensationa," and the suspended excitement that comes with it, affects the perception of the readers in different ways: it moves from a passing reference to a product, like in the case of ale and furs, to a more complex effect that defines a specific narrative strategy, like in the case of the visit to a factory and in the novel on the British expansion in India. While the first examples simply highlight the novelty and prestige of the items that would be missed in a general article on the market of specific goods, the other two engage the whole narrative structure of the pieces around an awaited sensational turn. In the case of the visit to a factory, an otherwise technical description of its machinery is transformed into a mystery. In the novel that fictionalizes the captivity of the British soldiers in the infamous "Black Hole of Calcutta," the history of the British presence in India reaches a harrowing peak of horror and generates associations with the more recent history of the Indian Sepoy rebellion and the rationale for a British presence in India.

A simple philological analysis of the semantic field marked out by the term "sensational" in the macrotext of *Belgravia* suggests that sensationalism can be identified with the intensely charged shocking effect of modernity. Modernity here represents the changes that affected the redrawing of the maps of the culture of industrialization, as seen here in new advertising strategies and in new patterns of consumption of products and ideas.[1] In order to chart the culture of late Victorian sensationalism I chose to study the whole run of the *Belgravia* magazine and consider it a "monad" in the benjaminian sense of the word; Benjamin's perception of history in terms of fragments subtracted from the "homogenous, empty time"[2] of traditional history applies to the fragmented experience of modernity I examine here. I place modernity specifically (but not exclusively) in the period that witnessed the widespread affirmation of a fragmented but not less systematic organization of industrial production, visual perception, and social order. In this light *Belgravia* can be seen not simply as a cultural product reflecting the new reality of industrialization but as a fragment containing in itself the whole structure of the system. By system I do not mean the unity of the romantic absolute as a complete and unattainable whole, but rather a fecund matrix informing several scattered remains produced by the nonlinear and rather circular whirlwind of history. My work juxtaposes several aspects connected to late Victorian sensationalism. First, it is a study of the material history of the *Belgravia* magazine: the book retraces the life of the magazine on the market of periodicals, its global distribution, and its demise. One of the purposes of this study is to present original archival materials that I found, which include the ledger books of the publisher and the list of agents scattered over four continents, which help draw a new global map of distribution patterns in the periodical press of the 1860s. The choice of the *Belgravia* magazine as the main focus is, I believe, particularly significant in the field of Victorian studies. While the study of Victorian magazines since the foundation of the Research Society for the Study of Victoria Periodicals has produced fundamental research tools, as well as a general agreement on terms and approaches to the study of Victorian print culture, *Belgravia* has not yet received a comprehensive analysis. Existing articles and book chapters dedicated to Braddon's *Belgravia* are interested in thematic questions such as sensationalism in science, the debates on the role of reading, and the work of Mary Elizabeth Braddon as an editor.[3] My research, taking its departure from sensationalism in the magazine, focused on several instances of sensationalism that appeared in contemporary Victorian culture. I shall return later in the chapter to sensationalism and the distinctive highlighting it offered to objects and people that animated the teeming life of London with an overflow of businesses, commodities, and new social agents demanding political and professional recognition. Besides presenting the documents associated with the history of the magazine, I chose to investigate other aspects of cultural history, like the new perception of temporality during the industrial age and the significance of space at large: the space of the Victorian London neighborhood that gave *Belgravia* its title, the localities covered by the articles contained in the magazine, and the global localities reached by the distribution of the magazine. I chose to consider these realities through the many types of discourses—visual, verbal, historical—that made them an experience of everyday life for readers of the press, art critics, entertainers, and political reformers alike. These apparently unrelated elements of cultural history—art, literature, popular entertainment, political theory—present, as I mentioned in my preface, specific discursive formations and recurrent patterns, like the polarity multiplicity/unity. Novelistic installments and the debates on political representation, subliminal messages contained in advertising and new configurations of the public sphere, the refined abstraction of the Belgravia neighborhood and the global readership reached by the distribution of the magazine all reflect a larger concern with unity that contemporary culture elaborated. In order to understand the wide impact of sensationalism on these different cultural formations I propose to define sensationalism as a *cultural trope* that shaped the experience of reality and its representation: sensationalism encompassed industrial production and aesthetic theory, reverberated in new expanding markets and new political agencies, shaped advertising strategies and the success of popular fictional characters. The practices of industrialization articulated through the trope of sensationalism had many reverberations, which I shall examine in my chapters: the nineteenth-century industrial age in which sensationalism flourished gave rise to a specific novelistic genre (chapter two), with transnational ties to the French novel (chapter six). The success of the sensational formula created also ways to imagine commodity culture through new fictional narratives (chapter four). Sensationalism provided a common denominator in the industrial age of exponentially expanding commodity capitalism that included print culture, aesthetic theory (chapter two), political theory (chapter three), and new forms of entertainment that catered to a new urban market (chapter five). The intensified peaks of sensory perception were by no means tied solely to a literary genre: sensationalism coalesced into a cultural trope originating in the reality of urban modernity. The impressionistic forms of perception that defined sensationalism had already marked the new experience of the industrial city and its new forms of entertainment before becoming a distinctive genre of fiction, and, most importantly, a self-conscious theory of culture elaborated on the pages of the monthly *Belgravia*.

Following the example of many historical excavations of nineteenth-century print culture that called for an intertextual reading of the fiction published in the periodical press,[4] I similarly want to redefine the idea of the text and extend the object of stylistic and historical analysis beyond the boundaries of the bound volume containing a novel. I include, therefore, on the one hand the paratextual elements of the magazine: advertisement, illustrations, articles, and poems all constituted the macrotext that I subjected to literary analysis. More distinctively, I chose to relate a particular genre of Victorian fiction, the sensation novel, not only to the specific means of its serial publication, but to the broader late Victorian visual and intellectual culture that was similarly affected by the trope of sensationalism.[5] As stated earlier, I do not intend, however, to simply enumerate the elements of Victorian cultural formation present in the texts of the novels or in the articles of the magazine. I am also interested in focusing on the historically specific aspects of the reception of the many forms of sensationalism that I outline. I shall highlight the dialectical relations that sensationalism created in the minds of the readers of the monthly installments of *Belgravia*. I call this psychological process dialectical because the stimuli the reader was subject to in *Belgravia* were by no means homogenous and the trope of sensationalism, particularly in a monthly issue, can suggest, however paradoxically, a critique of the dominant values of the Victorian ruling class. I take the term dialectic in the meaning employed by Henri Lefebvre when introducing his notion of the critique of the everyday: in his view, the category of the "everyday" is the ultimate textual production of a culture and its ideology.[6] I shall explore how reading practices of different sorts may have questioned dominant values or defused the implicit critique they contained. This approach allows me to reconsider twentieth-century mass culture and gain a more thorough understanding through its nineteenth-century early appearance, following in this the premise of Ann Cvetkovich's *Mixed Feelings*. Her work , which appeared in 1992, first placed sensation novels within the context not simply of a "long nineteenth century" ending with World War I but of a more lasting persistence of Victorian cultural formations throughout the twentieth century. The similarities that can be noticed between the two centuries indirectly question not only the conventional distinction of historical temporality in centuries but a fetishized sense of cultural otherness that is often associated to the Victorian age and inevitably projected in a selective view of the past that does not engage with contemporary history. I want to speak of sensationalism as a trope that elaborated the fragments of modernity into distinctive dynamics that cannot be ascribed to a strictly Victorian process of cultural formation.

THE CULTURAL TROPE OF SENSATIONALISM

The periodical press of the 1860s constitutes a significant case study in the history of the British publishing industry for several reasons. First, as I mentioned earlier, its system of production presents for the first time patterns and strategies that can be later ascribed to twentieth-century mass culture. Not only has the industrial production of literary artifacts reached a turning point in its numbers, but its marketing strategies have also shaped a new public of readers and, indirectly, created a persistent trend in the publishing industry with a lasting influence in the history of nineteenth- and twentieth-century mass culture.[7] Second, distribution patterns of periodicals from that decade exceeded the confines of the British and colonial markets, as I have discovered. The case of *Belgravia* illuminates a so far neglected aspect of the distribution patterns of late-nineteenth-century print culture that calls for a remapping of trade routes. Braddon's husband Maxwell, who ran his own publishing company and issued *Belgravia* until it was sold to Chatto and Windus, had established a network of dealers that was not limited to the confines of the British Isles nor to their colonial domains. Magazines and books by the publishing house Maxwell were part of a global market that reached out beyond the territorial categories of the nation and of colonial expansion.[8] A new map of the impact of Victorian ideology that breaks the typical categories of "British" and "Colonial" historiography can thus evoke and pave the way for the contemporary geopolitical territory of global trade we are familiar with. Third, the craze for sensational topics of interest and sensational practices of writing—and pitching—anything from novels to newspaper articles and popular shows, far from being a distinctive feature of the 1860s, reaches at this time the status of a cultural trope. By that I mean the conflation of literary narratives and journalistic rhetoric, the interaction of marketing calculations and induced demand for specific goods, the emergence of ground-breaking artistic innovations as well as a redefinition of what aesthetic theory was. Everything, in short, was sensationalized.

Sensationalism was the result of the impact of industrial production on print culture and also an agent in the widespread expansion of the new logic of the market economy.[9] The deep influence and lasting effect that sensationalism had is not simply the reflex effect of industrial output, advertising strategies, and massive availability of much demanded goods and sensations for an expanding market. If sensationalism lasted so long, up to our age, it is because it was a most viable trope and a most powerful symbolic rendition of practices that went beyond the literary. This trend in popular culture touches sensitive areas of public opinion at a time in which new pressure was exerted upon traditional society and its principles of political organization. The shock represented by the repeated use of exclamation marks in sensation fiction, often amplified by their paroxistic appearance at the end of the installment, signifies a sudden and compelling revelation that challenges the reader's understanding of the privileged status ascribed by birthright to the main character of a sensation novel. The sensational effect is not limited, however, to the narrative structure of popular fiction; the disturbing unveiling of secrets regarding upper-class characters opens the literary representation of inveterate and stable rituals of class identity to a world of social mobility, entrepreneurial calculations and maneuvers, reinvented and manufactured identities that went beyond fiction. What makes these revelations so disturbing is the shattering of preconceived notions caused by unmanageable forces and by unpredictable outcomes. It is the sudden, episodic nature of these revelations that contributes to the shattering of conscious assumptions about established structures of social order.

Fragmentation represents one of the key features of the cultural trope of sensationalism and is a telling symbol of the many atomistic perspectives that the process of industrialization introduced into the urban landscape. Some of the insights of Walter Benjamin have defined this kind of fragmentation as the shifting views of a *flâneur* in a changing urban space.[10] The literature of urban *flâneurie* is vast and characterized, ever since the early part of the nineteenth century, by a new perspective on crowds and city spectacles. In the case of Wordsworth's *The Prelude*, for instance, the stroller's perspective of city crowds assembled by the early stages of industrialization is opposed to the aesthetic of rural idylls unaltered by this process. Wordsworth's representation alternates between a realistic rendition of the fragmented stimuli of the urban sensorium and an aesthetic mediation of natural landscapes by means of Platonic categories. The percussive rhythm that the eye of the city *flâneur* registers is the rhythm of the visual "shocks" imparted by the fleeting glimpses at humanity in constant movement, by the passing look at signs, advertisements, and street scenes that rapidly parade in front of the stroller or the coach rider.[11] Their immediate reality, deprived of a contemplative elaboration, or of a narrative, levels out any hierarchical organization of perception and equals one view with the other until the contemplative mode of vision of Wordsworth's poetry implodes. Fragmentation is, therefore, an experience that goes beyond the aesthetic or subjective and acquires a new ontological value in the context of nineteenth-century industrialization. I want to stress that the many instances of the word "fragmentation" that I have used in discussing the editorial practices of the periodical press, the aesthetics of sensationalism, the ensuing political debate on political representation and pre-cinematic entertainment make fragmentation more than a useful metaphor for literary criticism. Fragmentation, like sensationalism, belongs to the reality of industrial cities while at the same time contributing to the elaboration of many formations that conjugate this cultural trope. Sensationalism, therefore, appears to be a social form that intertwines the real and the cultural, the material and the ideological.

When sensationalism became a matter of concern for physicians and preachers, Platonic art theoreticians and "avant-garde" intellectuals, the language that was used to refer to it dovetailed with a discourse of fragmentation. Sensationalism was associated with a specific apparatus, the nervous system, that offered an example of anarchic and unrestrained agency. Sensationalism, it seemed, targeted the impressionable public of female readers, in a trend to single out a dangerously aroused part of the whole society against the accepted norms of the whole. Critics such as Eneas Sweetland Dallas saw the time-bound episodic nature of sensationalism as a challenge to the Platonic tradition of transcendental intuitions of order that postulated a stable organization of society. Disparate cultural products, such as periodicals, had such an appeal that the sheer proliferation of specific magazines dedicated to one trade and its demands seemed to threaten the conservative hold on an immutable structure of power. The market of the publishing industry could thrive on creating niches and affiliated buyers by issuing a new magazine to cater to their demand. The increasingly fragmented market of readers, according to some commentators, inspired fears of a seemingly varied and active constituency that might be organizing in separate groups and even push for a new Reform Bill to demand political rights. It was not only the general public that was perceived as a fragmented constituency, as an unpredictable collection of individualities. Industrial production of literary artifacts changed the psychological experience of reading, too, as the perusal of newspapers and magazines was ultimately fragmentary. Serial publication of novels was not new; it was practiced in the nineteenth century by an industry that sought in the installment a source of profit and a form of advertising; circulating more copies of a novel in installments allowed the publishers to try out the marketability of a title and to monitor its impact throughout several months. Unsold issues could later be bound together for the book edition so that the publication in installments appeared to be a step in the production of the final commodity, the double or triple decker. An installment of a novel published periodically obviously could not reflect the cultural trope of sensationalism in the same way that a magazine might have. An installment was more a manifestation of sheer fragmentation of the industrial production of novels than an elaboration of a compelling constellation of symbols and social meanings that only the issue of a magazine might have evoked. Installments of different novels appeared in a magazine next to articles and illustrations, thus engaging the reader in a paradoxical dialectic alternating fact and fiction, sensational revelations and accepted notions of social order.[12] In all these cases, fragmentation appears as a cultural trope that extends beyond the subjective experience of reading or perceiving reality. The trope, in fact, defines practices of consumption as well as of production; it is rich with ramifications that go into the social and political spheres, redefining notions of subjectivity and political agency.

The varied articulations of the cultural trope of sensationalism recognized the tendency to fragmentation as inherent to the process of industrialization; they also envisioned, in the political arena, the emergence of new agencies that appeared with the changes brought about by market economy. While it is true that a new perception of reality surfaced in the consciousness of political theorists as well as art historians, intellectuals, and critics, it must be pointed out again that they often held on fast to their systems of knowledge and their political implications. Fragmentation, while being a signature mark of the culture of modernity and industrial capitalism, always existed in relation to firm, established structures of meaning. The many reverberations of the culture of sensationalism did challenge these established beliefs, as the artistic avant-garde of modernism later did, not unlike its isolated precursors in the history of nineteenth-century art and, to a lesser degree, literature. Isolated fragments, however, were never taken per se as the free-floating arrangement of chance encounters, neither were they juxtaposed by means of sheer association. A sense of episodic fragmentation was indeed perceived in the spectacle of urban life or forced through the paroxysmal ruptures of sensational fiction. One must keep in mind, however, that larger systems of meaning were introduced to account for them, either by rejecting them in favor of old systems or by rearranging them in new paradigms, as Marxist theory did by reducing them to entities leveled under the unifying system of exchange value.

The chapters in this book deal with the many tenses and tropes that articulate what I call the sensational mode. Chapter one presents a diachronic history of the roughly ten years in which Braddon conducted her "London Magazine," followed by a more dialectical examination of the reception of the genre of sensation fiction in the format of the miscellaneous magazine. I want to reconsider the claim made by Barbara Onslow and others that the perusal of the miscellaneous content of the magazine in question, or of any other title, was a simple, casual accumulation of different contents.[13] An analysis of the whole run of the magazine shows a consistent construction of an abstract understanding of space and of time for its global readership. This move toward abstraction and homogeneity is conveyed despite the sensational revelations of the fiction Braddon was popular for. The sophisticated London neighborhood in the title of the magazine suggests a world of secluded privilege and by doing so defines a certain kind of individuality that the plots of the novels constantly demystify by showing their proximity to crime. Social status is reinforced through advertising of precious items and locations for shopping, as well as through political views of the upper classes that emerge from the magazine's fragmentary coverage of the world. Braddon's magazine created a complex representation of contemporary culture by juxtaposing print image and text, mental picture and empirical knowledge, and, more specifically, thrilling revelations of the sensational plot and normative discursive formations that reconstituted a cohesive meaning in the minds of the readers. The perusal of Braddon's magazine had a dialectical component that problematized the dominant culture it represented in a unique way in the history of nineteenth-century literary magazines.[14]

Chapter two discusses more systematically sensation fiction. It outlines the narrative functions of sensation novels by Collins, Mrs. Wood, and Braddon. The chapter questions, as many interpreters have done, the critical viability of a genre such as the sensation novel, which was coined by the publishing industry largely *ex nihilo* to advertise its popular fiction. Existing scholarship on sensation fiction, when confronted with the wide array of applications that the term sensational had in Victorian culture, which signaled, in a smart marketing move, a call for the attention of the reader, ends up applying the generic definition of the sensation novel without due distinctions. In order to outline the discreet identities of some of the main sensation novelists that competed for readers during the sensation craze of the 1860s, chapter two defines the specific narrative and stylistic qualities of each, as evinced by some of their most popular titles. Braddon's fiction appears as the more consistent in employing the sensational turn as a kind of spasmodic suspense exerted on the linear narrative prominent in other novelists. I want to argue that Braddon was aware of the relevance of this mode not only in reference to the melodramatic model as many interpreters have done or as a set of narrative functions but as a defining feature of contemporary culture at large.[15] This is evident when considering that the intellectuals in her circle, largely in response to the establishment's attacks leveled against Braddon, elaborated a semiotic theory of culture based on the sensational that accounts not only for their view of art but of science as well, which I am going to pit in the second part of the chapter against the works of other cultural critics.

Chapter three examines the role the *Belgravia* magazine had in the history of the British press. I discuss the changes in British journalism that involved the status of readers on one hand and journalists and editors on the other. The *Belgravia* magazine, by imagining a target audience through the shocking sensations that were used to manipulate its response paves the way for the "new journalism" that appeared in the 1880s. The increased professional recognition demanded and at times expected by journalists emerges in the debate on anonymity versus signature that I examine next. This debate is important, I think, because its discursive formations overlap with the contemporaneous parliamentary debates on the first and second Reform Bill. The contemporaneous reflections on the role and function of the periodical press share with Victorian liberal ideology the same configuration of the public sphere. The idea of the public is imagined as a paradoxical construction that apparently allows for the growing presence of more individualized subjects while in fact being made to coincide with the interests of the status quo. A series of unpublished letters by Mary Elizabeth Braddon requesting to publish an article on Zola anonymously further illustrates the reconfiguration of the public and private spheres in the Victorian press with the specific example of the conductor of the *Belgravia* magazine. The letter indirectly suggests also that the resistance to the sensational mode in official British culture was an opposition to the introduction of a new kind of realism, naturalism, that was to take the place of the more accepted and moralistic tone of canonical realism.

Chapter four analyzes different degrees of fragmentation that appear to the reader of the periodical press. I start with a study of nineteenth-century advertising to show that the advertisements are not in this case the fleeting flashes of the spectacle of modernity that Benjamin described but rather the ephemeral appearance of recurrent and overall consistent discursive formations.[16] These formations appeared in extensive verbal narratives and did not rely on visual cues only, unlike later in the history of advertisement. I then proceed to examine how these common discursive practices inform also articles on specific commodities as well as the generic features of the narratives of industrial journalism contained in *Belgravia*. The chapter ends with a study of how global trade is fictionalized in a novel, *Bound to John Company*, that adumbrated the recent events of the Sepoy rebellion by means of a story set in eighteenth-century India. While the discussion of advertisements earlier in the chapter suggests a direct relation between products and consumers, this novel on the East India Company sensationalizes the Western fascination with oriental commodities. Since the mysteries of sensation fiction are oftentimes resolved through the use in the novels of oriental commodities that are crucial to the development of the plot, I want to argue that these objects are a *mise an abyme* of the sensational dialectic: they represent social status while at the same time linking it to a criminal trail so artfully hidden behind bourgeois respectability. This is the case of *Bound to John Company*, too. The novel, therefore, is particularly interesting because it reveals the colonial subtext of the bourgeois consumption of luxury items: it sensationalizes British history by uncovering the horror of colonial rule. In openly criticizing the British war effort in India, the novel questions and to some degree demystifies the prestige associated to the consumption of oriental commodities.

Chapter five discusses several forms of nineteenth-century popular entertainment such as magic lantern shows, peep-boxes, and phantasmagorias, which capitalized on the sensational effect both through awe-inspiring vistas and thrilling narratives. Existing scholarship on the sensational in literature has only explored the intertextual nexus between stage melodrama and sensation novels without considering these popular attractions that left a distinctive mark on many Victorian authors that goes beyond, I think, the sheer mentioning of some in their fiction: I believe that these spectacles did transform traditional notions of literary representation and affect the creative process in unprecedented ways. I want to point to these visual practices as they marked a shift in the history of perception from the transcendental vision of platonic order to the fragmented accumulation of sensory stimuli that characterized the new aesthetics of the sensational discussed in chapter two. I propose to see the history of these spectacles, and the history of the magic lantern in particular, as an apt correlative of the disjoined and yet cohesive experience of reading a magazine such as *Belgravia*, which meant to induce strong emotions scattered along the perusal of the magazine while at the same time defusing them through the normative effect of appeasing and moralizing narratives. I also want to propose an interdisciplinary reading of the social history of the magic lantern practice in relation to the history of the modern British novel. I then proceed to compare an example of sensationalism in the silent film Feuilliade's *Les Vampyres* (1916) with Braddon's brand of sensationalism to open up literary studies to the persistence of narrative models and characters of Victorian novels in the silent film industry beyond the sheer adaptation of popular novels. I want to point to an often neglected trajectory that links the vast repertoire of narratives circulating in the periodical press with the creation of specific genres and characters that were popular in the silent film era. More specifically, my analysis compares two examples of female characters to historicize the workings of gender at different stages of the development of the capitalist system of production.

Chapter six focuses on the popularity of the sensational formula in the British and French publishing industry past the peak of the sensation novel's craze of the 1860s. By choosing to discus the French sensation novels from the Vizetelly catalogue of the 1880s, the chapter aims to problematize the category of "detective fiction" that literary history has circulated; the specific narrative structures of the genre are based in the works of few authors, oftentimes in select titles by one popular author only. I am not interested in the diachronic and oftentimes teleological narrative that literary history has created to discuss detective fiction, which indicates the precursors of the genre, the transition figures such as Gaboriau (usually present only with few of his titles), and the final codification in authors such as Doyle.[17] I rather propose to read detective-sensation fiction within the broader synchronical context of popular fiction of the 1860s and 1870s in both England and France, where Braddon published two novels in feuilleton edition and where her works were regularly translated and reviewed. I shall also underline the different perception of what was sensational, scandalous, and thrilling on the two sides of the Chunnel in the 1870s and 1880s. The presence of criminal characters belonging not to the traditionally demonized working class but to the middle and upper middle class features prominently in the British sensation formula and in French popular fiction from the same period. While both the French and the British sensation novels dramatize an anxiety revolving around the notion of class mobility, the French examples do not cast the question of crime in general moralistic terms. The French examples point to a specific historical context, the new social order following the coup d'etat of 1850. Setting the novels during this pivotal historical moment reflects, I think, a crisis in liberal ideology that invests the traditional ethos of honesty that accompanied the rise of the middle-class and of middle-class characters in the first part of the nineteenth century.

Chapter 1

The Case of Mary Elizabeth Braddon's *Belgravia*: Research Methodology for a New Intertextual Reading of the Periodical Press

The historical method is a philological method based on the book of life

—Walter Benjamin, *Paralipomena to "On the Concept of History"*

In this chapter I shall present a description of the Victorian periodical *Belgravia* as it has been preserved at the British Library in London.[1] Any archival research focusing on the periodical press is confronted with fragmented findings: the single issues that originally circulated are often lost, together with the advertising sheets. Even the volumes of the bound collections are heterogeneous: each volume carries very unique traces of its own history. In the case of *Belgravia*, the whole series has been assembled through copies coming from libraries located in every corner of the British Empire. The book form is only the last step in a production process whose history entails shifts in price, design, and layout. These scattered findings exercise a centrifugal pull that resists the conventions of historiographical narrative.

In discussing the history of *Belgravia* under the direction of Mary Elizabeth Braddon I chose to arrange these findings into two kinds of narratives: one is conventionally diachronic and tells the history of the publication of *Belgravia*. The other is more synchronic: I want to retrace the modalities of reading *Belgravia* in separate monthly issues. Adopting a synchronic perspective means confronting the layered complexity of each issue without assuming it belongs to a larger unity like the bound edition. The material and intellectual content of the magazine—with its illustrations and texts arranged in a specific layout—appears to the reader not only fragmented but potentially aleatory. Readers may have flipped through each issue randomly or constructed a heterogeneous sequence of impressions based on momentary associations to the different contents of the magazine. The historically specific format of the magazine entails a likewise historically specific modality of reading shaped by the contemporary technology of periodical production. In the case of the periodical press, the aesthetic experience of reading the magazine is a combinatory juxtaposition of different elements of culture. While the possible combinatory sequence of articles, novel installments, advertisements, illustrations, poems read in any issue of the miscellaneous magazine may be endless, the *montage* effect juxtaposing literary and nonfictional narrative, text and image, is a constant that needs to be factored in when trying to understand the history of reading practices.

Weeklies and monthly publications are generally preserved in book form, the publisher's annual edition that collects the separate issues in one volume. Archival research, therefore, rarely allows a study of the separate issues of a magazine as they originally circulated. A serial publication goes through a process of reorganization of its material based on two factors: its marketability, that is, its necessary presence on the shelves of a bookseller in manageable book format, and the demands of the reading public. The history of the periodical press is the history of how scattered factuality becomes memorialized into a more homogenous artifact, going from individual issue to bound volume and to complete collection in a library. Every time the periodical circulates in one specific format the reading practices are affected in significant ways. A bound volume entails, besides the loss of important traces of its history, such as original cover with price, front cover illustrations, and advertisements sheets, a different perusal by the reader, who can proceed from issue to issue in reading a narrative that first appeared in installments. The methodology of reading that I followed reconstructs the *first* reception of the periodical issues, that is, the experience of reading fiction and newspaper articles next to one another within each individual monthly issue. This methodology recognizes an important aspect of the temporality of reading separate issues that the bound volume of the magazine and the novel published in book form inevitably alter. In an annual edition, or in a book edition of a serialized novel, any narrative originally appearing in installments joins in the sensorial continuum of the reader's attention protracted over a malleable period of time. By contrast, reading the monthly issues of the magazine separately creates a more pressing dialogue between the contents of each issue. The readers' attention and associations, which the montage effect of print publication complicates by juxtaposing different sections of the magazine, reveal a dialectic nature that opposes the contents of the magazine and transforms the meaning of fact and fiction under the motley stimuli the reader is subject to.

Scholars who have studied the Victorian periodical press have rightly spoken of the intertextual nature that defines the object of their analysis. Some, like Linda Hughes, speak of reading "sideways" when trying to suggest a methodological approach to the vast repositories of our cultural memory contained in periodicals collections. The term intertextuality does suggest that, from the perspective of the reader, perception tends to build some kind of continuity through the faculty of memory, spanning over a single issue or the traces of one's readings over time. Intertextuality, moreover, does suggest that knowledge proceeds by an intertwined accumulation of materials that are somewhat homogenous. In this regard, every form of communication appears to be interchangeable and to be reduced to the metaphorical understanding of a text as, literally, the material fabric that constitutes a given cultural product. I propose, instead, to use the term dialectical to define the practice of reading the periodical press. I do so for two reasons: one is to define the sphere of interest of this book, the dialectics of the "everyday," as Henri Lefebvre defines it. According to Henri Lefebvre, the "everyday" is the area that best facilitates an understanding of the workings of ideology. In this case, the dialectics of the everyday pertains to the specifics of a periodical publication. The content of a periodical publication is encoded in specific genres (fiction, scientific journalism, art criticism, colonial history, etc.). At the same time, the profoundly heterogeneous reverberations that these genres *together* generate indicate that *very* specific and distinct forms of representation are involved. A novel installment read next to a journalistic reportage or an illustrated advertisement implies different epistemological assumptions that the reader may rely upon in processing this information. Reading fiction next to articles means not, I think, reducing both to the universal textual nature of culture but realizing the contrast that lies within the experiential understanding of these cultural formations *together*. The temporality of reading an advertisement in a flash is not the sustained attention required by a novel installment, nor is it the focused belief in the words of a scientific article corroborated by a professional signing the piece. The lingering effects of experiencing each are part of a dialectical process of reading that, while perceiving each component according to specific assumptions, creates a *dialogue* between one cultural form and another, transforming each by virtue of the montage effect that juxtaposes them. The status of each cultural form is, thus, at stake in this exchange: literature may be less trustworthy than science but the lingering effect of reading a sensation novel, the genre more prominent in *Belgravia*, next to a scientific article may paradoxically transform the status of science. Science and literature, market forces and intellectual productions are indeed separate entities reflecting culture through their own prism, but they do produce a *new* dialectical meaning when experienced by juxtaposition from the pages of a magazine. Within the confined materiality of the magazine issue the textual segments of its contents do confront one another, transforming the perception of each cultural form.

This dialectics is twofold: it stimulates the production of new meaning through the juxtaposition of two components: *intellectual* and *emotional* content. The first type, the intellectual dialectic, brings together narrative segments, thus questioning the status of the literary narrative in relation to the scientific or journalistic narrative or vice versa. Each component is processed with different assumptions: the reliability of an article written by a professional specialist engages the reader in a process of absorbing scientific knowledge according to the accepted codes of a specific rhetoric and an unquestionable pretense to an authoritative voice. The simultaneous or slightly deferred viewing of the illustrations highlighting a realistic scene from the fictional narrative, as well as the early illustrated advertisements that I was able to locate, confront the intellectual content of an article according to the conventions of a different medium. The time necessary to process these pictorial representations, as well as the appeal to the reader's interest, are profoundly different; their relation does not link them metaphorically through an intertextual link, that is, through two forms of communication existing in a homogenous continuum. The different media and codes of meaning defining each present a stark opposition on the page that isolates each medium. This marked difference in epistemological status and rhetorical construction requires the reader to bridge the gap between them by reassembling their input in a new meaning that may privilege one over the other, fiction over science, image over text, or transform the understanding of each in relation to one another. This dialectical effect, as mentioned earlier, is not limited to intellectual content. The second type of dialectic effect that I think is important in understanding the practice of reading periodicals involves the emotions associated with the genre of sensation novels published in large numbers in the *Belgravia* magazine when edited by Mary Elizabeth Braddon. Shocking revelations that oftentimes close the installment of the sensation novels serialized in the magazine solicit an emotional investment on the reader's part that peaks at the end of the installment and is then dispersed, but not lost, among the suggestions coming from other articles/media that constitute a monthly issue. The reader cannot read further into the following issues or the following chapters. This dialectical experience is more complex: it forces the epistemological queries that a mystery plot elicits through strong emotional effects to be redirected on the rest of the magazine where other elements of culture reappear. The reader may be shocked by a story of colonial horror like *Bound to John Company* and alternate the emotional impressions recorded in one's memory with an article allegedly claiming the superiority of the British civilization or with an advertisement for a colonial product. At other times, a rhetoric of excessive emotions may pervade a scientific article such as "Is the Sun Dying?" in order to catch the attention of the reader and rivet it. In the latter case, the blurred line between fiction and scientific prose conflates two categories of writing that are distinguished in the table of contents as well as in the reader's understanding of which is a more trustworthy narrative. Can the lure of an advertisement for a luxury item be associated to the disruptive revelations of the sensation novel's plot that question the strict social hierarchy based on a presumed higher moral standard for the upper class, in opposition to the so-called lower classes? If that is the case, a narrative that spins the mystery of class identity and procrastinates its resolution by insinuating suspicions of criminal behavior implicitly questions the status of literature as an escapist pastime and at the same time reveals the fictitious nature of binding social structures. When I call the conflicting pulls that the emotional and intellectual content of the magazine may stir dialectical I do not mean to present an overdetermined tripartite dialectical movement in the representation of class dynamics in the magazine, also because the magazine does not offer a third step in a dialectical movement that may lead to a new phase in history out of the conflicts of class. I nonetheless want to use the term dialectic to point to the stark opposition that the conflicting narratives on class decorum generate in the pages of the magazine through a practice of reading that infiltrated the sphere of the everyday, affecting men and women, in the private and in the public space. I call it dialectical because the implications of the ubiquitous sensation novel's narrative that shapes the editorial choices of *Belgravia* bring together opposing perspectives on what is class distinction, and on the role of the ruling classes in world history; they also question the status of literature as an escapist pastime, thus eliciting a more critical response from the public.

Reconstructing the first reception of sensationalism in Braddon's magazine makes the modality of reading a periodical like *Belgravia* an important moment in the history of mass culture. This mode of assembling different stimuli coming from distinct media through the *montage* effect does not speak only through abstract and chaotic oppositions of fragmented sensations. The model here described relies on the manipulative power that each fragment of culture may have in provoking strong emotions in the public and in redirecting these emotions within the same system of values that guides the other contributions to the magazine issue.

I affixed an epigraph by Benjamin at the opening of the chapter, which says that the historical method is "the philological method applied to a book of life." The philological method does register a multiplicity of sources in an attempt to regress to the reliable text at the source of the transmission of culture. In adapting the philological method to the book of life, in this case print culture, one must imagine not so much the coexistence of variants leading to the most authoritative text through a process of *emendatio*, the process of correcting the flaws in the transmission of a text. A philological approach to the study of the periodical is still possible, albeit not in the terms of a discipline, like philology, that was originally created to read classical and biblical manuscripts. Classical philology, which has shaped the study of literature for two centuries, defines the object of analysis in purely textual terms and in limited number of exemplars; the end result of the philological study of the variants of a manuscript tradition is an authoritative text that is closer to the "intentions" of the author than to the reverberations in the reader's minds. A new philological approach that safeguards the primary methodological importance accorded to close-reading should posit not a single, authoritative origin but a more dispersed idea of origin. The reader of the text of the periodical can, so to speak, activate a text each time in a different manner. A new philological approach to the periodical press must "construct" the present tense of the constellation of meanings that the original reception of the periodical issue among its readers generated. Nineteenth-century media entail a more motley combination of stimuli than a select number of scrolls or a volume may have engendered. The coexistence of narratives and suggestions affecting the reader within and without the material text of the periodical issue are so ephemeral and aleatory that no *stemma codicum*, no chart of the transmission of a text, could map. Modernity has profoundly transformed the idea of the text; reproduction is no longer a matter of copying the source text but rather an instant dissemination of countless exemplars. This is why the methodology of literary studies shaped by traditional philology needs to be reconsidered in order to entertain the new intertextual and intramediatic experience that the industrial age has set in motion. I do not mean to suggest that the experience of the past inevitably escapes us or that no narrative can adequately convey the significance of the past. I want to suggest a new understanding of the text and of its reception, building on the methodology invoked by Linda Hughes, Michel Lund, and Laurel Brake. The media narratives at stake in the periodical press include fiction and fact, advertising and illustrations, poetry and newspaper articles.[2] The reader needs to retain the impression of the many scattered elements of the periodical text and be able to juxtapose and absorb them in what I call a dialectic experience opposing image and text, sensory stimulus and intellectual idea. I mean to subtract the history of the press from the selective linearity of many existing narratives aiming at tracing a theme in a publication; I am more interested in "constructing" the present tense of the reception of the periodical. It is a fragmented present that juxtaposes the input of visual, intellectual, and emotional stimuli in a montage effect that can be recognized also in modernist and postmodernist aesthetics, if we were to take Benjamin's insights on the fragmentation of nineteenth-century modernity into the future.

I do not want with this *caveat* to diminish the historical importance of doing research on the periodical press. Bound volumes or digitized versions of periodical titles build an understanding of the past strictly through the format of the book or the more questionable computer screen, which often does not match or make legible the original page at a glance. Bound volumes and digitized pages from a periodical reflect only one step in the history of the production and circulation of a magazine, and a most removed one from the individual issue that first circulated. The case of the periodical press, and of *Belgravia* in particular, is important because of the scattered elements of cultural formation, such as articles, advertisements, installments of novels, that originally circulated in loose issues that were not perceived as a book. While it is obvious that most nineteenth-century novels appeared in installments, I want to point to the case of *Belgravia* as a significant step in the development of new modalities of reading and of producing mass culture. The magazine, through the popularity of the genre of sensation fiction that spilled over the other media and genres of writing featured in the magazine has accelerated the spread of new modalities of production. Mass culture does not entail only the availability in large numbers of cultural products at increasingly affordable prices, but the creation of a wide network of sensations, often guided by commercial concerns, which transformed the psychological modalities of perception as well as the pri ority accorded to the written text and to the traditional hierarchical arrangement of cultural products. The sensation novels's craze that the magazine capitalized on in the 1860s and amplified throughout the 1880s benefited from the shocking effect of its revelations, in the same way that the culture of modernity as described by Benjamin insisted on episodic, intensified effects stimulating the *flâneur* on a city street. I do not want to simply argue, however, that what constitutes the experience of modernity is only a fragmented perception of chaotic stimuli. While it is true that the examples of Baudelaire read by Benjamin, of Poe in *The Man of the Crowd* and, more importantly, Wordsworth in *The Prelude* suggest a chaotic, impressionistic rendition of modernity based primarily on visual stimuli, the time-bound experience of reading a magazine is more complex. Together with the fleeting appearance of images from illustrations and advertising, the microcosm of the magazine also suggests to the reader a less chaotic sequence of intellectual concepts that appear in the novels or in the newspaper articles. This other kind of fragmentation is less random than it might seem.

The case of *Belgravia* best illustrates both the pervasive nature of multidirectional sensational communication in popular culture and the more normative discursive formations that are interspersed within its textual unit. The magazine was, to my knowledge, the only distinctively sensational literary magazine published during the sensation novel's craze of the 1860s that theorized on the sensational as a category of industrial modernity and arranged its production accordingly. Like some other magazines edited by celebrities of the literary industry, it capitalized on the name of its editor, Mary Elizabeth Braddon, which appeared on the opening page as the "conductor" of the magazine. The metaphor of the conductor implies a convergence of intents among its contributors who, in most cases, benefited from the increasingly widespread practice of signing their copies, thus acquiring both a professional status and a public identity. Dickens' *Household Words* and its sequel *All the Year Round* not only printed Dickens' name on each page, but, to the frustration of many of its brilliant contributors, had many of their articles appear anonymously as the mysterious work of an author that may as well have been Dickens himself.[3] Mary Elizabeth Braddon did brand her product as an extension of her popular persona of author of sensation novels, as the quotation in the front page of her magazine of two of her best-selling titles next to her name would imply.[4] At the same time, however, her successful formula of riveting the audience by overturning the established perception of the affluent class inspired other contributors and emerged throughout the overall editorial choices. *Belgravia* could, therefore, be singled out in the overpopulated market of periodicals as *the* sensational magazine, if not the mouthpiece of a movement, as the articles on the sensational that I discuss in chapter two suggest. Braddon's interest lay not in defining once and for all a sensational formula, or, for that matter, an editorial one, but rather in marking the experience of modernity that sensationalism skillfully represented as an excitingly motley one, at least at first glance. This is realized not only through the personal versions of sensationalism provided by scientists, cultural critics, and journalists who contributed with their articles to the magazine, but, more ostensibly, by serializing up to three or four novels, mostly hers, in each issue of *Belgravia*. The arousal of suspense that gripped the reader at the end of most installments became a trademark of the magazine. To prevent the audience from getting too accustomed to the thrilling effects of the sensation plot to the point of boredom, the fiction appearing monthly declined the verb of sensationalism in new hyphenated forms, such as the sensation-historical novel, the sensation-*bildungsroman*, as well as the more mainstream sensation-domestic novel.[5] Sensational fiction intensified the effects it created on the readers and shaped the experience of reading by transforming general curiosity into a series of fragmented sequences of exciting climaxes interspersed with articles of miscellaneous content, illustrations, and advertisements. What distinguishes *Belgravia* from the countless competitors on the market is that the interaction of literature and nonfiction, splendid illustrations and advertisements for items of consumption were not the product of a chaotic jumble of superficial impressions. The articles published in the magazine defused the intensified emotions deriving from fiction by bringing its demystifying and subversive revelations to the unquestioned order represented by the values of the dominant class, much as the closure of most novels, when read in bound volumes, would do. This applies also to the articles written in accordance to the structures of a sensational rhetoric: the excitement induced by the shocking revelations borrowed from bourgeois sensation novels is contrasted with appeasing generalizations and abstract notions of order that inform the "educational" closing remarks. The time-bound experience of reading a magazine such as *Belgravia* in monthly instalments, therefore, created a distinctive dialectic between text and image, newspaper articles and advertisements, fact and fiction, social order and shattering revelations. The magazine went beyond the visual juxtaposition of images and words, fiction and fact; it also subtly instilled a more normative dynamics that opposed upsetting revelations and more stabilizing abstract notions that the Victorian ruling class believed in. This dialogue between fact and fiction within the magazine paradoxically undermined the feared effects that sensation fiction might have had on its readers and thus reduced it to a disciplined pastime.

From Warwick House, Paternoster Row, to the Global Markets

I consulted the copies of the magazine preserved at the British Library in London, as well as at the University of London Library and at the National Library of Scotland. When I first viewed them, the libraries held the full run of the magazine, including the years following its acquisition in 1876 by Chatto and Windus. No individual issue of the magazine is preserved, except the annual issued around Christmas time: the monthly publications were bound in one volume and sold as part of a series. This practice of selling the magazine in a bound volume that contained all the issues published in one year came after the initial circulation of the separate issues. The magazine became marketable as a volume that had the same semblance of a high culture artifact.[6] The serial aspect conveyed by the publication of volumes covering the yearly production, moreover, stimulated a collector's interest in completeness and in temporal continuity. Bound volumes make a structured unity that extends over time and memorializes the past in a sequence that reproduces an organic view of the unfolding of history. Its pretense to historicity, however, comes inevitably with a selective process that overlooks the synchronic aspects of the publication.

What in fact is preserved in the annual series? The bound volumes create a continuum that is not interrupted by the separate covers of each issue. This sequence of articles and illustrations join in the new status of a marketed product without maintaining significant indicators of its production and reception, like cover illustrations and the fluctuations in cover prices. The apparently complete series creates, therefore, a selective pattern of historical preservation that is further confirmed by the archival holdings. What are left out are also the sheets of advertising that were stitched to the folios of the magazine and at times constituted the back cover of the separate issues. The narratives presented in the advertising, the images that were printed, as well as the kinds of objects that were marketed to the reading public made the perusal of the magazine an even more fragmented experience. By juxtaposing luxury objects, advertisements from shopping centers and private professionals with the already miscellaneous format of the magazine, the monthly issue constitutes a visual and intellectual experience of temporality that is dialectically more complex.[7] What is interesting here is to consider the scope of the distribution of the magazine. This allows me to point to the global trade routes of books and magazine that I discovered, which were already in place in the nineteenth century. A different configuration of the geographical extension of the market of the periodical press shall result from this study.

The full run of the magazine preserved at the British Library in London, which I want to focus on now, does not come from a single collection. What the library holds is a series made of volumes assembled from all parts of the British Empire. Only few volumes of the annual publications that are held at the British Library appear to have been produced and preserved in London. In many instances, the sequence is completed by means of volumes coming from other collections, parochial or public. Volumes ten–twelve, for instance, come from the Blaxhall Parish Library, while volume thirteen carries the stamp of the Public Library of South Australia in Adelaide, and volume nineteen that of the Dublin Library. The presence in the collection of these issues from other archives chronicles the history of the global production and circulation of the bound volumes. The map of circulation of the periodical press in individual issues interestingly extends beyond the borders of Great Britain and beyond the network of national syndicated papers that have been studied in recent scholarship. The intentional but partly accidental survival of these volumes draws a larger picture of the distribution of a finished product, the bound volume. What I want to discuss now is the distribution not of the bound volumes but of the separate monthly issues in an attempt to begin charting the map of trade routes that the initial phase of production drew. I want to stress that distribution, particularly of this magazine, was a global phenomenon that not only points to usually overlooked trade routes but hints to a practice of cultural formation that reached out to the English-speaking public in Europe as well as in India and Australia; it involved dealers and publishers in Jamaica as well as in Constantinople.

The bound volumes in a library suggest the presence of the periodical in a collection, whose aim is completeness in chronological order. Publishers, after circulating the issues of the magazine periodically, bound them in volumes and sold the series as a different product, exclusive of advertisements and covers. What I want to consider here is the circulation of the ephemeral product of each issue of the magazine. The case of *Belgravia* is interesting because, unlike other periodicals, records survive detailing the names and locations of traders and booksellers involved in the sale of the magazine on a global scale. By focusing on the product as it initially circulated in a competitive and expanding market, historical research can thus access the existing records on advertising companies, on fashion and consumer trends that made the publication of the magazine possible. The bound volume, by contrast, appears as an abstraction, a projection of what the magazine represented, of the status it gained; it is not an indicator of the economic and social process that made it possible. The whole run of the *Belgravia* magazine at the British Library, being completed by volumes from the far provinces of the British Empire, does hint at global distribution but eludes some of the questions posed by this research.

To my knowledge, the existing scholarship on the British and French periodical press that I consulted when I first started my research dealt only with the national distribution network. The commercial network of distribution reached, in the case of *Belgravia*, a wide array of centers in non-English-speaking countries in which booksellers and at times publishers were in charge of the sale of the magazine. *Macmillan's Magazine* of November 1867, for example, lists its distributors in the front page but the territorial expansion is limited to the United Kingdom with agents in Edinburgh (Edmonston and Douglas), Glasgow (James Maclehose), Dublin (W.H. Smith), Oxford (John Henry and J. Parker), the English-speaking colonies or former colonies with New York (William & Roger), Sydney (W. Maddock), Melbourne (George Robertson), and Adelaide (W.C. Rigby), and only one dealer from the European continent in Leipzig (Alphons Duerr). The list of distributors of *Belgravia*, instead, helps to draw a more global map of the book market. In Berlin, Braddon's and Maxwell's commercial partner was F. Schneider & Co.; in Vienna W. Braumueller; in Athens C.W. Wilberg; in Turin and Florence H. Loescher. Of these companies, only the latter has been publishing books up to now, focusing mostly on textbooks for primary and secondary education. In Paris, Giovanni Antonio Galignani and his English wife Anne Parsons ran a bookshop, which is still operating, and established a circulating library in the early part of the nineteenth century. As publishers they issued reprints of English books and tourist guides.[8] In Leipzig, Brockhaus's catalogue included medical books as well as books on the history of England. H.A. Kramers in Rotterdam sold together with *Belgravia* copies of *Frederick Douglass*. In Brussels, Muquardt offered a bibliography on European vampires as well as an 1870 edition of *Le Livre de Parfums* and the essay *Le Socialisme Contemporain*. Commercial routes extended overseas to New York, where Wilner and Rogers distributed the magazine. British trade reached Constantinople and the books that were distributed by S.H. Weiss included wide-ranging travel books for "Turkey and Asia." In Calcutta, R.C. Lepage & Co. had in stock the 1866 edition of *Rammohun Roy* by Kissory Chand Mittra, while Thacker Spink & Co. sold a *Liberal Education in India* by Nagendra Nath Ghose, esq. and *The British Jugernath* [*sic*]*: Free Trade! Fair Trade! Reciprocity! Retaliation!* In Adelaide, W.C. Rigby started a bookselling activity in 1859 on Hindley Street and included an 1861 edition of J.S. Mill's *A Plea for Democracy*. In Kingston, Jamaica, De Cordova Mc Dougall & Co. displayed *Belgravia* at 62, Harbour Street and in 1866 had also *The Report of the Jamaica Royal Commission* available.

The titles from the catalogues of these booksellers suggest that global trade circulated a wide variety of cultural products, reflecting the miscellaneous interests shown in the table of contents of *Belgravia*. The fragmentation of the market created a wide reading public that extended beyond the national borders of English society. *Belgravia*'s global distribution pattern complicates the model of a solely British middle-class reception or, rather, it carries, along trade routes, the discursive practices of the British bourgeoisie by means of a luring title that evokes an aristocratic neighborhood of London and projects social privilege and economic distinction on the world scale. The distribution pattern of the periodical press is of particular importance as it anticipates and tests the transnational routes of contemporary globalized economy.

Despite the obviously bourgeois political and social referent of the magazine, a closer look at the publishing and editing practices shows *Belgravia* to be a unique example in the history of miscellanies. The fragmentation of reading a magazine with fiction and journalistic articles, with text and illustrations, created a dialectical juxtaposition between the typically sensational plots of novels for which the editor was famous and the content of the magazine. Cultural formation in the magazine worked by endorsing a bourgeois ideology through advertisements and articles on upper-class life and at the same time by showing the construction of prestige in the sensational narratives that revealed the hidden origins of middle-class decorum. This dialectical opposition between amplifying the gilded appearances of upper-class distinction and deconstructing them by showing the proximity of upper-class characters to crime is unique in the history of Victorian periodicals of the 1860s. When *Belgravia* first appeared under the direction of Mary Elizabeth Braddon, the magazine was edited as a miscellany, in the long established tradition that comprises Dickens' *Household Words* and its sequel *All The Year Round*. With Dickens' weekly magazines the monthly *Belgravia* shared a wide range of interests in reality and fiction, and the attempt to create a wide and abstract reading public. While Dickens' abstract notion of social organization is defined in the opening remarks of the first issue published in March 1850, Braddon's magazine engages in a more dialectical definition of the reading experience and it does so by insisting on visual representation in a degree that Dickens does not.

Dickens' opening remarks specifically address a public that included men and women, the laboring classes and the affluent ones, while avoiding any specific issue related to what the opening remarks of the first issue called "the brutal facts" of any specific aspect of society. The solely material interest in reality is replaced by the abstract idea of all-inclusiveness that would make readers more "tolerant of each other" and more "thankful for the privilege of living in this summer-dawn of time." The acknowledged hope is that "the multitudes" could be "moved by one sympathy." The miscellany aspect of the magazine, therefore, offered a broad view of a panoramic society while projecting into future time the hopes for any improvement. Futurity, therefore, neutralized the "good and evil" by leveling the two opposites in a far-sighted trust in the "progress of mankind."[9]

The idea of progress is in Dickens a guiding principle and a symbolic vision of the mind that magnetically attracts all the scattered elements of the magazine and by extension of reality. This cohesive mind's view includes abstract subjects organized under the social structure of the household, as the title suggests, and extends its temporality into a cyclical time "all the year round." Named after the aristocratic neighborhood in London, *Belgravia* offered at the cost of one shilling both fiction, which was predominant with as many as three novels per issue, often by Braddon herself, as well as articles on science, politics, and economy. The miscellaneous character of the titles representing different elements of society is the key established aspect of the genre. The title chosen by Braddon, however, points visually and symbolically to the privileged space of an urban elite that is both the distant mirage of a rising middle-class reading public and a social construct. The magazine offers the trappings and views of a ruling class while deconstructing its dominance through the fiction published in it. Many of the novels of the sensational kind, in fact, present a distinctive narrative pattern that de-fetishizes the decorous rituals of the bourgeoisie. The thrill of periodical narratives that is repeated at every installment stages uncanny revelations that question bourgeois status by insinuating the close link between social distinction and crime. The narratives ultimately show the efforts at preserving decorum by a class that parades its exterior distinction through social mannerism and glamorous, polished glitter. *Belgravia* is a mentally recognizable image, a social symbol created by synecdoche, that is reinforced and at the same time deconstructed by the material and intellectual contents of the magazine. This configuration of the public of the magazine is unique, in my view, in the history of nineteenth-century British periodicals. In order to better explain what the reception of the magazine entailed, I now want to discuss the history of the publication of the magazine and underline the specificity of its layout.

Beyond the Miscellany: Fragmentation and Abstract Notions of Time and Space

The first issue of *Belgravia* was published in London in February 1867 at the cost of one shilling.[10] The name of the editor and popular novelist Mary Elizabeth Braddon appeared on the frontispiece of the magazine, together with a reminder of her most successful titles, namely *Lady Audley's Secret* and *Aurora Floyd*. The full description of the frontispiece of the magazine, with the name of Mary Elizabeth Braddon listed as "author of" followed by a couple of titles, appears to be similar to any of the listings in a bookseller's catalogue. In the same manner, in fact, a catalogue of a bookseller or of one of the many circulating libraries introduced a new item on the market by evoking an established and memorable success by the same author. Published by Braddon's husband's company, Maxwell, that was located at Warwick House on Paternoster Road, London, the magazine enjoyed a remarkable success for a decade, reaching a circulation that amounted to twelve thousand copies in May 1876,[11] and a much higher number for the annual editions, issued in December and August, the winter edition being more popular with a circulation of at times thirty thousand copies (see figure 1.1).[12] It was sold in 1876 to the publisher Chatto and Windus, with "all copyrights and unpublished MSS and woodcuts and desegns [*sic*]" for a "sum equal to the nett [*sic*] profits of the magazine for the three years preceeding [*sic*] the last number, to be payed by bills divided into twenty four equal monthly instalments [*sic*]."[13] A legal contention soon arose on the copyright of unpublished works, some of them by Mary Elizabeth Braddon. Chatto revised its initial offer to include in the deal all unpublished works, by committing to pay only for what he "may care to take" (March 16, [187]6). Following Maxwell's decision to be represented by Robertson & Sons law firm, Chatto deemed the settlement as "excessive" for material that needed editing (April 12, [187]6) and later in 1876 requested to be "furnished with a list and means of authentication" (November 28, [187]6) to sort out which of the articles were by Braddon. Their correspondence on this issue, on the copyright of woodcuts and on the preclusion to publish an abridged version of "Tom Sawyer," went on for years. In 1882 the argument was still on the grounds whether the sale of 1876 referred to the title of the magazine only or to the right to reprint also articles published in *Belgravia*. Maxwell's involvement in the sale of new works by his wife did not fare any better. In 1883 Chatto is willing to offer L 250 to purchase the serial rights of a new story by Braddon who initially requested 1,000 guineas, and was even willing to reduce it to 500, inclusive of the American and Australian serial rights.[14] At that point Maxwell dismissed any previous correspondence "all off as if never made," insisting that Braddon's increased popularity made her "the strongest weaver of plot-interest and the most consecutive and constructive story writer" (October 16, 1883). The year after, the publication of "Ishmael" was rejected due to the "large number of first class works [. . .] already in preparation, as well as the depressed state of business of the circulating libraries" (August 25, 1884). The new editor of the *Belgravia* magazine, which was clearly not Mary Elizabeth Braddon, changed the format and the generic features of the publication whose profits soon dwindled.[15]

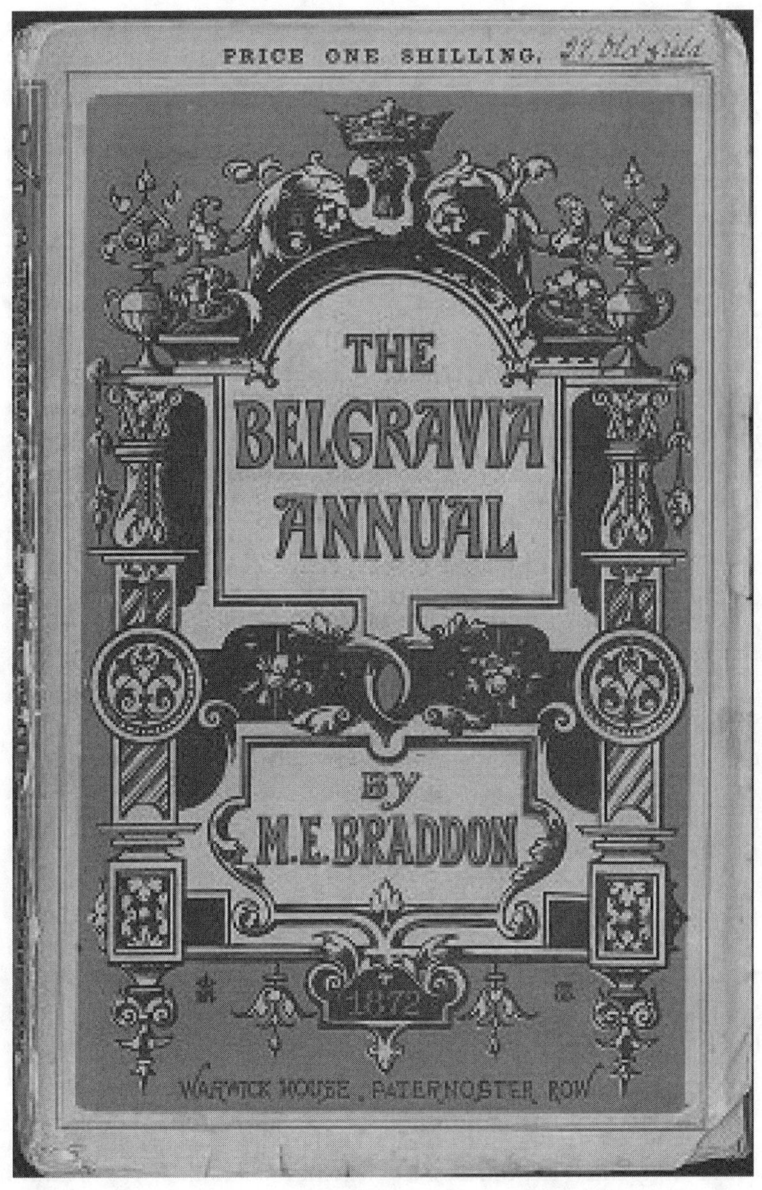

Figure 1.1 *The Belgravia Annual*, 1872—Cover.

What was the successful formula launched by Braddon? Each issue opened with a one-page plate illustrating a climactic moment in the plot of the first novel, usually by Braddon. A similar plate introduced the installments of long running serial novels. There were as many as three titles published in installments at times all by Braddon through her real name or her *nom de plume* Babington White. *Birds of Prey* by Braddon inaugurated the magazine in November 1866 and by June 1867 a new novel by Babington White was added, *Circe, or Three Acts in the Life of an Artist.* Two months after, another new novel by Braddon appeared, *Dead-Sea Fruit.* The order of the publication of the various titles allowed for the most recent novel to be given priority for few months, before the editor assigned a newer one the most prominent spot of opening the magazine. In some cases there was an interest in keeping a presumably successful title in the opening slot for months to come, as in the case of *Dead-Sea Fruit* that opened the issue even when a new novel by "the author of 'Lady Audley's Secret' etc.," namely *Charlotte's Inheritance*, closed the number of April 1868 with the first installment. Some novels were published with the quasi-anonymous marketable phrasing "by the author of," as in the case *Diana Gay*, attributed to the writer of "Bella Donna," "Never Forgotten" "etc. etc." This is also the case of *Stern Necessity*, attributed to the author of "Poor Humanity," "No Church," "Mattie, a Stray," "etc." and also the case of *Three to One, or Some Passages out of the Life of Amicia Lady Sweetapple*, by the author of "Annals of an Eventual Life." All of these quasi-anonymous novels were published in the second half of the magazine but *Bound to John Company, or, the Adventures and Misadventures of Robert Ainsleigh*, to which I will return in chapter four, opened the July 1868 issue anonymously.[16] Justin McCarthy is credited as the author of *My Enemy's Daughter* that opened the November 1868 number and his other works "Paul Massie" and "The Waterdale Neighbour" were listed on the title page. Short stories are usually credited, while poems, which, as I mentioned before, are usually illustrated, are either signed, initialed—there are some compositions by M.E.B., including the lyrics for a musical valentine—or anonymous.[17]

Mary Elizabeth Braddon's novels are the predominant contribution to the magazine's fiction. Besides the titles mentioned, *The Splendid Stranger*, *Fanton's Quest*, *Milly Darrell*, *The Lovels of Arden*, *To the Bitter End*, *Strangers and Pilgrims*, *Lost for Love*, *Hostages to Fortune*, *Joshua Haggard's Daughter* were all serialized in the *Belgravia* magazine. The magazine offers, therefore, significant material for a philological study of "how Braddon worked," for a close reading of the features and structures of her literary workshop. I am not interested here, however, in retracing the intertextual reverberations of Braddon's novels' plots as they appear in the magazine format by means of analogies, overlapping characters and situations that migrated from one novel to the next, presumably written about the same time. I want, however, to return to the master plot of sensation fiction in chapter two where I consider the massive output of this serial production of novels in terms of interchangeable narrative functions, a term I borrow from Vladimir Propp, which the wide public of readers could easily recognize and grow addicted to.

I want now to describe how an individual issue organizes the appearance of fiction—poetic and narrative—in the bigger unity of the magazine. The editing practices and the publishing technology used in *Belgravia* make the many separate elements that constituted the fragmented unity of the magazine more outstanding. The magazine layout isolates each contribution in a full page that is not arranged in more columns like in Dickens' magazines. *Belgravia* abolishes, therefore, the continuum in print that other publications, such as *Once a Week* or Dickens' *Household Words*, created on the pages of a two-column magazine. The miscellaneous format of other contemporary periodicals such as the *Fortnightly Review* share with *Belgravia* the juxtaposition of articles and novelistic installments but do not have in common with it the specific sensational referent that Braddon's magazine was associated with. In the *Belgravia* magazine, each fragment of cultural production stands out and, by doing so, it engages in a dialectical relation to the rest of the magazine. *Belgravia*, moreover, complicates the simply textual antithesis between fiction and fact that it shared with other publications, by means of its remarkable presence of visual stimuli of different kinds derived from several sources, such as the illustrations to novels and poems, the contemporary technology of print advertising and the social symbolism associated with its title. All these visual and intellectual stimuli shaped a historically specific kind of reading that is important in the context of late Victorian periodicals. I discuss the implication of the visual and narrative stimuli deriving from the advertising in chapter four, where I consider the only few surviving separate issues of the magazine that preserved the advertising omitted in the manufacturing of the bound volumes, and in chapter five, where I trace the parallel development of sensationalism in periodical literature and in pre-cinematic entertainment.

I am now going to address the mosaic of journalistic contributions to the magazine and the discursive practices that circulated through them. As diverse as they may be, these discursive practices were still condensed in the symbolic mental image of the Belgravia neighborhood that gave the magazine its title. This magazine is important for it exemplifies how spatial symbolism worked as an intellectual magnet that united the scattered elements of its content and brought together the variety of readers it targeted. The miscellany format of *Belgravia*, by addressing issues as scattered as patent inventors, guns manufacturers, lawmakers, and practitioners, built at the same time a symbolic system that allowed these fragmented views to converge under the cultural image of the eponymous London upper-class neighborhood. Cursory views at culture and society that focus on specific categories of social organization, such as the military, the clergy, and manufacturers, are published next to advertisements and illustrations depicting marketed items and realistic scenes taken from the life of the fictional characters. The visual cues contained in the magazine overall suggest a sense of cohesiveness, even though the editorial choices addressed a wide-ranging array of specific concerns meant primarily for a varied public of upper-middle-class readers. The articles published in the magazine offer, therefore, a panoramic view of a British urban and imperial society while pointing to a mental image of secluded privilege and fashionable social order that the title *Belgravia* would point to. This homogenizing effect is achieved particularly in the articles that redefined the notions of time and space; in such instances, a move toward abstraction and homogeneity supersedes the apparently fragmented coverage of disparate topics. The conceptualization that the Belgravia neighborhood entails goes from multiple perspectives to structured order. While the presentation of both time and space participate in this move, it is the mental visualization associated to space that makes the most cogent symbolism that brings together the many multidirectional aspects of the magazine.

Nonfiction contributions to *Belgravia* often present a descriptive report on exemplary samplings of scientific enquiry that ranged from meteorites and the life on Earth[18] to revised views of the explorers' accounts on wildlife in the colonies,[19] or to ethological studies on the life of animals. A more theorizing aim structures the articles on fixed notions of, for instance, psychological types, namely Escott's categories of "vacillating subjects" and "communicative persons."[20] An even more systematic view emerges from an article on the related effects of the 3 percent bank rate's increase[21] following the 1866 financial crisis, or on the uses of electricity.[22] What I have just presented in choosing to focus on different degrees of theorization that can be evinced in some of the articles published in *Belgravia* is a move from fragmented perspectives on specific topics (wildlife, meteorites) to general views confirming broad categories ("vacillating subjects" and "communicative persons," vagaries of the financial world). This move signals a shift from random samplings to structured systematic knowledge. I want to observe that a similar trend, a move to an abstract notion of order, informs the whole magazine despite its apparently miscellaneous content. This is especially true in the case of articles that discuss current events, which I examine next, and those that cover a large number of localities scattered over several continents.

Few of the articles in *Belgravia* deal with a specific historical event; the majority of contributions tend to disregard temporal specificity in favor of a more widespread and abstract notion of temporal continuity. The map charting places of interest for the magazine, similarly, offers a move from the cultural specificity of a distinct location in a foreign country to the domesticized space of established trade routes and upper-class tourism. Through the vagaries of journalistic prose, what emerges is an implicit structure of meaning that appears beyond the fragmentation of the superficial perusal of the magazine. The fragmented layout of the magazine apparently destabilizes a structured order of knowledge of reality by focusing empirically on a wide variety of topics; it does so, however, while repeatedly hinting at a symbolic cohesiveness that brings together the mosaic of perspectives and disparate stimuli that constitute the magazine.

In dealing with time, the magazine occasionally offers articles that are a response to current events, such as parliamentary sessions on reform bills, or debates on extended voting rights for women. Parliamentary representation is criticized in the reported cases in which elected MPs change their political creed while in office. The defeat of the 1866 reform bill is presented resignedly, while the parliamentary debate on extending suffrage to women reports in November 1868 the refusal of an attempt at proposing the word "person" in law-making procedures. International politics limits its span to unavoidable foreign news such as the feared experiment of the Paris Commune with its believed suspicious lurking allies among Charles Kinley's Christian Socialist followers, which are stigmatized in an article dating 1875 by T.H.S. Escott.[23] Imperial expansion puts Central Asia on the spotlight with the second Afghan military campaign of 1869. These are all the references to contemporary history that can be found in a ten-year time span. More than expanding the purport of specific events, however, the magazine creates a sense of continuity by establishing patterns of time consumption that insist more on the ahistorical temporality of leisure activities, considered to be an occasion for educational growth for all classes. Articles on museum schedules, Sunday lectures, shopping for furniture, and those on marketed objects are more frequent and they all suggest a more manageable and abstract dimension of time.[24] The specific event, therefore, is overlooked to make it disappear in a more malleable and continuous temporal extension. As in the case of time-specific issues of political debates, the magazine likewise privileges established practices mediated through routine and abstraction when it comes to presenting the diversity of places it addresses. The places of interest draw a map of renowned localities where British rule is a given. The territory charted is a homogenous land of global tourism that follows the schedule of a domesticized time made of wintering in Aegypt,[25] spending spring in Syria,[26] while bric-a-brac hunting in Europe all the year round. The leisured classes benefiting from this time free of the restraints of production can choose Japan[27] or the Bosphorous as their destinations,[28] Turkey[29] or the West Indies.[30] In all these locations where otherness disrupts established notions of cultural identity the traveler preserves an intellectual image of a structured space that is built on "national and imperial boast"[31] coupled with a "proud disdain for the conquered,"[32] a boast and a disdain that are pitted against ruins as well as plantations, monuments, and "subjected races."[33]

While the representation in the magazine of both time and space constructs a subliminal image of abstraction, it is space that makes the most prominent category of intellectual organization for the miscellaneous representation of sites and social practices of the Victorian age. Space is also the most recognizable category for the reader, considering that illustrations of bourgeois settings, as well as the title of the magazine, reinforce their obviously visual appeal. Space is the structuring symbol for a reading public that collects diverse perspectives in the articles and unsettling revelations in the fiction published within the magazine, while conflating the diverse stimuli coming from fiction and nonfiction under the title *Belgravia*. The London neighborhood that appears on the cover of the magazine helps not only to build an easily recognizable product identity but also serves as a magnetic spell for its target audience. Urban space is the focus of a series of articles that describe and retrace the history of several London locations. The series titled "London Squares," "London Palaces," "London Pubs," and "London Theatres," by Walter Thornbury, investigate urban sites to reveal their history, which has to do with aristocratic ownership, with urban development to accommodate new classes of dwellers, and with current attractions such as resident celebrities, exclusive club membership, or entertaining theater productions. These instances of urban planning, of selective gatherings at pubs, and of captivating theater productions all show that private class identity finds a natural extension of its status in public settings. The space of the city articulates a symbiotic relationship between subjects and buildings, between class formations and public places such as the square, the pub, or the theater. These places of interest constitute a material and symbolic expression of a dominant ideology whose teeming symbolic production circulates its discursive formations in the global market of the periodical press. The case of the pub and, better, of the theater are the best examples of the dialectical exchange between the material and the ideological, between public and private spheres that are formulated here in spatial terms. In the pub, the privacy of the interior reinstates a communal sense of belonging to its individual members; in the theater, the display of rank is instated in the disposition of audience members within the architecture of the building and at the same time reflected through the figurations on stage. The theater, with its ephemeral representations of class relations, constitutes a more porous dynamic between visual representation and the appearances of social status; the theater may be the best equivalent of Braddon's brand of sensational fiction and, one may argue, of Braddon's editorial practices in *Belgravia*. In the theater one can find a parallel of the impact that sensation fiction had on the Victorian reading public. Theater functions as a reminder of, and also as a metaphor for, the episodic appearance of status that sensation fiction and a magazine such as *Belgravia* capitalized on. This may be true not only because Braddon started her career in the 1850s as a poor actress when pressed by economic need to support her mother and sister, but also because the theater was also a training ground and background for some of its contributors, such as George Augustus Sala and Edmund Yates. The theater, however, is not simply a source for some of Braddon's tales. In a manner similar to the theatrical procession of characters on stage the magazine shows the fictional construction of social status; in insisting on the fiction of social distinctions the magazine deconstructs bourgeois decorum by showing its performative core. This is achieved not only through the plots of the sensation novels but through the dialectical exchange between representation and fact, intellectual structure and fleeting impression, fictional revelations and realistic mystifications. I am not underlining the theatrical quality of the publication and of sensation novels in general.[34] I want rather to call attention to the technological medium of the periodical press that made the intellectual juxtaposition of sensational fiction and journalistic articles, advertising and illustrations, a dialectical experience for the reader. The abstract space of a London neighborhood evoked by the title of *Belgravia* defines a certain kind of subjectivity and at the same time questions it through the sensational fiction published in it. The paradoxical associations inspired by *Belgravia* hint at the criminal making of the dominant structure of power. Social status is reinforced through the advertising of precious items and sophisticated shopping venues. The political views of the upper classes are filtered through the homogenizing representation of established ideas on time and space that emerge from the magazine's fragmentary coverage of the world. The fiction, on the other hand, offers realistic scenarios and weaves fables of an unsettling kind. The novels tell uncomfortable truths while advertisements and articles reinforce an image of society that is founded on appearance. In the pages of *Belgravia*, therefore, mental images of class decorum, represented by advertisements and illustrations, confront the suspicions of criminal workings that linger in the reader's mind after having read a novelistic installment. The normative power that *Belgravia* achieved through visual cues extends beyond the subliminal level of instilling social mores through the act of reading, which can be applied to other Victorian periodicals. Braddon's magazine created a more dialectical representation of culture by juxtaposing print image and text, mental picture and empirical knowledge, and, more specifically, thrilling revelations of the sensational plot and appeasing discursive formations. The format of the magazine had a predominantly visual lure that Dickens' abstract and blinded vision of all-encompassing universality of feeling had not. The experience of reading *Belgravia* was, again, more complex: the magazine alternated written text with pictorial stimuli from prints, casual associations suggested by the *montage* effect of its editorial choices, and symbolic condensations, like in the representation of urban and global space. The practice of reading the macrotext of *Belgravia,* with fiction next to articles and illustrations, confirmed the mental image of the upper-middle-class target audience while at the same time problematizing its status though the thrilling revelations of the sensational plot. I will return to the specificity of the magazine in chapter two where I discuss the narrative functions of the sensational plot in the macrotext of the *Belgravia* magazine.

Chapter 2

Abstract Order and Fleeting Sensations: The Aesthetics of Fragmentation in Mary Elizabeth Braddon's *Belgravia*

Just as the entire mode of existence of human collectives changes over long historical periods, so too does their mode of perception

—Walter Benjamin, *The Work of Art in the Age of its Reproducibility*

Scholarly work on the history of the practices of reading have stressed the importance, when discussing the reception of the periodical press, of the intertextual experience constituted by reading a periodical.[1] Rather than defining this experience as intertextual, a term that carries the implication that all materials, as texts, are communication acts, I choose to define this experience as dialectical, in order to take into consideration the specifics of each medium and the complex production of meaning that reading the periodical press through the process of *montage* entails. The "dialectics of the everyday" that the periodical press exemplifies presents a wide array of stimuli—visual and textual—that are encoded in specific media and genres. Each medium appears to the reader as a separate kind of communication that follows different conventions. The separate components of the magazine, therefore, require different forms of attention on the reader's part. A glance at an advertisement does not require the same attention as a scientific article. The lingering emotions elicited by one installment of a sensation novel, moreover, accompany the reader while the more reassuring voice of, for instance, a newspaper article defuses its emotional impact. The dialogical relation between the heterogeneous components of the magazine entails the constant negotiation of the reader's emotions and thoughts. From this opposition between different stimuli that are assembled in the reader's consciousness a new meaning is created, or, rather, the intended meaning of the novel or of the nonfictional piece changes in relation to the other components. Shocking revelations from sensation novels are redirected toward more reassuring articles that reinstate the dominant values of the culture they belong to. Taken per se, however, the sensational revelations in a narrative installment from a single issue of a magazine have the potential to demystify the very values that the rest of the magazine identifies with. When a novel appeared in *Belgravia* it took a whole month before the action could proceed, and several months before the closure of the plot could resolve the conflicts by reinstating dominant values. A periodical issue in its original form of circulation, therefore, creates a more complex and less overdetermined reception, a type of reading that constantly shifts focus, emotional involvement, and intellectual interpretation as the reader is dialectically confronted with the fragmentary components of the magazine issue. The format of the magazine, in other words, exemplifies the fragmentation inherent to nineteenth-century print and urban commodity culture.

The idea of fragmentation has a long history dating back to the scientific discoveries of the Baroque age that shattered the perfect unity of the Ptolemaic universe and created the first artistic landscape of obsessively repeated units or fragments of decorative motifs. This decentralizing poetics appeared in the organic-like decorations of an architectonic façade, in the complex trajectory of gazes in Baroque painting, and in the likewise painterly multiplication of foci of vision well known to the artists of the Northern Renaissance. Eighteenth-century and Romantic culture feature a persistent fascination with the landscape of archeological ruins and the fragmented mode, which informs both writing and the perception of history. While for many writers—Schlegel *in primis*—fragmentation entailed an intuition and an aspiration to a lost unity, the form of fragmentation that I discuss here applies specifically to the fragmentation that the process of industrialization and urban modernity introduced. Fragmentation surfaces in different artistic practices inextricably tied to the industrial means of production and signifies primarily a splintering of the many narratives of preindustrial culture. In the landscape of modernity, the scattered remains of this dynamic explosion of possible views lie in no random abandonment but are constantly reworked into the systematic meaning introduced by the universal referent of market economy. The apparently chaotic jumble of suggestions associated to the sensorium of urban modernity, therefore, is not completely aleatory. The sensational overkill of modernity does question the traditional understanding of narrative continuity, which relies on structured order; the juxtaposition of different media and suggestions, however, becomes a new, more dialectical narrative, which the minds of the readers grow accustomed to. The resulting *montage* effect of the new aesthetic experience of modernity that periodicals exemplify is not absolutely incoherent; the juxtaposition of heterogeneous stimuli within the pages of the individual issue calls for a renegotiation of the meaning, status, and reliability of each component of the magazine issue in relation to one another: the status of fiction and fact, image and text is constantly redefined. In the case of *Belgravia*'s individual issues, the content of the novelistic installment at first glance undermines quite directly the accepted norms of proper social behavior that the community of readers, attracted by the title of the magazine associated to an upscale neighborhood, shares. The demystifying effect of the sensational rupture, however, is constantly redirected and defused by interacting visually and intellectually with the rest of the magazine. The doubts the sensation plot casts on the official, constructed notion of propriety, however, are easily rearranged by the more reassuring narratives surrounding the fiction. Modernity produces aesthetic and emotional "shocks" that undermine traditional forms of understanding; this moment, however, is only a *pars destruens* (the deconstructive part) in a larger process that entails, as a *pars construens* (the constructive part), the circulation of new narratives that reconstitute a "new" sense of order and meaning.

The practice of reading *Belgravia* in monthly installments reveals an important link between the early forms of modernity introduced by industrialization and what scholars focusing on twentieth-century history have commonly defined as mass culture. Theodore Adorno, for instance, has rightly pointed out the normative quality inherent in many apparently spontaneous manifestations of popular culture. The explicitly sensational content of the literature published in the *Belgravia* magazine makes this publication a fundamental one in a discussion of the history of mass culture, at a specific time, the decade of the 1860s, which is usually overlooked to focus instead on the *fin de siècle* as the starting point of mass culture. *Belgravia* is a site of dialectical exchange between fact and fiction, illustration and text, constructed meaning associated to a London neighborhood and its global coverage. This cultural bricolage can emerge from reading other periodicals as well. Like other periodicals, *Belgravia* speaks through the *montage* effect that reading a single issue as a complete unit may create. What is peculiar to *Belgravia*, however, and significant in the history of the press, is that the magazine offers a self-conscious elaboration of what sensationalism means. The "sensational," a common denominator for many marketing strategies aiming to catch the reader's attention, is presented within a larger theory of culture that is semiological in scope.

I shall discuss here first the genre of sensation fiction through the recurrent narrative functions common to some of the most prominent writers in this tradition. Second, I shall read the defense of the sensational in relation to contemporary art criticism to outline the contrast between the fleeting impressions of the sensational and a traditional understanding of transcendental unity as the foundation of knowledge and art. The narrative functions capitalizing on the shocking effects of surprising turns in the plot are part of the same cultural system that the articles on the sensational attempt to theorize on. The sensational and fragmented features of the genre share their rhetoric with the contemporary communication media of the press, advertising, and popular entertainment. I want to stress here that the narrative functions of the sensation novel, the fragmented mode of its narrative, have two important implications. The first is that the fragmented mode is not only a reflection of the cultural forces of the age but also a premonitory anticipation of the modernist aesthetics of fragmentation, which is applied here, through a popular culture artifact, to narrative development. The second implication is that fragmentation in the late Victorian age was never experienced per se; it was always woven into a larger theory of culture. The double bind linking fragmentation on one hand and intellectual theorizing on the other one, thus, defines *the* epistemological model for nineteenth-century theorists of culture.

Fragmented Sensationalism

Before returning to the defense of the sensational I want to discuss the genre of sensation fiction through its interchangeable narrative functions. I use the term "narrative functions" borrowing from the study of folklore that Vladimir Propp has conducted. The popularity of the genre of sensational fiction and the massive output of titles went together in simplifying the plots of these novels to meet the tastes and demands of a larger public. Popular fiction, therefore, invites a formalist reading by means of a study of its narrative functions, which are usually associated with other forms of popular culture, like the fairy tale.[3] A distinctive function in particular, the fragmented peaks of emotional excess, borrowed from melodrama, became canonical with the popularity of the genre.[4] I want to underline, however, that the sensation novelists of the 1860s, while employing many narrative functions of the genre, presented specific stylistic features that distinguish each from being simply lumped into one category, "the sensation novelist."

"Sensation novel," before becoming a category of literary history, was originally a marketing label for the successful outputs of novels by authors as diverse as Mrs. Wood, Wilkie Collins, and Mary Elizabeth Braddon. The sensation novel came to identify in the 1860s a narrative form that blended traditional elements of popular fiction in a successful formula that the expanded market of serial fiction made fashionable for several decades, before migrating to newer forms of popular entertainment, like silent film. Two factors in particular contributed to the increase in the production and circulation of periodicals serializing sensation fiction: a cheaper kind of paper imported from North Africa, and the abolition of taxes on paper, advertising, and the circulation of print material. As a result, the production of periodicals expanded to an unprecedented degree.[5] The sensation genre thrived in the late-Victorian epoch that was reaping the results of its policies supporting unfaltering trade, imperial expansion, and parliamentary reforms that gave recognition to new political agents. The public discourse contributed to constituting a national identity that justified, not without being questioned, the nation's claim to imperial power, while the expanding networks of production and consumption infiltrated many aspects of the everyday, including gendered structures of social relations. Trade, empire, and social roles became pervasive discursive practices that circulated in every social stratum also through popular culture. Novels, magazines, and popular forms of entertainment elaborated and circulated coded behaviors while infiltrating the public and the private spheres with the luring visibility of commodity culture and the implications of the expanding and triumphant market economy. During the roughly ten years in which *Belgravia* was edited by Mary Elizabeth Braddon the magazine benefited from the extraordinary commercial success of a genre, known through earlier periodical publications, that broke the conventional progression of novelistic narration with unsettling challenges to the structure of power that these narratives implied. Authors such as Mrs. Wood, Wilkie Collins, and Mary Elizabeth Braddon, while differing significantly in their literary style and in the poetics of sensation, all shared the conventions of the nineteenth-century bourgeois novel. Their understanding of the sensational changed, as they identified it either with melodramatic codes of feeling, or made it more effective through references to visual narrative cues. The *incipit* of the novel typically presents a domestic scene of familial affect enclosed in the private space of the home or transcended in the abstract social value of the very same house seen and described from the outside. The view of the more or less splendid mansion, thus, anticipates the interest of the characters in the social status of the family and motivates their actions in the market economy of the marriage plot. The outlook of the house often might suggest a decaying economic splendor; the composition of the family unit usually includes an inheritor to an estate and title. In either case, the condensation of social value in the space of the home unfolds in scenes of quotidian interaction surrounded by the precious novelty of manufactured objects and exotic trappings that serve as reminders of world trade.[6] The characters are introduced in parenthetical excursus with recurring references to their education—especially for female characters—or to social status and entrepreneurial prowess in the global market for male characters. In doing so, their description takes a detour from the progression of the narrative to encapsulate the broader social relations that they build in the novel.

These narrative functions of domesticity constitute a comforting recapitulation of accepted generic and social conventions before the sensational turn hints at mysterious disappearances, suspicions of criminal behavior, or, before the sensational revelations evoke uncanny similarities among apparently unrelated characters. As it has been pointed out repeatedly in the early and more recent reception of the sensation novel, the unsettling revelations in the plot affect the constructed idea of an imperiled and sound bourgeois status.[7] These fictional revelations of uncanny truths innovate traditional narrative functions employed in previous genres, such as the classical novel and the gothic, which also relied on the surprising effect of their plots. In the classical novel, a genre that the British public was familiar with via Shakespeare's comedies, the ending miraculously reconnects the mysterious origins of the inquiring characters to their temporarily lost highborn status. In the gothic novel, by contrast, the suspenseful unfolding of the plot introduces an injustice that the unknowing victim suffers in an oppressive escalation of abuse. What makes the sensation plot unique is the disturbing association of bourgeois status and criminal activity that the classist discursive formations of the present and past age would tend to ascribe only to representatives of the working classes or would coat with the lure of an often aristocratic foreign origin. The proximity and interaction of representatives of both working and middle-class characters in the plot of sensation novels somehow levels out any difference between the two and suggests that the motivations of each—survival and upward social mobility at all costs—are universal. Upper-class inveterate stability emerges as the result of some original and repressed misdeed that the plot allows to surface, usually through the irruption on the scene of an outsider, excluded from the wealth of the main characters. The narrative function of this figure can either be the bearing of compromising information or the witnessing of a violent confrontation or an indecorous altercation involving one of the main characters. The narrative function of the outsider here has an all too *heimliche* and familiar meaning, being at times involved in the greedy and criminal plots, which the bourgeois characters try to hide in their decorous routines, or even related to them. In Braddon's *Aurora Floyd*, serialized in *Temple Bar* between 1861 and 1863, Steve Hargraves, the stables man, overhears Aurora screaming "2000 pounds!" in response to the newly introduced stranger menacing her bourgeois respectability with his knowledge of Aurora's past. Other unsettling remarks that break the continuum of bourgeois secluded order are operatic exclamations like "I hate you!," directed to the same newcomer, "You here!" at the appearance of a long-lost relative, or "I!" when Aurora is suspected of the murder of the stranger. These are fragmented instances of intensified emotion in which the fetishized decorum of middle-class social relations is questioned and its constructed stability faced with uncanny revelations.

In a similar manner, Mrs. Henry Wood's *East Lynne*, serialized in 1861, has one of the two plot lines, the assumed criminal responsibility of Richard Hare, the judge's son, in the murder of Hallijohn, fit in the sensational paradigm. The return of Richard Hare to the enclosed tranquility of the country village is met with intensified reactions of surprised astonishment, such as Carlyle's outcry "'Richard!'—'At West Lynne?,'" that peak in the trial scene with the sequence of exclamations "Richard the exile!" "The reported dead!". These paroxysmal condensations of the narrative speak of a return of the repressed content of a Victorian bourgeois propriety that is usually defined in exclusive opposition to crimes and misdeeds associated with the working classes. Knowledge of the main character's origins, moreover, can be shadowed in mystery when the narrative introduces elements such as an indecorous family line, only to inevitably reappear in the typical sensational fashion. It is the case of Braddon's *Lost for Love*, serialized in *Belgravia* in 1873, in which Flora's origins are kept a secret to remove from the child's familial history the notion of a mother's elopement and a father's conviction charge. The sensational turn appears also in the happy bourgeois marriage of the heiress Flora that is based on the attempted murder of a rival by her husband. It is the uncanny surfacing of this knowledge that alters the structured relations between the characters, while the narrative brings together apparently unrelated strangers.

What the recurrent narrative functions that combine in countless examples of sensation fiction indicate is that socially constructed identities such as servant and master might be made to coincide, while the stranger can be revealed to be a family member, as in *East Lynne*'s masked return of the eloped lady of the house as the disfigured servant to her own children. Similarly, in *Lost for Love* the sensational turn questions the assumed stable status of the family maid by revealing that she is actually Flora's grandmother. Identities are also manipulated through the orchestrated death of an opponent or by means of the internment of a usually female heiress to allow the completion of a hereditary scheme: the latter is the case both in Collins'1860 *The Woman in White* and in Braddon's *Lost for Love*. All these narrative strategies challenge the stable structure of nineteenth-century class relations and, while evoking anxiety about social mobility, demystify bourgeois pretense to moral superiority. This mystifying effect is particularly true in the serialized edition of these novels. The unavoidable teleology of the triple-decker edition that leads to an ending inevitably reinstating established values is here shattered and leaves all system of values in disarray. In discussing the literary fragment of novelistic installments in the context of the magazine, I am avoiding the inevitable teleological progression of the narrative that the reader can expect in a bound novel. The pretense to unity that a triple-decker or any contemporary edition of nineteenth-century novels implies has been a critical assumption that imagines a cohesive structure out of the more complex experience of reading that a periodical allows.[8]

The sensation plot's break with generic and social conventions is a mode of fragmented revelations that creates a shocking effect; this is particularly true in the fiction of Mary Elizabeth Braddon. Other sensation novelists differed in the way in which the stereotypical narrative functions were incorporated into their plots. Wilkie Collins in *The Woman in White* dilates the suspenseful astonishment of the reader in a slow unfolding of the mystery through a collection of first-person narratives by persistent and obsessive inquirers. Each chapter of *The Woman in White*, each installment published separately in Dickens' *Household Words*, shrouds the reader with the same ominous anticipation of catastrophic events, regardless of whose first-person account the reader is faced with. The oppression of the abuses inflicted on the female victims is associated with a villain whose omnipresent emissaries surround every move of the circumspect detective until the long-awaited demise of the devilish figure marks the end of the narrative.

Mrs. Henry Wood relies, in *East Lynne*, more on the power of excruciatingly condensed episodes of emotional intensity. The author does fragment her narrative with paroxysmal turning points that intensify the carefully studied emotional response of the characters. The novel, however, introduces shocking revelations that lead, within the narrative unity of the novel, to a stagnant and melodramatic resolution distinguished by still, even statuesque tableaux of two characters displaying their suffering. The scenes of the death chamber with Isabel assisting her dying child disguised as a servant, or of the final confrontation of the by then revealed Lady Isabel to the hostile Miss Corny are examples of a slow-paced apotheosis of the victim that show a theatrical inspiration, as Ann Cvetkovich has pointed out in her analysis in *Mixed Feelings.* Mrs. Ellen Wood, however, does not privilege the fragmented mode of narration that punctuates Braddon's novels. A classical inspiration keeps a sensational episode such as Isabel's train accident off scene; the narrator shows no interest in it. This event serves more as a narrative function advancing the narrative than as a chance to mimetically represent the traumatic experience in visual terms or through a shattered syntax of bits of information increasing the suspense of the readers.

Braddon's novels, by contrast, persistently employ a shocking mode that is amplified by their appearance in installments in the periodical edition on the pages of *Belgravia* where up to four titles by Braddon herself were serialized at the same time. The thrilling mysteries that motivate the peripateia of inquiring characters create a recurrent mode of astonishment that indirectly denounces and unveils the paradoxes of social conventions. The immobile time of upper-class decorum and coded behavior is questioned by the rapidly changing scenarios of class dynamism and individual, entrepreneurial prowess. Power relations are therefore negotiated in the open arena of market economy and bound to fluctuate due to their socially constructed value. Social recognition is conveyed through visible signs with an urgency that is concerned primarily with appearances.

The empathic excesses of the fragmented mode in Braddon, which is not as pervasive as in Collins and as theatrical as in Mrs. Henry Wood, can be juxtaposed in the reader's attention to the visual impact of advertising, which abruptly shifts from one segment to another, or to other forms of popular entertainment, as I shall discuss in chapter five. Similarly, the diverse mental landscapes evoked by the miscellaneous articles published right next to the exciting and suspenseful installments of the novels reinforce this sense of fragmentation. I stress, again, that the format of the magazine, as well as the plot of Braddon's novels, went together in creating a fragmented perception that questioned social structure and established conventions in the fleeting and constantly changing scenarios of an expanding mass culture. The episodic perusal of the magazine hinted at assumed responsibilities of the middle-class characters in murders, criminal plots guided by greed, in long-lost trails of mischievous dissimulation. Only the ending leads to their denouncement; the installment of the magazine leaves the reader without any reassuring standard of social practice. The stories published in the magazine deconstructed the narratives associated with social rituals and bourgeois decorum in a way that the bound volume would entail temporally only, since the conventional plot would lead to the expected happy ending that restored order and justice. By creating in the reader an increased awareness of the constructed meaning of social relations, the magazine therefore redirected the reader's expectations toward the rest of the magazine. Inquiry becomes a mode of knowing in the serial publication of sensation fiction; this epistemological side-effect of the sensation plot ends up questioning established narratives while finding more reassuring answers in the rest of the magazine. In the reading of periodical literature that I propose, one needs to consider the impact that the rest of the magazine has on the mind of the sensitized reader of sensation fiction over several months. The fragmented nature of the information conveyed in the installments of the novels deconstructed systematic knowledge—social and other. The articles published in the magazine, however, seem to have a potentially stabilizing effect in redirecting the puzzled implied reader through a more rhetorically structured and normalizing narrative. Sensational fiction published in the magazine had a temporary demystifying effect introduced again and again through shocking turns and revelations. Instead of making the demystifying claim an end in itself, however, Braddon's magazine defuses the shocking effect through the more appeasing articles that interspersed the novelistic installments. The value of sensation fiction as it appears in its original publication form must therefore be redefined. However disturbing the plot of sensational novels might be for the Victorian middle-class readership, the format of the magazine makes the installment in each issue paradoxically insinuate doubts about the criminal workings of a class whose values the rest of the magazine presented as a given fact.

Scholarship on the sensational has produced narratives that juxtapose the social context of Victorian time to a study of the novel. Critics have therefore been able to "reconstruct" the cultural climate of the age through a parallel study of contemporary legislation, through the *causes celèbres* of the divorce court or of the dispossessment orders for assumed unstable characters that were also rich heiresses. In all these instances the sensation novel appears as a site of conflict between the infiltrating discourses of the dominant ideology and the oppressed subjects that struggled to affirm their humanity. These readings stem from a reflective view of literature, from what is seen as a direct inclusion in the world of fiction of pressing contemporary issues. I want, instead, to point out to the macrotext of the periodical, and not the novel per se, as *the* historically specific site of this confrontation. A thoroughly descriptive attention to the reception of *Belgravia* and to its technologically based production reveals the periodical press as a "monad" reflecting and containing the whole of societal injunctions and historical dynamics of the age. The periodical press, therefore, becomes *the* sensation novel of the age. A reading of the fiction of *Belgravia* in the separate issues of the magazine contains the crisis of the bourgeois ideology and its resolution that the teleological arrangement of the book form leaves to the end. Reading sensation novels within the individual issue of a monthly magazine inevitably complicates the traditional understanding of the unity inherent to the text of the novel. A focus on the layout of the serial magazine and on the practice of reading through the montage effect makes the interconnection of fiction, fact, and market culture more apparent. A focus on the *montage* effect that the periodical press allowed reveals a strong link between literary creation and the urgency of market economy, between fiction and the simplified and recognizable impressions of advertising or popular entertainment. In other words, the poetics of the genre and the rhetoric of its progression share an economy of sensationalism with the techniques of a newly structured mass culture. Sheer shocks set the tempo of the serialized installments appearing in *Belgravia*, as well as constituting the experience of urban modernity in city streets and popular entertainment.

The importance that this fragmented mode plays in the history of the press is very significant. The sensational and fragmented progression of the genre, in sharing their rhetoric and cultural impact with the contemporary communication media of the press and advertising, signal the inception of what was later be called "new journalism." The sensational accumulation of sensorial stimuli, moreover, contradicts the aesthetic assumptions that privileged a contemplative unity inherent to the work of art, as exemplified, for instance, by the platonic model. I am now going to discuss the two models of aesthetic appreciation, the platonic and the more modern, if not modernist, one, which appears in the defense of the sensational in *Belgravia*. I do not mean to present the two in a simplistic stark opposition. The case of *Belgravia* is particularly interesting because the magazine that contributed to popularize the sensation novel paradoxically defends the ephemeral nature of any work of art and at the same time recurs to abstract intellectual schemes to support its claims. The disrupting force of the sensational, in other words, only temporarily challenges the assumed order invoked by traditional theorists and large quarters of Victorian society. Fragmentation and structure, fleeting impressions, and intuitions of order coexist in what is a reenactment of the market economy dynamics between distinctive commodities and universal fetish value, atomistic flow of discrete elements and constructed visualization of intellectual order: in other words, multiplicity and unity.

Abstract Order and Fleeting Sensations: A Theory of Modern(ist) Fragmentation

The poetics of fragmentation that reading a periodical reflects emerges first and foremost in the miscellaneous structure of the periodical, in the temporal experience of perusing a magazine made of disparate contributions. This aspect of the print medium affects sensation fiction published periodically by transforming each installment in a fragment of narrative that peaks toward the end with some surprising revelation or shocking event to be continued later. *Belgravia* makes explicit the relevance of sensationalism at a specific time in the history of the British press. A newly structured market economy permeated patterns of production, distribution, and social organization; market economy gained a massive visibility through the spectacular show case of commodities, and it informed editorial practices as well as the debates on political representation. The articles on the sensational in art and science, which appeared on the *Belgravia* magazine account for the social and cultural phenomena of the age by inscribing these phenomena, together with fiction, in a contemporary theory of art and culture focusing on the "sensational." I shall examine these articles in relation to some contemporary examples of criticism that investigate the epistemological relevance of perception and intuition in relation to the work of art. I am particularly interested in examining the contemporary theoretical views on culture that privilege notions of unity, or different degrees of static contemplation, as a means of attaining true knowledge in opposition to the sensational advocated by the writers of *Belgravia*. These models of representation coming with a judgment of value oppose quite openly, at times *verbatim*, the cultural forces defined by sensationalism, as I shall point to. In the selections that I include transcendental vision of order becomes the primary metaphorical elaboration of a theory of knowledge, artistic representation, and social organization. What in *Belgravia* appears as a realistic perception of modern culture coexists in Victorian culture with a persisting strive for abstraction that preserves a constructed sense of platonic unity. This intuition of unity supersedes the empirical perception of fragmentation and ultimately overlooks the import of the senses as a foundation of knowledge. Abstraction provides a defense of a unitary principle that persists in parallel and paradoxically next to the perception of the impressionistic fragment. The models of knowledge represented here alternate between multiplicity and intuitive construction of order similarly to other kinds of nineteenth-century theorization, such as value and political agency, as well as to some forms of visual practices to which I will return in the following chapters. The critics that I include here are salient points in a narrative arc that reaches the 1920s, thus suggesting the persistence of this model of abstraction at the expense of materiality.

* * *

The Victorian establishment attacked the sensation novel and more specifically Mary Elizabeth Braddon since the publication on the predominantly literary journal *Temple Bar*, edited by the *Times* journalist George Augustus Sala, of *Lady Audley's Secret* and of *Aurora Floyd*. The attacks on Braddon escalated after her inauguration of the *Belgravia* magazine.[9] In response to this, the magazine elaborated, in a series of articles by George Augustus Sala, a theory of culture that made the sensational a key symbolic referent of the culture of modernity. Sala's theory of culture hinging on the sensational poses important questions on the epistemological models that the contemporary age employed to read modernity. The net of sensationalism is widely cast to encompass many aspects of modernity that are filtered from the standpoint of a theory of culture that is semiological in scope. By reflecting on the place of *Belgravia* in the history of nineteenth-century and western culture, the articles on sensationalism cover literary creation and knowledge of reality, scientific inquiry and technologically based production of marketable goods. The breadth and the acuity of these reflections encompass every aspect of culture, art, science, and society, thus showing the limitations of a traditionally hierarchical view of art that distinguishes separate fields. In order to understand the cultural challenge that sensation fiction posed to an established tradition that posited an epistemologic approach to reality by means of abstract normalizing assumptions, it is important here to trace the presence in nineteenth-century culture of contrasting models of perception that structured vision as well as interpretation and, consequently, representation of reality. The two modes of visual perception, the contemplative admiration opposed to the fragmentary sensation, constitute an important contrast that can be traced throughout fictional and theoretical writings. If the novelistic forms of pictorial writing in the eighteenth century presented scenes and landscapes with the same still organization of forms of an idealizing painter of the sublime or the picturesque, nineteenth-century visual spectacles of urbanization—and the contemporaneous interest in optics and visual technology—grounded perception in empirical sensation, thus questioning the validity of any previous dominant model of vision. These two modes, the fragmentary and the contemplative, represent two currents of perception and representation that can be characterized in different degrees oscillating between the opposites of chaotic chance and structured order, multiplicity of perspectives and structured organization of representation, priority of empirical recording of impressions, and transcendental attainment of abstract truths. They both originate in different epistemological approaches to sensation, unmediated and atomistic in the first case, intellectual and deductive in the second. Wordsworth's *Prelude* is an example of this twofold model as it indulges in the paratactic and kaleidoscopic spectacle of the city of London only to refrain from it to seek refuge in the blinded vision of transcendent Platonic stillness.[10] Periodicals such as Braddon's *Belgravia* shared both in content and form a keen interest in episodic representation and in mobile perception with a century-long tradition of theoretical inquiry on movement and perception that paralleled the technological innovations examined by Jonathan Crary in *Techniques of the Observer* (1990). Studies on optics and the technology that illustrated them define the culture of modernity as a motley inscription of visual stimuli on the eye of the observer.[11] In this sense, the *montage* of sensations that the layout of a miscellaneous magazine suggests to the reader is no different, as I argued in chapter one and shall examine more closely in chapter five.

I now turn to a textual analysis of some nineteenth-century theorists that further elaborated this dichotomy polarizing unmediated and mediated perception not only in reference to the place literary writing has in an expanded system of the arts but in reference also to the structures of interpretation, and psychology of reading, at large. I shall examine the theories on art and criticism elaborated by E.S. Dallas in *The Gay Science* (1866). I shall also trace the persistence of such a twofold model of perception in the aesthetic theories expounded by Henry James in *The Art of Fiction* (1884) and in Percy Lubbock in *The Craft of Fiction* (1929). I intend to chart the semantic fields associated to vision as a metaphor for transcendental knowledge. I then want to retrace in the discussion of contemporary art forms the systematic preference accorded to established artistic practices like painting in opposition to drama or ballet, inasmuch as this opposition contrasts dynamism with stillness. Pitting movement in opposition to stasis marks a dominant trait of a critical discourse that privileges transcendental intuition to the detriment of episodic sensationalism. Such a discourse is important in this history for it is in direct opposition to what Mary Elizabeth Braddon and the most mimetically experimental trends of nineteenth-century culture were committed to. A tendency toward abstraction that dismisses and finally erases the episodic and the fragmentary from aesthetic appreciation signals the pervasive import in the Anglo-American context, in the time span that goes from the 1860s to the 1920s, of notions that privilege order, transcendental unity, and a deductive mode of thinking.

The Gay Science (1866)

Eneas Sweetland Dallas wrote his treatise on poetic theory, whose title echoes the Provençal idea of *El Gai Saber*, to advance a new definition of art and consequently to reform the conventional foundations of criticism. His work reviews the classical and modern tradition of poetics with one agenda in mind, that is, to support his point that art's aim is pleasure and criticism can only be a science of pleasure.

His definition of pleasure does not revive, however, the philosophical epicurean tradition that saw pleasure in dynamic terms, as a moving away from pain, as a striving to reach the fulfillment of desire. The pleasure that he discusses has to do with a static and transcendental purity of an intuitive impression beyond both knowledge and science. To support his claim, Dallas recuperates Simonides' definition of poetry in visual terms, later adapted by Horace in his phrasing "ut pictura poesis." The visual image suggested by this theory places Dallas' position along the line of a transhistorical continuity with the traditional ordering of the arts. "Pictura," however, means here a unity in abstract terms of all the scattered elements of reality. The mental image to be created is the picture of the perfect unity of all the arts, the idea of an abstraction that refutes the particular fragmentation of what Dallas calls disparagingly the "separation of the arts" carried out by an empirical disposition of certain criticism. Art aims at the "sensible possession or enjoyment of the world beyond consciousness." Pleasure derived from art lies in "conceit" and is a creation of the mind that transcends materiality.

Diametrically opposed to Dallas' theory of art as a still, ecstatic intuition stand two aspects of perception and artistic representation: on the one hand, the episodic and the fragmentary; on the other hand, the dynamic movement of a time-bound action unable to transcend itself into intellectual stillness. The examples of periodical literature and drama serve Dallas as the manifestations of the aspects that escape his theorization of a static ideal. Periodical literature, through the proliferation of "detached essays," is responsible for a "tendency to fly system and so to underrate it."[12] Drama, in the forms of tragedy and comedy, relies, according to Dallas, on a transition of sensations based on movement from one state of being to the other, on a progression from pain to pleasure, from need to satisfaction. The aim of art, however, eludes the empirical fact or the unsettling movement of uncontrolled states of being. The pleasure of art is free from the "painful pleasure" of dramatic action; it aims at peace of mind and contemplates harmony of still forms. Dallas uses visual metaphors that contrast stasis to agitation, transcendence to relativity. He elaborates two terms of comparison, the pictorial image of the mind and the dramatic chaos of experience, deriving them from the established tradition of classical theory. Painting and drama serve as fixed semantic definitions that exclude any analysis that would let loose other uncontrolled implications. The pictorial and the dramatic exemplify the two polarities, contemplation and fragmented experience, which can be traced in contemporary culture. Only the first one, however, is recognized as epistemologically viable and is granted a trustworthy indication of stability inasmuch as its aim is an abstraction that avoids a confrontation with the scattered and the transient.

The discussion, covering two volumes, restates this dichotomy between pure pleasure and action, still image and ephemeral sensation, while at the same time insisting on the superior value of intuition against sensation, of beauty against becoming. True knowledge dismisses the exterior reality of the episodic, since the latter only attains fleeting glimpses at dynamic shapes moving through space in time. At the end of the second volume, Dallas applies the organizing rules of his system of values to the contemporary reality of social progress, cultural production, and gendered relations. The lofty tradition of intellectual stability that Dallas establishes is opposed to the episodic manifestations of history in order to test its validity and, by doing so, to memorialize what is compatible to it own homogeneity. The first realization is that "throughout all the art of the day, and much of its thinking, we are troubled with a sense of disorder."[13] Dallas recognizes in a situation of "change" and "movement" a possible explanation for the loss of transcendental unity in the proliferation of incidental products of mass culture. He proceeds to include in his survey groundbreaking inventions such as the railway, the telegraph, the penny postage, but also factual events such as the Reform Bill or social phenomena such as the "race between the press and the pulpit" in gaining the attention of the public. Not surprisingly, any spectacle of unmediated ephemeral expressivity is targeted as an element that contradicts his theoretical elaboration. Spectacles such as "pantomime," "farce," "rope-dancing," "jugglery," and "the ballet" are acknowledged for their popularity but dismissed for not being "intellectual." We can now see how these amusements in his view partake too much of the periodic nature of performance, of the multiplication of ephemeral entertainment, of the prevalent sensation of passing impressions they stir in the public. In Dallas' terms, these shows belong to the *dramatic* as opposed to the *beautiful*. Change and movement, however, do not challenge the system of ordered representation only through the spread of popular art forms. There is another tendency that is deplored together with all the practices of reading and entertainment that reach at the time more strata of the population and induce more marketable sensations: it is the "feminine" presence in countless novels and among the number of authors incessantly publishing books. Dallas employs here the same dichotomy of intuitive purity versus unstructured progression to chart femininity according to the same categories of visual abstraction:

> Woman embodies our highest ideas of purity and refinement. [...] And now, when the influence of women is being poured into literature, we expect to feel within it an evident access of refinement. We find the very opposite. The first object of the novelist is to get personages in whom we can be interested; the rest is to put them in *action*. But when women are the chief characters, how are you to set them in *motion*? The life of women cannot be described as a life of action. When women are thus put forward to lead the action of a plot, they must be urged into a false position. To get vigorous action they are described as rushing into crime, and doing masculine deeds. Thus they come forward in the worst light, and the novelist finds that to make an effect he has to give up his heroine to bigamy, to murder, to child-bearing by stealth in the Tyrol, and to all sorts of adventures which can only signify her fall. (Emphasis added)

This passage that condenses the linguistic semantic field that Dallas has drawn throughout the book is particularly significant for two reasons. First, it shows, once again, that the visual categories of his system imply an essential definition that refutes and eludes the challenges of unrestrained dynamics animating the social and the intellectual realm. The unquestioned idea of womanhood is relegated to the moral empyrean of purified abstraction. This iconic idealization has the same stability of a manageable intuitive truth that sets the standard for what is considered compatible with his system of knowledge and is worthy of gaining historical status through the memorializing effort of the appreciative critic and the approving historian. When elaborating on the negative effects of the "feminine" presence in literature,[14] Dallas resorts to the same semantic field that defined motion as a disruption of the still contemplation of abstract truths and action as a theatrical, unmediated, and therefore imperfect experience of the real. Dynamic motion is discredited when present in social phenomena, dramatic writing, and psychological sensations because motion, by revealing its want of stability, implies a necessary movement toward a better state of being. The second and more obvious reason why this passage best exemplifies Dallas' visually biased reading of contemporary reality is the clear reference to the plot of sensation novels and the equation of crime and dangerous behavior of any female character attempting an unsolicited and, because of that, criminal break with the essential celestial order of beings.

The Art of Fiction (1884)

Henry James, a more empirical critic, sensed the historical relevance of sensation fiction since his 1885 review of Mary Elizabeth Braddon's *Aurora Floyd* published in *The Nation*. In his analysis, sensation novels stand out in the tradition of English fiction because their plots dispel the gothic mists surrounding medieval castles in the Apennines to reveal the "domestic mysteries" of familiar dwellings such as "the cheerful country house and the busy London lodgings." Mary Elizabeth Braddon's preeminence in the field is recognized by Henry James because she has "done her work better than her predecessors," that is, "with a woman's *finesse* and a strict regard to morality."[15] It is not my aim here to focus on the critical reception of Mary Elizabeth Braddon's production, which, by the way, has been echoing James' views throughout twentieth-century scholarship on the sensational. I would rather investigate a broader array of critical theories in order to single out any instance of the paradigmatic opposition between an empirical approach to fragmentation and the persistence of idealized notions of an ontological ideal. The case of Henry James allows me to recognize a symptomatic condensation of the critical discourse around the crystallized notion of a coherent unity of a work of art. Unlike Dallas, Henry James here sets a distinctive model of an artist's individualized experience not by means of a deductive irradiation on reality of preconceived notions. In his example, perception negotiates a transmigration of sensual data into an artist's work, in an attempt to be a rhapsodic weaving of sensual stimuli. Composition is achieved through a selective and symbolic, thus cohesive, arrangement of suggestions coming from experience to set up the complete unity of artistic creation. If the infinite potentiality of experience is the starting point of fiction, the impressions deriving from it never constitute the episodic recording of random sensations. A novel is first and foremost "a personal and direct impression of life" in which definition the immediate perception is entangled with an individual point of view, and the empirical sensation with an individual "mind." Only the union of the two can make the alchemical transmutation of the "pulses of the air" into "revelations." Perception tends significantly to the absolute, and filters through the "finest silken threads" the elemental stimuli entering consciousness. The selective aggregation of impressions disregards the lowly "infinite rubbish-yard beneath the back-windows of the world" and aims at the reflections of light emitting from the most perfect examples of fiction. James refers to the traditional comparison of the novel with the art of painting, primarily in order to support the novel's claim to truth and not to revive the exclusive model of metaphorical coherence of Dallas' theory. Perfection of mediated consciousness may stem from a novel, a statue, or a painting, as long as all their parts reflect one another in a metonymic anticipation of the critical appreciation of unity, which comes after and condenses the secret trajectories of the artist's sensitivity.

The work of art, therefore, projects numinous epiphanies that are previously collected and invented by the artist's mnemonic technique of assembly. Artistic invention reaches this ideal, however, only when it attains the fully rounded abstraction of individual unity. The demiurge-like operation of the artist recognizes and catalogues the elements perceived as equal to itself, consonant with the aspiration to truth and beauty of an absolute inspiration that is finally severed from empirical ties. Intellectual sight is again privileged in the act of criticism and in the preservation of distilled perfection that comes with it, while the rubble of the fragmentary accumulation of history is only marginally constitutive of the perfect order established on a different level of being.

The Craft of Fiction (1929)

While E.S. Dallas is an example of a distinctive delimitation of the field of the episodic to be sharply pitted against the field of the transcendental and the intuitive, Henry James exemplifies a more osmotic exchange of tensions between the two fields, an assemblage of impressions salvaged by the structuring order of symbolic creation. Percy Lubbock in his 1929 *The Craft of Fiction* expands Henry James' stress on experience into an aesthetic principle of *durée* (duration), while at the same time embracing an idealistic and antimimetic skepticism toward representation. His theorization of art follows a paradoxical path: on one hand "form, design and composition" are the sole interests of the literary critic; on the other, form escapes perception, design unfolds aimlessly, composition is eroded by any mnemonic—and therefore unreliable—attempt at coherence. Perception exists on a temporal level that records an ever-changing sequence of impressions that can never constitute a perfect unity. The experience of the reader is grounded on too feeble a psychological foundation to leave a recognizable mark on a vaporous memory.

Interpretation is a flow of stimuli that can and must try to construct a stable concept—"that a book *has* a form, that is not disputed"—but conceptualization is at the same time contrasted by a deconstructive pull.[16] This is due to what Lubbock elaborates as an illusory foundation of readership:

> The form of a novel—and how often a critic uses that expression too—is something that none of us, perhaps has ever really comprehended. It is revealed little by little, page by page, and it is withdrawn as fast as it is revealed; as a whole, complete and perfect, it could only exist in a more tenacious memory than most of us has to rely on.[17]

The intellectual and illusory perception of form mediates between a necessary stability of concepts and an inevitable fluidity of perception. In doing so, the fleeting perspective of passing phenomena appears as a distinctive element of literary theory. It is not, however, transcended, like in Dallas, or woven into a large tapestry, like in James. The reference to the episodic here involves the essence of reality as well as the perception of it. What seems to be a recognition of the episodic element constituting reality actually undermines any material definition of it. Factuality dissolves in a skeptical fantasy and is not distinguished from illusion. If form is the result of a questionable and uncertain intellectual process, it can adumbrate also a reference to the unreliability of existing reality. This is made possible by the extension of perception in time. Since perception is rooted in time, a plastic and still outline of reality, which is the aim of form, is not achievable. It is time that dissolves any intellectual construction, making words and concepts open to a fluid progression. A discussion of temporality in Lubbock is important because temporality makes traditional definitions lose their validity, transforming them into a crystallized occurrence of definitions so common in the conventional language that they inevitably lose their reference. I want to point out here how Lubbock, by recurring to the traditional distinction of the dramatic and the pictorial, while paradoxically contradicting it through the primary role accorded to the temporal perspective, best shows the move from definition to ungrounded convention, from designation to skepticism, from factuality to illusion. The terms used by Lubbock to define, however skeptically, the transient nature of perception in osmotic opposition to the fixed elaboration of structure reenact the traditional separation between the dramatic and the pictorial. The term dramatic, or "scenic," refers to the manifestation of unmediated perception and unpolished representation. The term posits a situation in which the subjectivity of the author disappears and identifies with the subjectivity of the casual spectator. The author of scenic inspiration does not connote a chunk of perceived reality through stylization but is rather lost in the surrounding overflow of reality that overwhelms the casual reader/spectator, too. The critic or any future writer is not to prefer this kind of nonsystematic representation: "on the whole, no doubt, the possibilities of the scene are greatly abused in fiction, in the daily and familiar novel."[18] Not only is the scenic too immediate and unrefined, but it prevents the superior order of reflection granted by the intervention of a reflective mind. Only the agency of a creative subject can safeguard the structuring workings of a centering mind. The term "picture" represents this artistic intervention on the unpolished collection of casual sensations. Given the questionable status of image, structure, and form in Lubbock's theory, it is clear now that the traditional distinction partakes in the fluidity of language and undermines any fixed elaboration through the temporal element of perception. Words elude meaning, definitions fail to encompass the time-bound experience of reading and interpreting reality. The significant role played by time in this example of literary criticism upsets the model of perception and representation elaborated by Dallas and James, among others. The time of the empirical and chaotic recording of impressions that cannot be fully managed by the ordering function of the mind cannot build a perfect picture and cannot preserve a systematic arrangement of any notions because of the limited faculty of memory. Time constantly challenges intellectual and linguistic elaboration; moreover, it undermines any trustworthy representation of a reality that is deeply immersed in the subject's fluid grasp on reality.

BELGRAVIA (1866–67)

E.S. Dallas, Henry James, and Percy Lubbock discuss empirical sensation and intellectual construction by recurring to a model that allows, when it does, for an account of different degrees of reality that complicate the system. The range of possibilities go from Dallas who dismisses the value of empirical stimuli in his transcendental contemplation, to James who recognizes the importance for invention of a temporary access to factuality, to Lubbock's only concession to reality as a phantomatic appearance that mirrors the equally immaterial fabric of art. Mary Elizabeth Braddon makes an interesting case in this history for her dedication to the aesthetic of the periodic and the sensational. She representes the fragmentation through her editorial practices and through the intensely charged revelations that punctuate her periodical literature. The issues of *Belgravia*, moreover, reproduce the fragmentation of urban modernity through the ephemeral association created in the reader's minds by scattered findings about world exhibits, bric-a-brac treasures, historical neighborhoods of London, satirical poetry, fashions of the day, installments of serialized novels, and episodic narratives contained in the advertisements. Some of the articles, however, self-reflexively discuss the aesthetics of sensation. They do so in two distinctive ways: on the one hand they defend the genre of sensation fiction with a series of theoretical articles; on the other, they achieve the same end by discussing with favor art forms such as the theater, which were associated by elitist criticism to the discredited sensational.[19] Sensation fiction is not only adumbrated by the magazine's interest in the theater as a contiguous form of expression, "the sensational" is also defended in a series of articles appearing between 1867 and 1869 that define a broad notion of sensationalism, which is not limited to literary production only. Literature is only one of the manifestations of sensationalism, since sensationalism appears also in history, painting, and science, thus contradicting any system of criticism that privileges specific literary genres and indicates suitable contents for each. The first article in the series that follows the attacks against Mary Elizabeth Braddon orchestrated by the *Pall Mall* magazine appears in the February 1868 issue. Written by George Augustus Sala, "On the 'Sensational' in Literature and Art" attempts to place sensation fiction in a longer tradition of world literature that includes Shakespeare and Dickens. Sala continues his comparisons by extending the notion of sensationalism to the field of history, with sensational patriots such as Garibaldi or sensational historical figures such as Napoleon III, Bismark, or General Grant. Sensationalism becomes, therefore, a mode of writing that shares its electrifying immediacy with life itself and other nonliterary forms of production, such as painting, with the inclusions of Goya, Fuseli, and Hogarth. Literary mimesis is only one example among others that conjugates the mode of sensationalism. Reality itself—Sala argues—is sensational or has been sensationalized by the innovations of nineteenth-century modernity. The mimetic empiricism at the root of the sensational encompasses technology, entertainment, and science, too: Sala's lists of what can be defines as sensational include the telegraph, Darwin, the singer Nolaton, *Belgravia* itself, and Braddon.

Literature, thus, loses the centered and hierarchically ordered position as the art that channels the privileged expression of ideal truths of the mind. With sensationalism, popular literature takes a semiological relevance, becomes a process of signification that, like other intellectual pursuits and technological innovations, absorbs the episodic and makes it a programmatic statement of a new poetics. In partaking of this protean force, which animates several fields of production that include history, science, and technology, sensational literature appears as a form of art rooted in the culture of nineteenth-century market economy. Sala recognizes the fleeting status of the sensational, which he likens to the rumor of traditionalists that singles out, while chastising it, everything that is "vivid, and nervous, and forcile, and graphic, and true."[20] He condenses the workings of the sensational in the cry, the slogan-like uttering, the simplified and exclamative statement that circulates in the public when facing an unexpected novelty, such as the unprocessed flow of sensations that the irruption of any innovation entails. The claim that sensationalism belongs to the addictive excitement brought to the senses by the culture of modernity implicitly redefines the status of the work of art and the mode of reading that can best appreciate it. The defense of the sensational on the pages of the *Belgravia* magazine is not only the first historical discussion of the important role sensation novels play in the context of Victorian culture. These reflections implicitly undermine the aesthetic assumptions that privileged a contemplative unity inherent to the work of art. By revealing the nonexclusively literary nature of the emotional stimulus associated with the genre, the defense of the sensational in the *Belgravia* magazine demystifies the role of art as a transcendental path to the intuition of an ultimate truth. Revealing that the sensational effect can be artificially created and built into the fabric of a structured novel offers a view of fiction as a craft that is immersed in material history and engaged in a dialogue with many other disciplines and art forms. Literature is not, therefore, a representation of a refined, quasi-religious reality to be accepted blindly. Sensationalism is, therefore, the result of an individual agent's involvement in a world of contingency. This sensational fragmentation per se is obviously not advanced as the ultimate new poetics in the same way in which later avant-garde movements did, but rather perceived as the building block of a structured work of art. Fragmentation is the filigree trace within the work of art, reminding readers that the final work does not grow out of an intuition of higher order, nor means to approach it: art shares its functioning rules with the world of science, history, and industry. The sensational peak that fragments experience, while perceived as the building block of many cultural productions, never prevails over the literary, theoretical, or temporal structure that contains it; fleeting impressions coexist with a perception of order that shapes interpretation. Sala, however, never goes as far as invoking transcendental intuitive qualities as being a prerequisite of interpretation: his criticism derives from a non-hierarchical sensitivity to analogous phenomena in several fields of human activity.

If appreciation is no longer based on intuition only, the modalities of knowledge itself no longer seek the ontological, transcendental foundation of all. Experience registers the dispersive nature of multiple perspectives that modernity sets in motion; being immersed in temporality, however, inevitably leads to the construction of narrative, causality, theory. Atomistic fragmentation is perceived through the sensational index and entertained in an all-encompassing theory: this double bind becomes a psychological and epistemological paradigm that surfaces not only in scientific disciplines and literary production but in many aspects of everyday life. The atomistic overflow of discrete elements—commodities, political agents, parceled urban views—that signal industrial modernity is not a clash of chaotic empty signifiers; these aspects of nineteenth-century culture are processed under the terms of a constructed visualization of intellectual order. The same dynamic that entertains parcels and unity finds other incarnations in contemporary culture, like political theory, advertising, and studies of vision and movement, as I shall examine in the following chapters.

The commitment to the ephemeral and the new demonstrated by the *Belgravia* magazine, while registering the fragmented and imposing reality of artistic, historical, and scientific novelty, finds a counterpart in a more traditional and intellectualized approach that manages fragmentation through traditional forms of thinking. This is evident, for instance, in the articles on science that I wish to discuss here but has already been noted in chapter one for what pertains the representation of global geography and temporality. The perception of the fragment opposed to the structuring order of abstract knowledge coexists in a paradoxical bind that unites representation and intellectual construction of meaning, disruptive sensations and laws of the universe, novelty and tradition.

"Is the Sun Dying?"

The kind of scientific journalism that I am going to discuss here shares with sensation literature the function of revealing awesome phenomena through a very studied temporary thrilling effect aimed at capturing the attention of the reader. Scholars such as Richard Altick, Patrick Brantlinger, and Dallas Liddle have shown the direct link between newspaper reporting of *faits divers* and the narrative technique sensation novels.[21] I would like to point to the pervasive influence of the sensation narrative formula in other, more coded genres of journalistic prose like scientific journalism, in a trend that anticipates the more captivatingly commercial forms of journalism of the 1880s. In six articles on "Sensationalism in Science," which appeared between June 1868 and February 1869, various aspects of the universe are described and presented to the larger public as sensational, thus making sensationalism, in the intentions of the writer, a primordial force animating matter, but also a winning formula in manipulating the attention of readers. Starting with pressing questions contained in a title, such as "Is the sun dying?" or "Are there more worlds than one?" or opening with feared scenarios of limited resources of national coal, the articles anticipate catastrophic outcomes of interstellar disasters and likely shortages in natural resources. The sensational narrative mode employed here shocks the reader only to allow the rest of the article to dispel doubts and fears of apocalyptic endings and of economic crisis. This calming effect is achieved by introducing the rectified knowledge of the scientist, or the more abstract trust in the process of history or, even more abstractly, the "system of Compensation which pervades creation, testifying alike to the goodness and to the wisdom of the great Creator."[22]

While Sala recognizes the sensational as a realistic form discredited by traditional critics and, moreover, broadens its scope by including all categories of human endeavor, Patterson, on the other hand, discusses the sensational only to dispel its disruptive effect. His articles employ the sensational mode by imitating the structure of the novelistic plot that goes from shocking menace to appeasing order as the plot unfolds and reaches its end. These articles deal with the sensational as a constituent part of existence, as Sala's did; the narrative strategy they share with sensation fiction, however, paradoxically supports a quite different argument from the one that the sensational revelation insinuates first. Patterson's narrative strategy employs the sensational only as a preliminary warning that should shock the reader into accepting a notion of true knowledge and, ultimately, the religious concept of providence. Sala demonstrates a commitment to the novelty introduced by modernity; his defense of the sensational defends the ephemeral in the new order of market economy. Some other contributors, nonetheless, take the model of the sensational narrative and employ it to better support a move toward the abstraction of accepted values. The articles by Sala present the sensational as an aspect common to history as well as to art, to advertising as well as to science.

Sensationalism is a given fact identified with reality, nature, and history. Inasmuch as the sensational acquires a natural status that has the power to dazzle and manipulate the reader with its awesome shocks, Patterson uses it more as a rhetorical technique than as a matter of fact to be simply reported. The visual layout of the magazine and the reassuring knowledge coming from the articles published next to the installments of the novels belong to the same paradoxical rhetoric of the sensational. I wish here to reconsider Barbara Onslow's observation that the table of contents of any of the *Belgravia* issues is simply a "wonderful, eclectic mix."[23] Scientific articles in the *Belgravia* magazine not only share the thrilling mode associated with sensation fiction; in offering reassuring conclusions they inevitably defuse not only their own thrilling rhetoric but, within the context of an intertextual reading of the whole magazine, the shocking revelations of sensation fiction as well. The sensational mode, therefore, operates in a dynamic system that organizes the fragmented impressions associated with the culture of modernity into an overall structure confirming dominant values. The articles on science from *Belgravia* are also important because the literary, almost fictional component of their rhetoric (and not only the mix of genres as Barbara Onslow suggests) anticipates a new kind of commercial journalism that historians have ascribed to the 1880s.[24]

* * *

Dallas, James, and Lubbock base the origins of fiction in perception and theorize an epistemological status to the products of literary writing. The readers imagined by Dallas, James, and Lubbock filter exterior stimuli, respectively, through the abstract grid of intuition, through individual invention or fluid notions of subjectivity and objectivity. The material, fragmented aspect of reading is generally overlooked or translated into a mode of abstraction. They dismiss the empirical raw material of sensation in favor of abstraction and extend the purport of sensation to comprehend a broader field of analysis. The episodic readings of reality and fiction in their elemental aspects, which they all acknowledge but not favor as the ultimate goal of representation, parallel the fragmentation of visual practices and the challenge to a single perspective and to a Platonic order that other competing epistemological models were beginning to elaborate in the nineteenth century. The many practices of vision and the many perspectives of the Victorian experience challenge the unity of pictorial linear perspective: kaleidoscopes, magic lanterns, taumatropes, the moving perspective of the flanêur set in motion the reliance on a single, stable perspective in painting and in photography. Some optical toys such as the phenakistiskope or other early experiments with the moving image paradoxically combine still frames and the construction of a seemingly coherent abstract unity that supersedes fragmentation. The sheer registration of a wide array of discrete stimuli, while paving the way to the more experimental works of modernism, constitute the empirical counterpart of a lurking abstract and essentializing mental view that entertains particulars to supersede them in narrative forms of coherent unity. The two ends of the epistemological spectrum, the fragmented sensation and the structuring order of abstract knowledge, coexist in a paradoxical bind that unites representation and intellectual construction of meaning, disruptive sensations and laws of the universe, novelty and tradition. In this view, the cultural debate on the arts that I outlined here is similar to other nineteenth-century attempts to theorize, for instance, economic value or political agency, through and beyond the reality of fragmentation.

Chapter 3

The Redefinition of the Public Sphere in the Nineteenth-Century Periodical Press: Mary Elizabeth Braddon and the Debate on Anonymity

In a speech addressing the Members of Parliament in 1866, Gladstone opened his remarks by stating that the periodical press was an example of the improvements introduced since the Reform Bill of 1832. What he called the "emancipation of the press" allowed for a broader circulation of papers that covered political life "in numbers almost defying the powers of statistics."[1]

> As regards the press, an emancipation and an extension have taken place to which it would be difficult to find a parallel. I will not believe that the mass of Gentlemen opposite are really insensible to the enormous benefit that has been effected by the emancipation of the press, when for the humble sum of a penny, or for even less, newspapers are circulated from day to day by the million rather than by the thousand almost defying the powers of statistics to follow, and carrying home to all classes of our fellow-countrymen accounts of public affairs, enabling them to feel a new interest in the transaction of those affairs, and containing articles that, I must say, are written in a spirit, with an ability, with a sound moral sense, and with a refinement that have made the penny press of England the worthy companion—I may indeed say the worthy rival—of those dearer and older papers that

> have long secured for British journalism a renown perhaps without parallel in the world.[2]

The penny press, in other words, had become a public forum.[3] It was through the massive output of papers and periodicals, Gladstone argued, that the public constituted itself as a dynamic entity engaged in exchanging ideas and debating contemporary issues. In the second half of the nineteenth century the number and accessibility of printed matter reached an unparalleled peak: this increase in numbers was due to the repeal of taxes on advertising and on the circulation of printed material and also due to a cheaper kind of paper imported from Africa.[4] The increase in literacy rates, moreover, contributed to the expansion of the market of readers and to the oftentimes successful launching of new magazines and papers edited by experienced journalists and popular writers.

Gladstone's remark is significant for two reasons. First, because it recognizes the political importance of a public of readers outside of the institutional place of the Parliament. Gladstone's statement implies that public policy-making benefits from a wider and more informed public that finds its views reflected on the papers. Second, the speech is important because his interest in the public space of the newspaper press suggests that a link can be made between the shaping of a mass culture of marketed products and political representation. Readers make the fortune of a publication and their choice of one product over a competing one has a political connotation, in that they contribute to the financial success of a publication and its ideas.

Gladstone's view is obviously tinted by the politician's aspiration to massive publicity and political recognition, by the belief in the importance of printed material for the success of one political party over another. What it does not take into account, however, are two important aspects pertaining to the contemporary print industry and the political culture of the age. First, the concept of the public was being reshaped, inasmuch as the public did not necessarily coincide with an abstract formulation including all citizens nor did it coincide with limited groups affiliated along party lines. The public in the second half of the nineteenth century started being elaborated as a fictional target of marketing strategies devoid of political motivations.[5] Editors of magazines like *Belgravia*, in fact, devised strategies not only to attract more readers by means of content, as partisan papers had been doing, but to create an idea of readership by means of a certain tone of the writing independent of political party loyalties. Second, in concomitance with the reshaping of the concept of the public the notion of subjectivity was being transformed, particularly due to an increasing individualization of participants to public life both in the market economy and in the political institutions affected by the expansion of market economy.

My discussion in this chapter of the significant role played by *Belgravia* in the history of nineteenth-century journalism considers two aspects of this reconceptualization of print culture that entailed changes in production and consumption patterns. I focus, first, on the new public of readers created by the editorial practices of periodicals such as Braddon's sensational literary magazine. I then study the transformations in liberal ideology that witnessed a redefinition of the profession of journalism and of the redrawing of the boundaries between the public and the private sphere. More specifically, I retrace the political and historical implications of the century-long debate on anonymity in journalism. Braddon's case will again be introduced to shed further light on the debate through one unpublished letter that she wrote to an editor of a literary magazine in which she requests that one of her articles be published anonymously. I want to argue that the two symmetrical new trends in publishing, one concerned with producers (editors and journalists), the other with consumers of print culture (the public of readers), partake in a cultural dynamics that redefined the public sphere at large. All these aspects are linked to the expansion of market economy in several areas of nineteenth-century culture. These cases also suggest that a paradoxical recognition of new individualities and social groups was allowed in as much as they seemed to contribute to the construction of an overall sense of unity coinciding with the established status quo. The diversity of views and class interests was a paradoxical formulation that reinforced the binding force of unity and conformity.

THE (AN)ESTHETIZED PUBLIC OF *BELGRAVIA*

Before turning to the debate on anonymity and to the professionalization of journalism in the market economy of publishing, I want to discuss the likewise market-based reconfiguration of the public of periodicals. The ability of editors to pitch a magazine that readers could recognize and grow accustomed to found in the sensational mode a decisive factor for the commercial success of newspapers and magazines. The sensational tone in news coverage and in the content of magazines made strong impressions familiar to the readers, thus creating a distinctive feature that allowed the publication to stand out in a market swarmed with printed goods. The case of *Belgravia*, whose circulation reached in the 1860s and 1870s twelve thousand copies,[6] shows how the shocking revelations typical of the sensational mode not only impressed the readers and created expectations for the next issue of the magazine but also how sensational narratives that challenged notions of class decorum, when published in a miscellaneous magazine, thrilled the audience into absorbing, through the articles published in the magazine, new patterns of upper-class time consumption, oftentimes in luring localities abstracted from the everyday life of most of its readers. *Belgravia*'s attention to trend-making habits of upscale consumption and its insistence on fashionable sites for the leisure class exemplifies a relation between the printed text and a malleable audience that is seminal in the history of periodicals. Instead of privileging a public to be defined along political lines, the editing practices of *Belgravia* grounded its success and its marketable visibility on the effect produced on its readers. The target of the publication became therefore an audience defined by the fascination for the controversial issues that the novels appearing in installments provoked. The expectations of the readers on the one hand, and the generic features of the publication on the other one coincided, thus shaping a notion of cultural production in market terms of supply, demand, and profit. *Belgravia*'s appealing layout and its equally flashy content anticipated, I want to argue, what historians have defined as a later development in the history of journalism. Gaining more visibility the 1880s, a new trend in journalism gave priority to commercial interests, appealing subjects, and not always to the expression of a political side in the partisan sense commonly associated to earlier phases of the history of British journalism, even though that did not disappear.[7] The miscellaneous format of *Belgravia* was able to reach a wide and differentiated audience and to base its success on the commercial appeal of its content before more newspapers and magazines followed the example.

If the decade-long experiment of the *Belgravia* magazine was possible it was due to a symmetrical transformation in journalistic practices. The origins of this change can be observed in a parallel development in the history of journalism that affected not the construction of a reading public but the professional status of contributors to magazines and newspapers. A century-long debate had advocated and in the end established the independence of individual journalists, which could be defined by their intellectual value on the market.[8] The nineteenth-century discussion that I examine in this section opposed the reasons of anonymous, partisan journalism of old with those of a new kind of professional journalism independent from the abstraction that anonymous articles in a partisan paper would entail.

Given the extraordinary proliferation of periodicals and the assumed power that the voice of the press was gaining, according to many contemporary commentators, in constituting itself as the "fourth estate" capable of influencing public opinion as well as parliamentary representation, it is not surprising that the debate on anonymity engaged contributors in a reflection on the ever-changing definitions of political representation and agency. This is not the only reason why this debate is particularly interesting for the history of periodicals. The discussion on signature in newspapers, which was carried out on the pages of magazines, circulated new discursive formations affecting the perception of the political sphere and the paradoxical relation between abstract social order and fragmented individual participation. The debate, moreover, shows the importance of nineteenth-century periodicals for the history of journalism: periodicals were a testing ground for practices later adopted by the newspapers. If this innovation extended to newspapers as well it was as a result of two factors: the practice of signing articles in periodicals and the larger political implications that individual or group identity had in the configuration of the public.

THE DEBATE ON ANONYMITY IN THE PRESS

The earliest examples of articles advocating for a reform of anonymous journalism that I consider here date back to the 1830s. Both *The New Monthly Magazine*[9] and *The Fraser Magazine for Town and Country*[10] express a need for a revised policy on authorship. These articles encourage the recognition of each individual contributor as the avowed author legally accountable for the ideas presented. Examples of articles from the end of the century, on the other hand, present the claims to signed articles as a way to advocate for a professional status to be granted to journalists.[11] In between the articles addressing the issue of legal responsibility and the articles that state the necessary monetary recognition of the work of contributors, a series of articles cast the discussion as a larger issue of political theory. Appearing in the mid-nineteenth century at the time of repeated and cautious attempts to expand voting rights, questions of legal responsibility and professional recognition were formulated through discursive practices pertaining not only to debates on political representation but also to nationalist concerns for the preservation of an English character.

The 1959 anonymous contribution published in two parts in *The Blackwood Magazine*, attributed to E.S. Dallas by the Wellesley Index, is a most representative example of this trend. Eneas Sweetland Dallas offers a thorough overview of the contemporary publishing industry by observing its massive output that had been unparalleled by preceding decades. He notes the proliferation of magazines and newspapers of all sorts, for all trades and all classes together with the growing influence on society that the press, in his view, had achieved. In commenting on the success of these papers he argues that literature is no longer a specific labor but had become a "cultivation of a trade" universally present in every class independently of cultural hierarchies. According to E.S. Dallas the varied content of the periodical press makes its presence ubiquitous: any article in the periodical press might report on all aspects of life, be present in the parliament, and compete with the pulpit and with the theater in gaining the favor of the public. In response to the view that the press had become representative of a growing number of class interests widely circulating, Dallas resorts to the argument in favor of anonymity. Only anonymity, according to him, can preserve the integrity of the press and give "continuity of thought and sentiment" (p. 183), which is the press' "life and power." Only unsigned articles, he proceeds to argue, can keep "unanimity" as the press' highest goal and can preserve its power precisely through the mysterious quality of the authoritative anonymous voice.

Anonymity, Dallas contends, also guards against what he perceives as the dangers of the contributor's unchecked egotism flowing into a signed article and also against attacks based on personal grounds. Signature, therefore, is not a prerequisite invoked to introduce the public responsibility of the journalist but a feared breach of the anonymous "we" of an established public voice representing specific class interests. With the enforcement of a signature practice he claims that "public talk will swell with pride, glitter and tinsel" (p. 188); he also fears that nothing would stop the press from making each individual's life a publicized "photographic life." Signature in his view would, therefore, alter the tradition of British journalism that privileged the expression of class interests anonymously in a space distinguished from the private sphere of individual interests. An article is therefore the expression of an individual inasmuch as the author gives up individuality to conform to the harmonious representation of class identity. Signing an article would imply a breach of this abstract notion of power as well as the intrusion into the public sphere of personal interests that would question the uniformity of an anonymous formulation of public identity.

In articulating his views, Dallas draws a comparison between the practice of signing articles and a representative casting a vote in matters pertaining to the interest of a district. Since this vote is the expression of an individual representing a whole district, Dallas argues that it should be known publicly.[12] The large numbers of people affected by that decision pressures an individuality out of personal agendas into an identification with a public abstraction. The opinions expressed in an article, by contrast, do not require the individualization of the speaking voice: since the press, in his view, already identifies with an abstract class, the opinions presented in it should remain anonymous and tend to uniformity for the sake of a collective identification. The public sphere of newspapers offers to Dallas the best example of an abstract, impersonal space that may check the unmanageable multiplicity of individualities in contemporary life. Individualities can have a representation but only through the election of a district representative that supposedly would speak for all of them. The fact that at the time local elections were the expression of a limited fraction of the population shows how paradoxical Dallas' argument is. The article surveys approvingly the rightful expression of diversity in trade reflected by the proliferation of the periodical press while advocating for a harmonious convergence of all diversities in the class-based interests of the newspapers press that matched the system of political representation of the time. His defense of anonymity is presented as a response to the proliferation of periodicals multiplying instead of standardizing the interests of specific subdivisions of the public that he perceived as a homogenous construction. In his article he carefully surveys the market of periodicals and parades all the possible subdivisions of a targeted readership:

> [T]here is the *Builder* for architects, there is the *Art Journal* for artists, there is the *Mechanics's Journal* for artisans; there is the *Economist* for merchants. Lawyers have the *Law Times*; medical men the *Lancet*; chemists and druggists have the *Pharmaceutical Journal*; Churchmen of every shade—high, low and broad—have their papers; Dissenters have theirs; Catholics have theirs; the licensed victuallers have a daily paper.... Then there is an Agricultural Journal, a Shipping Gazette, a Bankers' Magazine, a Statistical Journal, a Photographic Journal, a Stereoscopic Magazine, an Illustrated Journal of all new inventions, a Musical World, a Racing Times, sporting newspapers without end, Railway Times, a Mining Journal, a Journal of Missing Friends in Australia, a Journal for Notes and Queries, an Educational Journal, a Scientific Journal, an Astronomical Journal, a Numismatic Journal, a Journal for Spirit-rapping, for Mesmerism, for Insanity, a Civil Service Gazette, a United Service Gazette, a Family Friend, a Lady's Newspaper, a Classical Museum, a *Follet* devoted to fashion, an Englishwoman's Journal devoted to the rights of the sex, a

> Chess Chronicle, an *Illustrated London News*, a *Punch*, a Biographical Magazine for those who are interested in memoirs, a Weekly Novelist for those who like fiction, and to show how limited is sometimes the sphere of a periodical, we may give the title of one which we picked up the other day at a railway station: "More sympathy between Rich and Poor; a monthly periodical, price 1d." (I, p. 103)

Dallas does not see the fragmentation of the public along market and political lines as the emergence of conflicting interests that call for a redefinition of the public space of social institutions but rather as an endless list representing diversity to be bridged with an uncritical belief in a sovereign rationality. Only in moving away from multiplicity into a type of abstraction can one create an intuitive harmony of one order that goes beyond the individual power of each group. Dallas views approvingly unison in public opinion when it replaces conflict and achieves the goal of "creating a public opinion in the main so true to reason, and therefore, in spite of differences and distortions innumerable, so unanimous in the end, that the authority of any individual journal is forgotten in the universal sentiment" (p. 195). If this result comes with a reduced power of the press that does not concern Dallas at all, since in his view " it is the victory of reason—it is the triumph of opinion—it is the perfect achievement of all that journalists have ever sought for."

Not only is the unwavering stability of a rational abstraction the intuited sign of progress, but the appeal to national identity becomes the corollary to this move toward the comfort of abstract notions that are seen as a consequence of natural course. The debate on anonymity in British periodicals frequently makes references to foreign practices and legislations, such as Napoleon III's decree of 1852 introducing compulsory signature—which led to massive arrests of journalists in the prison of St. Pelagie—or the American long-established signature practice. Many contributions to the debate on anonymity engage in a dialogue with leading journalists such as Zola, in reviewing, often with hostility, his speech on anonymity in Britain and France that he made in 1893 addressing the London Institute of Journalism. Many British commentators praise the British practice mediating between the American and the French model by coating it in national pride. The extremes of what is referred to as American "egotism" on one hand and French dictatorial tendencies on the other one are equally stigmatized as "un-English," while the English practice strives to construct itself as a conciliatory position postulating a middle ground between them.[13] This expression of national identity is all too paradoxical if one considers that by the end of the century a double standard in journalistic practice became dominant transnationally. French, American, and English journals eventually agreed on preserving anonymity for political editorials and signature for criticism. The fiction of nationhood appears to be an abstraction that encompasses both the ideological construction of national identity and the equally abstract production of a professional identity negotiating the borders between the private and public spheres. The middle ground of the British case is also a middle ground that advocates for a definition of the individual as a porous entity partaking in the fictions of the separate public and private spheres. The abstraction of a national character essentializes a structural formation of the public sphere that can exist paradoxically only through the symbolic production of discreet individuals that give up their individuality in the larger construction of the public sphere. The abstract public sphere of uniform subjects is separated from the private sphere of private gain through a fictional demarcation between the two that serves the double purpose of both allowing such a distinction and of sustaining the larger construct of the public sphere. The fictional demarcation between the two recognizes and encourages an individual's personal interest inasmuch as it conforms to the larger structure of a more uniform public space. Private gain is imagined as *de facto* separate from the public; its existence is necessary in envisioning, paradoxically, the public sphere as a "disinterested" gathering of anonymous subjects. A public, political voice, therefore, maintains its claim to universality precisely by relegating the interest of the more individualized identities to the margins and by keeping their demands as "private," that is, not necessarily worthy of public recognition. At the same time, the abstract configuration of the public political voice preserves its autonomy from these demands, together with its righteous justification in order to represent the alienated interests of all.

What the debate on anonymity suggests is that political representation had lost its traditional formulation, or, rather, had transformed the interests of partisan politics into a new fiction of the public space. The new symbolic productions supposedly did include more individualities but it did so while making them constituent to the abstraction of social order that disregarded their claims. The market of periodicals increased the individualization of new specific targets and inevitably multiplied different views and perspectives while making them a buttress to its more normative claims supporting a univocal structure of power. *Belgravia*, too, redefined the concept of the public as a malleable entity independent of political affiliations. Visual stimuli and intellectual reminders of class distinction scattered throughout its pages helped to build a public identity for the magazine as a uniform entity despite the seemingly demystifying effect of the revelations of the sensational plot. Only the debate on anonymity, however, and Dallas in particular, elaborated this paradoxical configuration that preserves the unity of a public identity within a fragmentation of views and individualities: Dallas felt the need for the construction of a common voice among differing voices as the more fragmented reality in his view posed a threat to the status quo. The notions of subjectivity implied in this specific epoch of expanding markets and of unparalleled cultural production functioned as a double-edged symbolic production that aimed at abstraction through and beyond the specificity of individual agents demanding recognition in the public sphere. While discreet individualities were indeed entertained and allowed some visibility, their more political demands somehow dissolved in a public voice that stood above and beyond them, thus contributing to a conceptualization of the public sphere as a supposed convergence of discreet forces.

"Must This Article Be Signed? This is a Serious Question for Me in Writing of Zola"

The separation of public and private spheres that appears in the debate on anonymity, specifically in the separation between the public anonymous voice of political articles and the private individual voice of the essays and criticism, resurfaces in the unpublished correspondence between Mary Elizabeth Braddon and T.H.S. Escott, the conservative journalist who collaborated with Braddon's magazine and was the editor of the *Fortnightly Review* after G.E. Lewes. Mary Elizabeth Braddon was asked to write an article on French literature, on which—she confesses in her letter of December 6, 1879—she was already thinking.[14] She refuses to adopt the somewhat dismissive angle suggested by Escott. In the same letter written from Brighton, in fact, she acknowledges her debt to French literature: "I owe so much to French literature and I am such an ardent admirer of the great French novelists that to depreciate their work would be to turn upon my chief benefactors."[15] Later on in that month, she proposes her project on Zola but insists that having the subject matter somehow dictated a "bold" kind of writing, which she refers to as "masculine"; hence, the anonymity of her publication must be imperative. The letter that accompanies her article on Zola a few months later, when she had relocated in the "rustic heaven" of Lyndhurst, even suggests an old *nom de plume*, presumably the Babinghton White, which had been unmasked by her detractors at *Pall Mall* magazine.[16] Her resolution on preserving her anonymity is unquestionable: "Should you like to use the paper please kindly let the authorship remain a secret between you and me." I was not able to trace her article, which must have remained unpublished as she requests after months of waiting for a response from Escott, when her husband's intercession was to no avail. Her letters, signed Mary Maxwell, show an ambivalent admiration for Zola, which she calls, one may imagine to please her editor, "a perverted genius." She also presents the question of style in gendered terms; her hesitation derives from the inevitable boldness of the content matter, requiring a "masculine standpoint" she evidently finds disreputable.

It is not my aim here to assess Braddon's reasons and explain how the author of sensation fiction that demystified class decorum could be intimidated by her association with a name like Zola's. Nor would I want to justify why an envied and disparaged popular author who experienced public attacks directly and indirectly from several papers (and from *The Pall Mall Gazette* specifically in reference to her newly launched *Belgravia* magazine) would prefer anonymity.[17] I find interesting that the issue of anonymity surfaces in a letter that reverses the established model of signed reviews opposed to anonymous political articles. The separation of private and public that I outlined earlier as a separation within the redrawing of the discursive boundaries between public and private reveals a further dimension, that of class and gender. While contemporary journalism often found ways to attack Braddon's work, and Braddon's contemporary historians of the press avoided altogether the magazine *Belgravia* or if they did mention it the reference was to her husband Maxwell the publisher, this letter points to a voluntary erasure of her name from periodicals. What this letter can suggest is that by requesting to be anonymous she guards her name from any publicity and any association with Zola. Her private character here would represent a specific voice, a visible presence in the market that she prefers to dissolve in a public anonymity that reiterates the underlying social structures. Anonymity, we have seen, served as a check on "strong minded" individualities and obtained an almost mysterious authoritative power from its established practice, precisely because this authority remained a fetishistic projection of added value that masked assumptions on class and gender.[18] It seems that for Mary Elizabeth Braddon publicity would have entailed a notion of impropriety. Even a signed review in this case would have to fall into the broader category of public anonymity; the author would have to give up its personal worth to the protective and uncompromising fiction of the anonymous voice. More than complicating the model I outlined earlier, this instance shows how the reconceptualization of the public and private spheres was superimposed on other conceptualizations of the British social structure, like class and gender, without dovetailing with them. I therefore propose to avoid an essentializing approach to the question of class and gender and to see both as shifting cultural polarities in relation to the ongoing redrawing of the boundaries between the public and the private spheres, as I shall do also in chapter five.

The debate on anonymity, therefore, which I retraced through a selection of voices expressed in nineteenth- and twentieth-century periodicals and newspapers, exceeds the purported controversy on whether articles should be signed or published anonymously under the general name of the publication or of the editor responsible for it. The discursive practices that circulated the spectrum of varying arguments in favor of one view or the other had historical implications that dovetailed with a redefinition of the public and private spheres and of the notion of authorship. Individual recognition and group interests were allowed in as much as they did not interfere with the unquestioned voice of the public, that is, established class interests and coded behavior. The author was expected by common editorial practices reflecting specific political views to conform to the voice of the public in political matters and was allowed visibility only in presumably apolitical matters of aesthetics, only to seek, sometimes, anonymity when aesthetics were perceived as overtly political or improper for the social status of the author.

Periodicals such as *Belgravia* mimicked the process of imagining unity within apparent fragmentation by creating a public of readers that could be manipulated by the overall enticing effect of the publication named after a London neighborhood whose ideology permeated the magazine. The magazine did so, one must remember, despite the sensational revelations that made its success. *Belgravia* exemplifies an important trend in the history of journalism in moving away from classical notions of party allegiance, thus beginning to shape, together with other papers, the later practices of some representatives of the "new journalism." Political affiliation did not matter as much as the marketable viability of a distinctive product whose practices mirrored the paradoxical configuration of the public sphere as an abstraction that the preservation of varied individualities did not question but made possible. The fragmentation of the public was more visible at this time precisely because the fragmentation of the market of goods and of their political counterparts not only preserved the prevailing ideological structural organization but was a product of it. Aspects such as the layout of a magazine, the editor's stance on the debate on anonymity and the personal choice of a contributor were under the constraints of the forces of market economy that were shaping the discursive formations on which these choices relied. The reconceptualization of the boundaries between the private and public sphere that accompanied the changes in the history of journalism found justification in the cohesive ideological formation of the nation opposed to the vagaries of the policies enforced in neighboring countries. In this case, the nation serves as another element of unity that each individual can easily adopt. The imaginary boundaries of a natural character seem all the more fictional and purely representational if one considers that the actual practices that became dominant on a transnational level made the fictions of national identity irrelevant to the larger global uniformity going past the individual nation's identity. Anchoring social practices on a national basis when in fact transnational practices were becoming the norm was only a mystification that nullified the belief in the exceptional nature of each nation. These fictions of nationalism could and did foment strong allegiances without ever realizing that the global transformations of trade and social practices were devaluing the claims to uniqueness that many national discourses made. In a sense, nationalism appeared as a fantastic visual projection that preserved unity within the geographical extension of each country; national identities, however, were blind to the growing influence of a larger global unity that was being superimposed on their apparently fragmented and differentiated territorial extensions. The new entity of global trade was beginning to seep into the social structures of each nation without relying on any discursive formation but, paradoxically, by leaving in place existing fictions and beliefs, to the point that this new entity went unnoticed. The unacknowledged presence of this new force was largely invisible, coated as it was in a national rhetoric of progress and innovation that maintained national identity only as an empty signifier that indirectly made the global dissemination of many trade practices stronger.

Chapter 4

The Cultural Trope of Sensationalism: Advertising, Industrial Journalism, and Global Trade in *Belgravia*

He had been brought up amongst people who treated literature as a trade as well as an art;—and what art is not more or less a trade?

—Mary Elizabeth Braddon, *Birds of Prey*

The cultural trope of sensationalism reflected the process of industrialization that invested many aspects of Victorian culture. In this chapter I shall examine the impact of sensationalism in the rhetoric of advertisements, newspaper articles, and in a novel on the East India Company that appeared anonymously in *Belgravia* in 1868–69. Sensationalism acted as a powerful social and cultural force upon which separate cultural practices of Victorian England hinged: text-based advertisements for new commodities, newspaper articles, and serial fiction, all circulated self-contained and apparently unrelated narratives that helped spread and naturalize the logic of market economy and the ambitions of imperial expansion. I shall start by focusing on advertising in *Belgravia* and in other nineteenth-century periodicals, basing my research on the sheets of advertisements or on the rare covers that contained advertisements, which in most cases were lost when the magazine issues were bound in annual volumes. The exemplars that I discuss are from the collections of the British

Library in London and the special collections library at New York University. I shall first analyze marketing strategies to outline how the rhetoric of novelty, expanded availability and irresistible lure of the commodities advertised targeted specific identities of consumers such as women and a new democratized "public" of buyers. I shall then consider a series of articles on individual commodities from the *Belgravia* magazine. I want to stress how the same rhetoric served not only to create a market niche but to naturalize consumption by inscribing a demand for specific commodities within the coordinates of Victorian traditional culture. A riveting rhetorical strategy, the rhetoric of mystery that made the success of the sensation novel appears in a report on a factory visit: narrative strategy here constructs a fictional, sensationalized lure associated to industrial production. Both the advertisements and the articles can serve as telling examples of how the narrative structures of sensationalism drawn from popular novels orchestrate a new type of relation between things and people: consumption is naturalized and the mysterious secret behind the accumulation of wealth unraveled through the sensational trope. The distinctive presence of commodities in Braddon's novels, which are often necessary to solve the mystery of the plot, further confirms that the cultural trope of sensationalism informed literary, journalistic, and commercial narratives. In order to point out how the sensational element in fiction did not question only notions of class and gender but also the telling of contemporary history, I shall then discuss *Bound to John Company or the Adventures and Misadventures of Robert Ainsleigh*, an anonymous novel published in *Belgravia* in 1868, which is set in eighteenth-century India and has been attributed to Mary Elizabeth Braddon.[1] I want to show how global trade was fictionalized and how the sensational rhetoric demystified the lure associated with colonial commodities. I shall also analyze the gendered discourses that accompanied the British expansion and the recent territorial acquisition of India, following the military repression of the Sepoy mutiny of 1857–58, which meant the termination of the territorial and commercial rule by the East India Company.[2] To my knowledge, there are two versions of *Bound to John Company*, one published in the magazine and one, largely revised, entitled simply *Robert Ainsleigh*, which was issued in 1872 under the inscription "by the author of 'Lady Audley Secret.'" I want to discuss the changes made to the earlier, more sensational, narrative that accuses the East India Company of being "an accursed monopoly, opposed to the law of justice and common sense." The first edition of the novel is an example of how sensationalism affected the perception of past history and disrupted established assumptions of the role and mission of the East India Company. The fierce attacks leveled at the Company and the realistic descriptions of the horror of the war served the purpose of sensationalizing the history of the East India Company in the eighteenth century, at the time of its expansion in the Indian continent. The scenes of colonial horror appearing in the novel break the generic expectations of the picaresque novel that structures the early part of the narrative while at the same time questioning the rationale for the colonial "adventure" that the young protagonist is involved in. The novel, therefore, shows how the sensation plot questioned not only accepted notions of class and gender, as it has usually been argued, but also the telling of British history. Mary Elizabeth Braddon's revisions in the book edition of 1872 are significant for, in refashioning the earlier version presumably to meet the demands of the large public, she removed the most historical parts from the main text and rewrote the second half of the novel to fit a more standardized and palatable narrative set in the context of eighteenth-century society.

Advertising in the Late Victorian Periodical Press

In my study of periodical literature I retraced the history of the ephemeral fragments of print culture that contributed to the multifaceted experience of reading the novelistic installments in the larger unit of the magazine; I also considered the ways in which contemporary culture rearranged the fragments of industrial modernity in cogent narratives and cultural syntheses. Advertising is another example of the cultural move from multiplicity to unity that editorial practices, art criticism, political theory, and studies on optics shared. In this section I shall analyze the surviving advertisements appearing in the bound volumes of serials such as *Belgravia*, *English Woman's Journal*, *Macmillan's Magazine*, *Victoria Magazine*, and *Colburn's United Service Magazine* between the 1860s and 1890s.[3] In contrast to previous forms of advertising these advertisements attempt to create a demand for specific products and consequently to shape a precise kind of consumer. Advertising employed marketing strategies to manipulate the public much in the same way in which periodicals like *Belgravia* employed the trope of sensationalism to create a niche catering to a specific market of readers. My interest in the predominant rhetoric of written advertisements is another monadic remnant, or, to use a term adopted by Giorgio Agamben, a *signatura*, pointing to the larger cultural forces that shaped late-Victorian ideology at large. I am focusing on the written text, since strictly visual representations became standard forms of advertising with a coded language of their own at a later time.[4] This period in the history of advertising, which has been often overlooked, is fundamental in the study of commodity culture because it exemplifies an important shift from descriptive advertising to brand-name advertising, which imagined—and created—target niche markets.

The advertisement sheets that survive in the bound magazine issues often employ written narrative techniques, mixed with visual ones in different degrees, to market specific products. The narratives accompanying a commodity on sale have often the tone of a personal account by a customer who can attest the quality of the product, or their own satisfaction. At other times, a quasi-scientific writing details the distinctive components of the product or the process of its production, while recommending it to the public, in the same manner in which a new cosmetic product is promoted in Balzac's novel *César Birotteau* (1837), thanks to the work of the journalist Finot who is hired to write the text to follow the brand name and logo for the new "huile cephalique." The established technique of listing the name of an item together with the address of its dealer persists throughout the 1860s and 1870s in periodicals and on billboards posted on city walls. The communication strategy structuring the more narrative-based advertisement does not privilege the descriptive presentation of a commodity or of the service and address of a professional.[5] Some of the simpler, enumerative advertisements, which seem more prominent in earlier serial publications, have the same function of a billboard in that they limit the communication essentially to the type of object advertised and to the address of a dealer. In the most traditional examples, the advertisements simply list the product and the producer, like EPP'S COCOA or HEAL & SON's BEDSTEADS. The more individualized advertisements of specific brand-name products aimed at creating an unmistakable association between a name brand, not just a general object of consumption, and its exclusive value. The name of dealers was less important and could change from city to city. The written narrative of varying complexity that accompanies some advertisements attempted to inscribe the use of a certain commodity in the reader's mind through rhetorical means. One of these strategies attempted to create an association between a name brand available to buyers at a reasonable price and excellence. In most cases, this fictional paratext met with a demand in the public, but in some cases it contributed to the creation of a consumer's identity, which was often gendered (figure 4.1).

Lent for the Evening.

MAGIC LANTERNS & DISSOLVING VIEWS.

Also SLIDES for the same, with or without Apparatus.

Catalogues of more than Two Thousand Slides free by post on receipt of one stamp.

E. G. WOOD, OPTICIAN, &c.

74 CHEAPSIDE, LONDON,

MANUFACTURER OF

Apparatus for Exhibition by Oil Light and the Oxy-Hydrogen Light.

Catalogues free by post on receipt of stamp.

MATHER'S ORIENTAL ROSE CREAM, extracted from the choicest rose-leaves, removes scurf, strengthens and imparts a gloss (without the use of pomades) to the hair, and prevents baldness, even restoring the growth in many cases which appear hopeless. Sold by all Chemists in Bottles, at 1s., 2s. 6d., and 5s. each.

WILLIAM MATHER, 14 Bath Street, Newgate St., London, E.C.; 19 Hanging Ditch, and 109 Chester Road, Manchester.

(Established 43 Years.)

STANTON'S CELEBRATED COUGH PILLS are universally acknowledged to be the best for the speedy cure of Coughs, Colds, Asthma, Influenza, Bronchitis, Consumption, and all Diseases of the Chest and Lungs. W. MATHER, 14 Bath Street, Newgate St., London; and 109 Chester Road, Manchester. In Boxes, at 1s. 1½d. and 2s. 9d. each.

Caution.—"W. Mather, Chester Road, Manchester," on the Government Stamp round every box.

Sent post-free for 16 stamps.

MATHER'S ROYAL BALSAMIC PLAISTERS (as supplied to the Army and Navy at Scutari Hospital). Sold by all Chemists at 1d., 2d., 4d., 6d., and 8d. each.

Caution.—Every plaister has the proprietor's signature, trade-mark, and address on the back.

REGISTERED.

MATHER'S NEW INFANTS' FEEDING BOTTLE, THE PRINCESS, is unique in shape and possesses advantages over all others; is a combination of the flat and upright feeding bottles; is perfect in action and simple in construction; can be placed in any position without danger of leakage; can be emptied of its contents to the last drop.

Sold by all Chemists at 1s. each.

BRITISH COLLEGE OF HEALTH,

EUSTON ROAD, LONDON.

MORISON'S

VEGETABLE UNIVERSAL MEDICINES.

Sold by the Hygeian Agents and Medicine Vendors, in boxes at 7½d., 1s. 1½d., 2s. 9d., and 4s. 6d.; family packets, 11s. each. Also the Vegetable Aperient Powders, 1s. 1½d. per box.

Read the Works of James Morison the Hygeist.

DR. ROBERTS'S POOR MAN'S FRIEND

is confidently recommended to the Public as an unfailing Remedy for Wounds of every description—Scalds, Chilblains, Scorbutic Eruptions, Burns, Sore and Inflamed Eyes, &c. Sold in Pots at 1s. 1½d., 2s. 9d., 11s., and 22s. each. Dr. ROBERTS'S PILULÆ ANTISCROPHULÆ, or ALTERATIVE PILLS, proved by sixty years' experience to be a cure for Scrophula, Leprosy, Glandular Swellings, and all Skin Diseases. They form a mild and superior family aperient, and may be taken at all times without confinement or change of diet. In Boxes at 1s. 1½d., 2s. 9d., 4s. 6d., 11s., and 22s. each. Sold wholesale by the proprietors, Beach & Barnicott, Bridport; by the London houses; and retail by all respectable medicine vendors in the United Kingdom and Colonies.

Figure 4.1 *The Belgravia Annual Advertiser*, 1872.

One of the rhetorical strategies that I mentioned is the publication, within the space of the advertisement, of personal narratives. These narratives are often first-person accounts of how the product was discovered, and they are written in the colloquial style of a letter or in the plain style of a journalistic article, like in the case of a quote from "American notes," published in the Belgravia Annual of 1872.

> "We visited, during our sojourn in London, last year, the General Mourning Waterhouse of MESSRS. Jay, 243, 249 and 251, Regent Street, the most noted Establishment of the kind in the world. In looking through its numerous Departments, we were able appreciate the true cause of the **distinguished success** which has attended the Establishment for many years. MESSRS. Jay receive large supplies of READY-MADE SILK DRESSES, direct from the first houses in **Paris**, and they are sold at **much more moderate prices** than ladies can procure them on the Continent. We take pleasure in directing the attention of our fair readers to this time-honoured Establishment, where we are sure they will be loyally and honestly dealt with."[6] (Bold characters mine)

In other cases of textual advertising, an excerpt from a scientific journal or the words of an expert serves the purpose of guaranteeing the efficacy of, for instance, a medical product; these quotes mean to defend its inventors from fraudulent imitations. Starting in the second half of the nineteenth century, commercial validation derives also from the participation in world fairs and from the reception of first prize medals that became another indication of exclusive value. In all of these cases, the authority of a testimonial has the twofold effect of, on one hand, singling out a particular product in the vast market of competing ones, and on the other, of preserving the copyright against counterfeited imitations. Advertisements for some products mention also their prestigious clients to add privilege to their distinctive line of business, especially when serving as purveyors to the royal family or the army; the advertisements also quote positive feedback from distinguished clients such as Earl Russell, who purportedly benefited from a cure against cholera when in Manila.[7]

I want to focus here on medical advertisements because they constitute an interesting case in combining marketing interests, like the previous ones, and evolving gendered discursive practices. One of the most distinctive patterns in the advertisements appearing in the periodical press is the marketing of a single remedy applying to a wide range of conditions. With time, the conditions constantly changed to cater to the demands of the time or to the shifting definitions of the medical discourse. While Keating's Lozanges aimed to alleviate specific affections of the respiratory system, namely "cough and throat troubles,"[8] some other more versatile products sound like the all-purpose concoctions of a quack. In a late-seventeenth-century example from the *Mercurius Publicus* the list of curable conditions included "Consumption, Coughs, Catarrhs, Lungs" and claimed the product to be "sovereign antidote against the Plague."[9] "Clarke's World Famed Blood Mixture," advertised in 1892, guarantees a cleansing effect against "Scrofula, Scurvy, Eczema, Skin and Blood Diseases, Pimples and Sores of all kinds" and is highly recommended against "Gout and Rheumatic Pains."[10] Dr J. Collis Browne prescribes his own patented CHLORODYNE for "Cholera, Coughs, Colds, Asthma, Bronchitis, Diarrhea, Dysentery, Spasms, Cramps, Neuralgia, the Vomiting of Pregnancy, Epilepsy, Colic Palpitation, Hysteria."[11] The panache affect extend to nervous conditions of all kinds. Toward the end of the nineteenth century, medical advertisements indicate a specific niche of female buyers that was made to identify with any of the many symptoms so as to conform to the persuasive diktats of the marketed remedy. Beecham's Pills would offer, for a guinea a box, a relief to "Bilious and Nervous Disorders such as Wind and Pain in the Stomach, Sick Headache, Giddiness, Fullness and Swelling after Meals, Dizziness and Drowsiness, Cold Chills, Flushing of Heat, Loss of Appetite, Shortness of Breath, Scurvy, Blotches of the Skin, Disturbed Sleep, Frightful Dreams and all Nervous and Trembling Sensations." A "WONDERFUL MEDICINE"—the ad proceeds in an exclamatory mode—adding how well indicated it is for women: "For Females of all ages they are invaluable," and "No Female Should Be Without Them." Advertisements for Liebig's bullion guarantee its genuine product imported from South America, and seek to protect its brand name by informing how to recognize the signature brand in blue ink across the label of each jar. Cook books are offered with each purchase, and are claimed to be "Indispensible to Ladies."[12] The medical and household industries insisted more than others in creating a specific gendered consumption of its products and a specific sphere of action for its buyers. One advertisement shows a woman involved in the private labor of polishing shoes with S.H. Harris' Ebonite Blacking.[13] By comparison, the cosmetic industry was not as gender-specific in devising advertising strategies for its products, as the example of the London-based WV Wright & Co.'s soap shows. The advertisement from 1867[14] is more concerned with creating a habit of using its brand name soap approved by the scientific community;

it insists more on linking its beneficial effects to continued use than on envisioning a specific market of buyers:

> SAPO CARBONIS DETERGENS/ PURE COAL TAR SOAP/ (Registered)/ This unrivalled Soap, if constantly used, will produce a healthy appearance to the skin, while at the same time it acts as a preservative of infectious diseases—See Medical Testimony, Lancet etc. etc/ to be had in tablets 6d and 1 s each/of all chemists, and wholesale of manufacturing Chemists.

"Beetham's World Famous Corn and Bunion Plaster" pitches its remedy by relying, in an indiscriminate manner, on the "thousands" who have been cured of "enlarged Great Toe Joints." A language that is not gender-specific characterizes other advertisements from the 1860s, for instance, for a household fixture such as the family sewing machine. FLORENCE Company promises to exchange the machine were the "purchaser" not satisfied. Wheeler and Wilson reproduces in the space of the advertisement the medals awarded at the Paris 1867 and London 1862 expositions to its brand name lock stitch sewing machine, reporting favorable comments by its users: "It is easy to work/ Mechanism is simple/ Does largest variety of work/ None so useful." Some medical advertisements envision a similarly undistinguished public, like the one from the *Belgravia Annual* of 1872 marketing the unfailing remedy of a pill that is "recommended to the Public." The marketing strategies of universal remedies for countless conditions is not alien to other businesses, such as the publishing industry. In the *Belgravia Annual*, Bentley novels are recommended for the "alleviation of hours of languor, anxiety, age, solitary celibacy, pain even and poverty."

The marketing strategies of medical products that I retraced are particularly interesting for several reasons. They combine medical discourse and commercial interest in trying both to create a gendered identity of the beneficiary of miraculous multipurpose pills and to expand the marketability of their pills in a scenario of constantly reinvented ailments and marketing targets. In addition to that, medical advertisements are a telling example of how, in a *mise en abîme* of the practices of the periodical press, they similarly shape certain notions of subjectivity and thus affect mass consumption. This does not mean that the language of advertising, while calling the attention of a circumscribed group of consumers within society, would dispense with the broader definition of "the public". The broader term "public" is simply superimposed on the privatized sphere of the new communality of buyers that appear now as a public, with no explicitly political undertones. A discreet group of buyers is made to coincide with a more universal notion of the public. The repeated insistence in these advertisements on catch phrases indicates how the fragmented perception of the multidirectional stimuli contained in a magazine was less chaotic than it may seem at first glance, since the recurrent terminology became a subliminal form of communication that the reader would easily recognize and retain in his/her memory.

"Luxury for the Millions": Advertising, Industrial Journalism, and the Narrative Structure of Sensational Novels

The language of advertising creates more than one system of meaning. The discourses of medical or household advertising that I outlined earlier are only one example of the possible relations between the fragmented item of consumption and the specific public of consumers whose consciousness advertising targets. Medical advertisements develop a system of meaning that changes over time by means of renewed marketing strategies, while never dismissing completely the old ones. I now want to consider the semantic field elaborated around the notions of value and cost. This inquiry is important, I think, because these advertisements I consider illustrate how the overarching tenets of liberal ideology in Victorian England infiltrate the representation of market economy and support its expansion in the sphere of the every day. Another example of the ramifications the discourses of value and cost had in everyday life are the narratives on industrialization, like the journalistic reports, that I am going to discuss later in the chapter. Fragmentation and abstract theorization, the two ends of my focus in this study, coexist. Discursive formations become dominant through repeated and recurrent appearances of fragmentary catch phrases, which are present in countless units that subliminally point to a more unitary message. These units, which may seem chaotic and contradictory, inevitably construct a manageable coherence through the reader's daily exposure to the seemingly scattered products of print culture. Few words in an advertisement, a narrative turn in an article, a reference in a novelistic plot are fragmented units, which are retained in the memory of readers and taken as a whole belonging to a larger and more elaborate discourse. A cursory view at advertisements, billboards, and shop windows in industrial cities of the nineteenth century has suggested, in the literature of *flâneurie*, a sense of threatened subjectivity, an objectification of perception at the expense of a centered human agency, a free-wheeling sequence of stimuli, an implosion of meaning: in a word, a sense of shattered alienation. The spectacles of *flâneurie* appear to the individual observer as a thrilling inquiry guided by the rhythmic movement in the crowd; they have been read as an aesthetic reflection on the disappearing schemata of traditional vision. A more attentive and focused view at the written texts of the advertisements published in the periodical press and also appearing, more concisely, on the walls of city streets shows, however, a hidden symmetry of recurrent phrases. Whether the advertisements involve pudding preparation, cough pills, electric belts, and mahogany desks, Irish friezes or French coffee, the frame of the introductory remarks, the exclamation-mark rhetoric, the reinforced injunction to consume, all speak one language. This language speaks of an increased availability of products, of purported thrilling novelties, and of fabled universal access to luxury. Several interconnected factors make possible this democratization of consumers' access to commodities: the industrial output of commodities in countless numbers, the logic of market economy, and the reduction of status to monetary value in a nonhierarchical structure— the structure of accumulation. Watches on sale are "first class" and also the result of an improvement in the "science of Horology"; paper is pitched to "all classes of consumers," pens are not simply a dazzling "wonder and delight" to behold but become a "luxury for the millions."[15] Poplin is "genuine" and made of "extra superior quality," medals can be now purchased at a "greatly reduced price," novels are at the same time "the best, cheapest and most popular," German wines "pure and selected." French coffee can now be afforded as a "luxury no longer unknown."

The charm of the commodity in these examples of advertising from the periodical press lies not only in the mysterious and mystifying lure of the image of the admired fetish; the fascination commodities have do not appear to the city stroller as an immobile social hieroglyph that entails a more complex reality. Both metaphors of the fetish and of the social hieroglyph, which are used by Marx, speak of a fascination with African lore that functions as a transfigured reminder of colonial power. The fascination of the commodity that emerges here has, by contrast, the thrilling, momentary quality of a passing sensation that reinforces temporary impressionistic notions, not necessarily still ones like the idea of the fetish, or intellectualized ones, like the social hieroglyph. The sensationalism of the commodity in the psychological perception of the urban consumer lies in the passing notion of uniqueness, in the constructed feeling of refinement, in the malleable view of status that appears to be up for grabs. The inscription of meaning is made possible not through the isolated and completely random flashes that the literature of *flâneurie* has insisted upon, but rather through notable repetitions of recurrent phrases. The cultural trope of sensationalism in the examples of the advertisements from the periodical press of the 1860s reveals the perception of commodities, and the textual advertisements that accompany them, to be fragmented, resisting any still intellectualized view. Both text and images are experienced in rapid succession and the perception of both repeated over time. A still, contemplative view, such as the analogy of the fetish or the metaphor of the social hieroglyph would imply, builds upon an earlier, more immediate and empirical perception of the commodity, which is what these examples help identify. Perception in the textual advertisements from the periodical press of the 1860s processes discreet sensations intended to build an intellectual concept through repeated exposure of fragmented units patched together by sheer accumulation *over time.* Reconstructing the "present tense" of everyday-life practices like reading a periodical or walking a city street entails imagining the reception of these advertisements by the contemporary buyers to be an impressionistic registering of specific recurrent catch phrases and images through a montage effect that gives them consistency and unity by sheer repetition. A sustained, musing attention on any one, which may have produced the analogy of the fetish or the social hieroglyph, belongs to a form of processing sensory stimuli through a transfiguration of the same impressions in the realm of ideas, which is what modern painters and critics defending "the sensational" and impressionism in art and criticism were beginning to transform.

Industrial Journalism in *Belgravia*

The examples of industrial journalism I analyze next show a recurrent narrative strategy aiming at naturalizing the consumption of commodities within the coordinates of Victorian religious and classical culture to make the claim that Victorian society has reached a peak in Western civilization. These articles reinforce the thrilling value of industrial products, which is also a *leitmotif* of print advertising and of the trope of sensationalism at large. Many examples of industrial journalism, more specifically, justify the consumption of these newly available exciting products through the use of a common narrative strategy. Articles on varied and unrelated items such as pins, bracelets, candles, and guns typically sketch the history of a given commodity by tracing back its production and use to remote times, only to complete the excursus with the latest exciting innovations of Victorian England that surpass any predecessor. This shift from classical and biblical examples to contemporary society implies that the latter constitutes a more complete and at times superior achievement. Frequent are also the references to an increased availability of commodities that market economy can provide in large numbers. Another genre of industrial journalism that naturalizes the consumption of industrially produced commodities is the visit to a factory. This kind of writing offers a passing glance at all the steps involved in the production process, which are enumerated with the scientific curiosity of showing "how" given commodities are made. In both the case of the articles on the history of specific commodities and the narratives detailing the production process of a factory the style chosen is the expository style of popular instruction, which shares its rhetoric with some examples of textual advertising from the same time. In the case of an article on condiments from *Belgravia*, for instance, the excursus through past cultures and faraway civilizations ends with a direct reference to the contemporary brand name of Epson salt, linking a product with a brand name as contemporary advertising would do.[16] Dr. Scoffern's article "Cartridges," likewise, structures the *exposé* in a teleological manner, by reaching, toward the end of the article, the discussion of the qualities of the current brand of cartridges used in the British service, that is, the Snider cartridge.[17] "A Visit to Schultze's Gunpowder Manufactory" by Cadwallader Waddy ends, much in the style of contemporary advertising slogans, with the assurance that the production process so carefully described allows for a policy of low price, thus making the commodity "available to the millions."[18]

The scenario of world trade appearing in these articles is one of international competition for innovative improvements to be patented and protected by national laws. While the invention and perfection of the sewing machine is credited by M.R.S. Ross to the equal contributions of American, French, and British inventors, in more than one trade sector the competition with France features prominently.[19] That is the case of the manufacturing of chamber-loading guns, a field in which Cadwallader Waddy assures the reader that by 1872 the long competition with the French counterpart can be set firmly in favor of a "British claim to originality," because the British products are supposedly "the strongest and best breech-loaders."[20] In the case of the standards for gold manufacturing, however, the comparison between France and Great Britain opposes a largely free market of insular goldsmiths to the state-controlled practices of continental France. The economic freedom of the British market appears as a deeply rooted tradition that shapes national identity. The common feeling on the matter is wary of, if not opposed to, the necessity of taxation, and therefore refuses, in the name of "personal freedom," the model of French Contrôle institutions. The winning factor in the competition for lower prices is perceived as the "self-correcting" policy of free-trade, and not a system of restrictive laws. The British system, it is argued, is consequently responsible for a better quality of gold. According to this logic, if business is unregulated by controls and taxation there is no need to adulterate the quantity of gold to meet low-price expectations.[21] Free-trade and excellence, accompanied by a more substantial quality of the products, constructed a proud image of industrial production that permeated the cultural representations of this age.

As the rhetoric of advertising described earlier has indicated, the tenets of free trade and the logic of the market insist that the industrial age has a democratizing effect on the structures of society. The purchase of once sophisticated and expensive objects at a reasonable price defines a new, less exclusive notion of status that is possible—it is claimed—only in the contemporary age. The spread of this discursive formation infiltrates also the writing of articles on specific commodities. A survey of past history in an attempt to make the discussion more authoritative often ends with an assumption of supremacy to be recognized in the Victorian age. In writing on the history of pins, an anonymous contributor to *Belgravia* finds examples of pins in nature and in past history, from Egyptian antiquity to British Renaissance. Only the contemporary age, the author concludes, can witness the massive output of low cost pins, due to the unfettered workings of "competition, free-trade and open markets" unfettered by any *ad hoc* legislation.[22] The late Victorian period is perceived as the reign of prosperity but also of peace. Cadwallader Waddy parades through the massacres of British history in an article that, while telling the history of guns, makes the carnages of past wars a somewhat natural phenomenon related to the evolution of the gun industry. He indicates that preparing for war can be a guarantee of peace, ascribing the latter, in 1871, to the reign of Queen Victoria: "'Victoria the Good' left more guns of every shape and pattern in her arsenals than any other queen that was, or is to come."[23]

The impressive and tangible results of industrial production inspire more than nationalist pride in H.T. Wood's article on the improvements in the manufacturing of sewing machines. Wood claims in the introductory paragraph that in the time from the Exhibition of 1851 a "revolution" in the household made possible the abolishment of the "old slavery of the needle," which is described as "worse than any galley work or *gabelle*," thus allowing the former "slaves to be emancipated."[24] The assumed benefits of industrialization that affected social and political structures extend to other institutions such as the military: C.J. Stone expects a regimental captain to be "a man of very strict business habits, [someone who] must go through a considerable amount of dry, matter-of-fact work."[25] The articles considered earlier share a pervasive optimism and a genuine belief in the symbolic productions of Victorian ideology: a common language structures the countless products of print culture that reiterated the message.

The insistence on recurrent discursive formations instilling optimism is not the only contemporary approach to Victorian commodity culture. The reverse side of this faith so forcefully projected into a future of certainty expresses some doubts on the historical process. Alternative views of a more complex reality do appear without being veiled, like in the former cases, by blind enthusiasm. This more realistic attitude perceives the world in terms of overwhelming numbers of commodities, quickly outdated models, disappearing practices, as well as by manifesting a mistrust in any attempts to influence nature through man-made artifacts. In William Duthie's opinion, his contemporary age can be viewed as an age of "counterfeits and adulterations; an age of outward show, of gloss, and of inward rottenness."[26] To some other commentators, like M.G. Watkins, commodity culture has the mischievous and vain quality of a despised colonial Other; the trappings of contemporary fad for bracelets calls to his mind the idea of Eastern "magnificence" that "plants the seeds of corruption while dazzling the eye."[27] Scoffern, in an extended introduction to his scientific treatment of cosmetics for the hair elaborates on the perfect but fragile harmonies of nature and discourages any attempt of the industrial age to alter it artificially.[28] He objects to the practice of dying one's hair with poisonous compounds on medical grounds.[29] The age of largely available commodities that so many articles and advertisements insist upon does not preclude the expression of doubts concerning one of the most lucrative careers, colonial service, which might not be as rewarding as common opinion would suggest.[30] These views of commodity culture, however skeptical about the tenets of the new faith in market economy and in the resulting progress of civilization, do nonetheless reflect the same facts of the industrial age that other commentators noticed, namely the thrilling effect of abundance in the marketplace and the rhetoric of easily attainable results. The difference lies in a change of tone in treating modernity, which goes from spellbound excitement to disenchanted realization.

The profits of manufacturers are, in any case, unquestioned. Some articles relate the evident profits to the fact that the industrial age made available, besides piles of things, larger amounts of capital in the form of credit. The industry of beer and "spirituous liquors," for example, seems a stable source of wealth, in the hands of an "oligarchical monopoly" that extends to "broad acres, seats in Parliament, a possible baronetcy."[31] In a report by Henry Lake on a visit to the Edinburgh-based brewer Younger and Co. the language reiterates the common formulations of industrial journalism and contemporary advertising. It refers to the higher quality of the ale, the constant improvements of its production process, the owner's ability to adapt the product to a diverse market, such as the Indian one. What is interesting in this article, however, is the use of a narrative strategy derived from sensation novels. The writer does not simply present the factory as labyrinth in which the visitor moves with the help of a necessarily mythical guide, as other examples of this genre in the *Belgravia* magazine show. From the very beginning, what assails the visitor is a sense of "anxiety" produced by the exceptional chance to "penetrate into the secret," the production process. A suspended curiosity and a feeling of awe inspire the visitor as the author enumerates random appearances of workmen and elaborate machinery. The architecture of its departments seems to belong to the "baronial" style of nearby buildings, thus suggesting continuity between aristocratic power and industrial fortunes. At the very end, however, the secret is only partly disclosed; there is both an avowed attempt to reveal the causes of this commercial success and the impossibility to do so, since its "secret is a secret still, and will ever so remain."[32]

SENSATIONALIZING COMMODITIES IN BRADDON'S FICTION

The rhetoric of sensational novels and possibly even of its earlier literary precursors is, therefore, a driving structural principle in the narrative of industrial journalism I examined earlier; following this rhetoric, the workings of a reputed and successful factory seems complex and unfathomable as one of the characters from a sensation novel by Mary Elizabeth Braddon. Sensationalism informs the many cultural productions of the industrial age as well as being shaped by them. This osmotic exchange between fiction and market economy cannot be reduced to a simple chart of philological genealogy tracing the influence of one over the other. Both sensational fiction and the many aspects of the culture industry of the late Victorian period appear to be entwined under the shaping pressure of the new system of commodity capitalism. It is not a coincidence, therefore, if Braddon's fiction swarms with objects and with recognizable commodities to a degree that I have not noticed in other "sensational" authors such as Wilkie Collins and Mrs. Wood. *Aurora Floyd*, for example, abounds with lists of objects and descriptions of interiors furnished with the fashionable imports of colonial trade, like "Madeira wine," "moroccan case and pouch," and reference is made to the intoxicating Indian drink "bang."[33] Lady Audley, too, is surrounded by luxurious furniture; her clothes and jewels mark her identity as a lady and guarantee her social status in the highly regarded rich existence she is now leading. Scholarly criticism has argued that the fast and glamorous female characters in Braddon's fiction represent the projection of the riveting mysteries of commodity fetishism on the objectified female body and on female consumption practices instated at the time.[34] Braddon, however, does not describe the mystery surrounding her female characters only through items of consumption. The use of more traditional narrative tools, like the description of works of art, conveys the same sense of prestige and mystery to the characters in Braddon's fiction. One may think of the significantly unfinished portrait of Lady Audley that the investigating character of Robert, her nephew, discovers and peruses in the drawing room of her house together with his friend and former husband of Lady Audley's, George Talboys. This painting suggests that the identity of Lady Audley is being constructed through the symbolic objectification of her appearance. Aurora Floyd is also the site of imaginative projections, in her case of colonial fantasies. She appears not only as a beautiful, smartly dressed woman; she is also sketched through the figments of mysterious colonial suggestions: she appears as a Cleopatra, a Semiramidis, a Sultana, even as a hieroglyph. Many of the objects used are identifiable name brands: Fortnum and Mason wares, Collard and Collard pianos, Berlin wool and Eugene Rimmel, are all mentioned.[35] The superimposition in the literary plot of alluring commodities and mysteries has a realistic touch deriving from easily recognizable locations of contemporary London city life and from known name brands. Sensational fiction merges industrial production and literary imagination, advertising rhetoric and realistic reminders of enchanting commodities, mysterious female identities, and marketing strategies. The narrative functions ascribed to objects in Braddon's fiction partake of the trope of sensationalism. Objects, in fact, often allow the plot to unravel and mysteries to be untangled; things are the means of ascertaining the identity of a murderer or function as evidence to unmask a scheming manipulator. In *Aurora Floyd* a brass button is traced back to its dealer and to the suspected murderer who bought it and unwittingly lost it at the scene of the crime. In *Bound to John Company*, the much sought-after will that might make the fortunes of the villain—if kept undisclosed—or damn him—if discovered—is kept in a "Japanese cabinet." The protagonist, moreover, receives the necessary information to identify the possessor of the will from a milliner who appears after an elaborate description of a "quilting" of red satin hung in her studio, from behind which she appears. In these last two examples from *Bound to John Company*, the presence of "modish" commodities such as a "Japanned case" or a satin quilt, which were the staples of the East India Company trade, signals the end of a suspenseful quest to unravel the mystery of the character's threatened stance in society. The compelling narrative links world trade and commodity culture, objects of consumption and personal destiny. Things are an essential part of the typical sensational narrative that discloses the workings of greedy plotters caught in the struggle for power between their ambition and the unbending characters they think they can manipulate. The plot typically demystifies the fictions of upper-class distinction by showing how class is neither a stable category nor a guarantee for a model behavior since recourse to criminal maneuvers or self-fashioning performances can alter one's stance in the world at any time. Precious objects, colonial commodities, and recognizable items from advertised city businesses all share the function of representing the appealing trappings of bourgeois status and of thrilling the reader—as much as the buyer—with their symbolic suggestions of rank. These objects do not have the narrative function of the objects appearing in romances; they are not the signs of recognition that in classical romances and Shakespearian drama put to an end the wanderings of misplaced scions of royal families. While objects might serve the same narrative function in abstract structuralist terms, in that they help identify a character by their possessions, in sensation fiction objects provide a distinctive mark of historical specificity. Objects and oriental commodities suggest a broad field of references to the symbolic productions of contemporary industrialization and commodity culture, while at the same time losing their appeal due to the demystifying effect of the sensational narrative. In linking the identity of the characters to fashionable objects, the suspenseful revelations that untangle the intricate plots of the novels indirectly suggest that the fictions of personal destiny can be as convincing and alluring as the undisputed charm and hyped value of colonial objects and industrial commodities. In both cases status appears to be a fluctuating fiction; its power becomes a matter of performance.

Bound to John Company: Global Trade and the New Order in India after the Sepoy Rebellion of 1857–58

Advertisements, by multiplying signs and at the same time dispersing common catch words, introduce a dichotomy between fragment and unity that is parallel to a widespread perception of unity past fragmentation in other aspects of Victorian culture such as periodical fiction, pre-cinematic entertainment, art criticism, and political theory. The industrial supply of goods, which offers in large numbers a rich variety of models and functions, makes commodities available supposedly to all, thus constructing a shared sense of distinction. I have discussed, so far, only the construction of value and distinction appearing in advertisements and newspaper articles. I want now to focus on the category of space to trace the interaction between center and periphery, consumption and production of precious commodities, private home and colonial territory. How does global geography feature in these advertisements from the magazine? The advertisements indicate that the geographical origins of the commodities promoted is scattered all over the world map, thus contributing to create a unifying perception of the world by the sheer consumption of these commodities in London, at the center of this system of production. Foreign territories appear next to the listings of ever-new commodities: rose cream is an "oriental, botanical preparation," Liebig extract of beef is a "prime" South American product," Plumbe's "Genuine Arrow Root" is imported from the South Sea Islands.[36] The "ottoman" is introduced in common usage as a noun at the beginning of the nineteenth century, as the Oxford English Dictionary attests; advertised goods in a furniture store are "japanned"; "French coffee" is a fashion imported on High Street in Islington.[37] While appearing as separate entities, as fragmented territories, these places actually join the geographical common space of a global market that they hint at. "500 patterns in all colours" can be mailed within the UK and, as an extension of its system of communications, to "any other part of the world," only where "pattern post applies." Pens, likewise, are sold by all dealers "throughout the world." Dr. Collis Browne's CHLORODINE has a widespread reputation "all over the East" to cure anything from cholera to epilepsy, and its efficacy is also testified by a quote from Dr. Gibbon, of the Army Medical Staff stationed in Calcutta. The fragmented differentiation of places and commodities is countered by a move toward the unity of a constructed common space that has the center of its trade in London.

The publication of *Bound to John Company* appears in this extended, symbolic space of colonial trade naturalized in the reader's consciousness by products used in everyday life. The novel presents an uncanny story of the eighteenth-century victorious war against the French that reminds readers of the recent victory of the British against another foreign enemy, the mutinied Sepoy army. The result of the eighteenth-century war depicted graphically in the novel signaled the first territorial expansion of the East India Company trade in the mainland. The war to crush the Sepoy rebellion, on the other hand, signals a transfer of power from a much maligned East India Company to the rule of the crown and its military apparatus.[38] The new space that emerges from the telling of an eighteenth-century conflict in the geopolitical context of the 1860s is the space of imperial geography in which the recent native enemy of the Sepoy army could be superimposed on the old, here vanquished, French one. The early history of the East India Company as told in *Bound to John Company* has the sensational effect of denouncing the making of an "accursed monopoly" through a revelation of the horrors of war and exploitation under the rule of the Company. On the paradoxes of the sensational effect that used the shocking elements to actually serve the purpose of the Crown and the powerful sectors of British society that demanded an end to the Company rule I will return later in the chapter.

* * *

Before discussing the novel I want to briefly sketch the history of the East India Company in order to show the stages that allowed it to dominate trade with the East and consider the political effects such an expansion had on British society. Queen Elizabeth, in a letter patent dating December 31, 1600, granted London merchants the right to form "one Body Corporate and Politick, in Deed and Name, by the Name of the Governor and Company of Merchants of London." She also allocated for its first voyage an amount not higher than thirty thousand sterling, six thousand of which was coined in the royal mint at the Tower of London. The petitioners therefore:

> [A]t their own Adventures, Costs and Charges, as well as for the Honour of this our Realm of England, as for the Increase of our

> Navigation, and Advancement of Trade of Merchandize, within our said Realms and the Dominions of the same, might adventure and set forth one or more Voyages, with convenient Number of Ships and Pinnaces, by way of Traffic and Merchandize to the East Indies, in the Countries and Parts of Asia and Africa and to as many of all the Islands Ports and Cities, Towns and Places, thereabouts, as where Trade and Traffick [*sic*] may be by all Likelihood be discovered, established or had; [. . .][39]

Four ships left for the first expedition: the Malice Scourge, weighing 600 tons, the Hector, weighing 300 tons, the Ascension, 260 tons, and the Susan 240. They were put in the charge, respectively, of James Lancaster with 202 men, John Middleton with a crew of 108 men, and William Brand with 82 men.[40] They returned in 1603 with 210,000 pounds of pepper, 1,000 of cloves, 6030 of cinnamon, and 4080 of gum lacquor.[41] The Lord High Admiral demanded a contribution of one-tenth and 917 pounds were paid in customs dues. Subscriptions to finance the coming voyages rose over the years,[42] with a sharp increase starting in 1609 when the right to hold and alienate land was granted.[43] According to the data published in 1898 by R.W. Frazer, lecturer at University College, in the early years of its activity, the East India Company sent 79 ships in several voyages, of which 34 came back with 356,288 pounds in wares that produced a stock of 1,914,000. By the end of the seventeenth century, the Company had lent 2 million sterling to the Crown at an interest rate of 8 percent, in 1702 1 million, in 1730 4 millions at no interest. By 1758 the total debt accumulated by the crown was 4,200,000 sterling, while a yearly sum of 400,000 was owed by the Company to the Exchequer. In Frazer's narrative of a splendid trading company supporting the demands of a profligate crown, the subsequent bankruptcy of the Company comes as no surprise.[44]

The parliamentary bills and royal acts documenting the Crown's interest in the East India Company trade actually tell a different story. In 1693, King William allowed for an additional subscription of 744,000 due to the debts that the company incurred in; in 1698, moreover, a parliamentary act raised the stock to 2 million.[45] The East India Company had also been borrowing money from Indian merchants without, however, honoring the conditions of their agreements. In a letter addressed to Edward Littleton at the end of the seventeenth century[46] Muttredasan, a merchant from Hugley, requires the return of 50,000 rupees, which were lent eight years before. The merchants had also gained large sums of money by plundering territories, as is the case of the destructive rampages during the latter part of the seventeenth century that Sir Humphrey denounced.[47] The disastrous finances of the Company, whose transactions were often kept secret, were one of the most strident contradictions of the "free" trade with the East. Despite that, trade was considered to be one of the most lucrative ones and therefore coveted by many.

From its early years, the history of the company shows the traits that were to characterize its operation until its demise in 1858 at the end of the Sepoy rebellion that started the year before. The Company, while being provided its initial capital by the Crown, conducted trade exclusively of other competitors and without any political control from the Parliament. The fortunes of the territorial expansion of the eighteenth century, moreover, brought additional income through the exorbitant interest rates that were imposed on local rulers for the loans they contracted with the Company.[48] As a result of the Seven Years War fought on the Indian front between France and Great Britain, the British victory allowed the Company to infiltrate the local structure of government. In 1765 the Company obtained from the Moghul a diwani, or right to exact taxes in the territory of Bengal. The increased commercial power of the Company's merchants was not easily monitored, since many of its transactions were not recorded. The Company's decisions, moreover, were not subject to Parliamentary debate and the questions were resolved within the internal governing structure of the company. The monopolistic anomaly of the Company's governance had from the beginning caused discontent among competing sectors of the British economy that argued that the national principles of free trade were not being upheld. The growth of the manufacturing sector, as well as the claims to power of the military and the groups affiliated with the Crown ended this exceptional rule. The Indian Sepoy Mutiny of 1857 became the excuse for this transfer of power. The opposition to the Company, however, had been building up since its inception as an association of London merchants.

Concerns that the operations of the East India Company were not beneficial to the British nation were raised throughout its history and can be traced to surviving documents from the end of the sixteenth century. The trumpeted "Advantages to the whole Nation" of many propositions supporting the company did not cover the interests of merchants who were trying to get into the trade with no success or were excluded from maintaining previously obtained rights in dealing with one territory, which was the case of the Turkey Company.

In other cases, manufacturers protested the competition of the East India products and demanded the expansion of the whole national industry and not just the businesses of the Company servants. Sir Humphrey openly attacked the company by reporting its predatory tactics,[49] while others denounced the horrific conditions of labor of its native employees. Moral outrage often pressed for the necessity of an unspecified better and more humane organization under the proposed change of rule. The objections to the Company and its practices were also due to the preferential consideration shown to the cadet sons of Gentlemen who looked for a respectable position in society without necessarily being worth it.

The Company appeared to many critics to be a monopoly "with one Buyer and one Seller"[50]; its practices, moreover, openly infringed, according to many petitioners, the "Birth-right of the Subject" to trade[51]: it served the private interests of few.[52] Fears that the money lent at no interest or at the "inconsiderable" interest of 3–4 percent would never be returned were also raised after the subscription of 1694. A weaver, signing his petition as Coquille, insisted that exporting bullion would result in a great loss for the nation, since money, he adds, is the "Sinews of War" and, "in the Body Politick," it "is as Blood in the Body natural, giving Life to every part."[53] Some of these petitioners pleaded to open access to trade via an admission fee or a variable percentile to be paid to the Company, usually 5–4 percent on imports or 20 on exports. The purported unfair sale of national goods was seen as detrimental to national manufacturers: the increased profit benefited a limited sector—that of wholesalers and retailers. Manufacturers also lamented the loss of a considerable number of jobs in an industry that hired "weavers, throwsters, winsters, yarn-men, wool combers, hot-pressers, callenders, fullers, spinsters" and was suddenly overcome by Indian commodities produced at much lower production costs. Some felt it useless to set "Work-Houses for the Employment of our Poor, whilst the East India Trade is left at full Liberty,"[54] often paying Indians one penny a day.[55] In a publication from 1720, a defender of the beneficial effects of the East India Company thus articulates the gains of the company's wage policy in India:

> The Labour here in England bears proportions to the Wages that are given for it, it must be measured by the price, so that the Labour of less price must be accounted for less Labour; Indian Manufactures are procured by Labour of less price, and therefore by less Labour than equal English manufactures.[56]

The weaver Coquino, in an effort to stop the competition of Indian-made textiles, such as wrought silks, bengals, and calicoes, which had replaced British "silks, half silks, worsted stuffs, Perpetuano's" as well as German "linnens" and "Silesia Cambricks," proposes protectionist measures like the ones enforced by the French King's edict that prohibited the consumption of "Callacoes" from East India. An anonymous reformer proposed to make the Company national, to save it from the feared Dutch expansion and from the Scottish Company, too, which authorized, by act of Parliament, subscriptions from "Jews, Hamburgers, Hollanders, English and some of other Nations."[57]

In the early history of its expansion on the Asian continent, the East India Company had to face not only the opposition of some of the sectors of the British economy that ultimately led to its suppression, but the commercial and territorial competition of other European nations. Portugal had founded its Estado da India in the sixteenth century and its main ports were based in the Deccan; Holland created a consortium of merchants in 1595 but by the 1700s its company was losing its commercial power.[58] France in the eighteenth century controlled the trade to and from the port of Pondicherry on the Coromandel coast near the British post at Fort St. George. Both Great Britain and France alternatively played the role of allies to local rulers that were waging wars to expand their territories at a time when the central authority of the Mughal was diminishing. This epoch marks the beginning of the British territorial expansion and the increasing British power over local governments. The British achieved a dominant role by two means: on the one hand, by providing financial help through high interest loans, and on the other by guaranteeing military protection against neighboring rulers. Not surprisingly, *Bound to John Company* adumbrates the recent victory over the Sepoy rebellion against the background of the hard-won victories against France and its Indian allies in the eighteenth century. The recent rise to imperial power under the rule of Queen Victoria follows the earlier path of the victories of the British in the eighteenth century. The novel was published anonymously in *Belgravia* between July 1868 and May 1869. The July 1868 issue launching it contained also an illustrated poem entitled "Awaiting the Conqueror" in which an ancient Roman setting provides the backdrop for more contemporary new colonial fantasies that the reader of *Belgravia* could entertain (see figure 4.2).

As reported in the existing biographies of Mary Elizabeth Braddon, the successful novelist suffered a nervous breakdown in October 1868.[59] The new titles appearing in *Belgravia* were by

Figure 4.2 Tomas Gray "Awaiting the Conqueror." Illustrated Poem, *Belgravia*, 1868.

different authors. Justin McCarthy's *My Enemy's Daughter* was serialized starting November 1868 and M. Spanswick's *Stern Necessity* opened the July 1869 issue. *Bound to John Company*'s installments kept on appearing monthly as did the remaining chapters of *Dead-Sea Fruit* and *Charlotte's Inheritance*, both by Braddon, which closed, respectively, in September 1868 and February 1869. *Bound to John Company* was presumably taken up by an unspecified writer after the fifth installment.[60] It reappeared in bound edition in 1872 as *Robert Ainsleigh* under the inscription "by the author of 'Lady Audley's Secret.'" The new edition was much revised: not only was the reference to the John Company taken out of the title, but substantial chunks of the most historical parts were expunged from the main text. Chapter XIV appears without the long excursus on Indian history that might have been deemed a difficult read. Chapters XVI and XVII of the serialized edition are conflated into chapter XVI of Braddon's version. The book version breaks the extended historical episode of Robert's imprisonment in the infamous Black Hole of Calcutta into two chapters, the second one referring explicitly in the title to the overnight interment of the British army in a pit where many perished.[61] The episode was known as the Black Hole of Calcutta and a monument had been erected in Calcutta to honor the memory of the dead and the stoic endurance of the Captain. The incident caused quite a stir in England and, according to Kate Teltscher, struck the public as a "justification of the British military intervention and the establishment of political and territorial control."[62] I am using the first periodical edition for my discussion because Braddon's later version, besides highlighting the British losses in the Black Hole of Calcutta, restructures the narrative by including easily recognizable and marketable tropes of eighteenth-century fiction that make the ending of *Robert Ainsleigh* more of a popular adaptation of stereotypical scenes of aristocratic ethos than a biting critique of colonial expansion that emerges from the periodical version. The earlier edition, moreover, best exemplifies how sensationalism applied to the telling of history and to the perception of global trade and not only to the perception of gender and class stereotypes in Victorian England.

Bound to John Company is at its inception a picaresque novel á la *Tom Jones* set in eighteenth-century England. The narrative opens with the idyll of countryside life, a secluded space of aristocratic peace, which is opposed to the city of the new professional classes. The story narrates the adventures of Robert Ainsleigh, a foundling who grows up in the country mansion of a refined and liberal lady, raised by her gamekeeper who accepts him in his family. After the young aristocrat

Dora is betrothed to her peer M. Everard Lestrange who always disliked the favors Lady Barbara lavished on the young foundling and the affection the latter shows for Dora, Robert moves to London to study law. Befriended by a former gentleman who turns out to be an accomplice of Everard, he is convinced to marry a masked woman, believing her to be Dora. Following the sensational discovery of the ruse, he awakes numbed and finds himself forced into the service of the East India Company by Lestrange's scoundrels who kidnap him. His education is now provided by the Company's ethos that is referred to as "an accursed monopoly opposed to all laws of justice and common sense" in the words of a fellow servant of the Company, who adds that upon joining it Robert, too, has become a "a valuable commodity."[63] Robert is then saved from being flogged for reacting to the insistent abuses of Sergeant O'Blagg; his savior is Captain Howell himself who remembers meeting Robert's father. Robert then becomes a soldier and fights the wars of 1756–63, during which he is imprisoned in the Black Hole of Calcutta and survives to meet his father, who is a mercenary in the French army. Having heard upon his return to England that Lady Barbara's will is actually in his name and the original document to prove Lestrange wrong lies in her former waiting lady's "Japanese cabinet," Robert will have to obtain the will, confront his enemy, and unmask his criminal plotting.

The *Belgravia* magazine theorized "the sensational" as a system of communication and of historical action that may apply to earlier examples in the history of art, literature, and theater, as well as to present and past historical figures. This novel elaborates fully on the notion of the sensational in history. "Sensational," having become a popular catch phrase to express surprise, or at times a shocked reaction, is used in the novel, too. I am interested here in analyzing the narrative construction around the functions of sensationalism, more than the semantic field of the word sensational as I have done in the introduction. The novel in its serial version repeatedly employs some of the narrative devices of sensational fiction, in a hybrid form of picaresque-sensation novel. A generic definition through a hyphenated category is necessary for many other examples of popular fiction published periodically; hybridity is not so much an essential feature of sensation novels, as it has at times been argued, but of periodical literature at large. I will return to the hybridity of periodical "detective" fiction in chapter six. In *Bound to John Company* startling revelations, intensified by an exclamation mark, close some of the installments, such as chapter eleven in the september issue. An intricate plot full of mysteries is carefully orchestrated to create paroxysmal moments of suspense, to use two aspects Wolff defines as the staples of sensation fiction.[64] In this novel, unlike many other ones, the narrative progression of the plot sensationalizes not only the discovery of the identity of its characters but the construction of a national history that includes the Indian campaigns. While Sala proposes in his article to define some historical figures as sensational, in the novel it is the telling of history that adheres to the sensational paradigm: the novel employs sensational narrative functions to deconstruct the tenets of British history that were arranged in a way to build a proud colonial narrative to identify with. Not only does the narrator intensify the effects of the distressing narrative of the war, as in the case of the imprisonment of Holwell and his soldiers in the Black Hole of Calcutta, but the novel also introduces uncanny revelations that undermine the rationale for the British expansion in India that was taken for granted by contemporary and later historians.[65] The horrors of the war of expansion seem to erode a previously unfaltering sense of exemplary moral standards upheld by the British: "I know not whether the treachery of Mohametan revolutionaries in this Eastern hemisphere is much darker than the plots and stratagems of the so-called Christians at home!"[66]—one character remarks. The breach in middle-class decorum that sensation novels achieved by insinuating doubts about its middle- and upper-middle-class characters has a shocking effect in a society where status is no longer a given but could easily be gained by various means. This novel, quite interestingly, brings the supposedly honest workings of colonial power to the critical fore. The narrative opens up the refined world symbolized by the Belgravia neighborhood in the title of the magazine to the war effort in the colonies. The realistic representation has an ever more temporary distressing effect by implying that the root of the Victorians' peaceful enjoyment of new commodities lies in the horrors of a war fought on behalf of the East India Company. *Bound to John Company*, therefore, not only undermines the status of the "Honourable" East India Company but openly associates its practices with slavery when the sufferings of the main character who is being "translated" to India are compared to the "helpless African bondsmen."[67] The several instances of suffering depicted in the novel, such as Robert's voyage or the episode of the Black Hole of Calcutta, are examples of a sensational treatment of history that uses the "politics of affects" to invite an empathic participation in the plight of the victimized character.[68] This strategy, while succeeding in intensifying the sensations of the readers, can easily manipulate the feelings thus evoked to support the claims of a nationalist agenda. The resonance of the recent Indian Sepoy war does not make the passing critique of British expansion a lasting one. The adventures of Robert in the end reinstate a British national identity and the consequent obligation to patriotism. At the very end of *Bound to John Company* the protagonist reunites and finally marries Dora. On their wedding day and while hearing rumors "of the war and glory imminent in Bengal," Dora remarks: "A brave soldier is faithful to his flag in the time of his wealth, as true husband is faithful to his wife in the time of their poverty and misfortune. You are not more surely bound to me, sir, than you are bound to John Company."

These are the last words to be spoken and printed in the serial edition of the novel, which Mary Elizabeth Braddon expunged from her later edition. However wretched the forms of exploitation enacted by the East India Company, its activity is finally aligned with the military duty of a loyal soldier and with the definition of masculinity in clear nationalist and imperialist terms. Thus, the eighteenth-century soldier under John Company merges with the late-nineteenth-century soldier who belongs to the new colonial order under the rule of the British crown. The novel retrospectively tells the story of a triumph that signaled the shift from commercial to territorial power. Its publication a decade after the Indian mutiny of 1857, however, suggests another turn in the British rule over India, that is, its imperial annexation. The implied accusations against this move are, therefore, not a humane cry against injustice, but another kind of glorification of the new rule of Victoria that ended the former rule of the Company after the constant criticism it was put under, as I showed earlier. The novel harshly criticizes the workings of the Company in many instances: another one appears when a letter from Robert's servant Mr. Swinfen reaches him in response to his own account of the events that brought him to India. The letter deplores the practices of the company, and wishes the public to know by involving the press. He concludes, however: "The Directors of the E. I. Company are numerous and wealthy, and these slavish journalists do not care to offend so influential a body. There will, I hope, come a day when the English press will be more enlightened, and a British subject may find a prompt hearing, if not a swift redress, for his wrongs."[69]

To the serial reader of *Belgravia* world trade and the ensuing flooding of new commodities coming from colonial territories are presented as a consequence of the horrors of war. The teleological structure of the novel leads all the episodes to an end that reinstates the allegiance to an imperial and nationalist ideology, which equates loyalty in marriage to service to the nation. Gender roles here are the structural working of an imperialist and nationalist ideology. Robert's discovery of his father in India where he is a mercenary soldier fighting with the French stresses the nationalist overtones of the narrative even further. The story pits Robert's identity against France, the country his father serves, in yet another nationalist affirmation. Robert appears as the loyal British soldier who comes of age during his service in India; his "baptism of fire" and initiation to adulthood implies overcoming the mysteries and gaps of his family history in the newly formed identity as a British soldier. The happy ending that typically closes nineteenth-century British fiction with a quiet scene of domestic life here resonates with the echoes of the language of nationalist rhetoric, of a sculpted monument from Victorian London that invites to obedience and sacrifice. In this light, all pieces fall into place, scattered commodities and the process behind their production, disturbing revelations and the unifying logic of Victorian ideology.[70]

Chapter 5

Sensationalism and the Early History of Film: From Magic Lantern to the Silent Film Serial Drama of Louis Feuillade

When sensation novels became popular during the 1860s the literary industry was quick to recognize a lucrative line of business, so much so that twenty years later Vizetelly could promote a whole series of French "detective" novels by marketing them as "French sensation novels." Publishers of books and periodicals were able to swarm the market with countless, readily available titles that supplied a strong demand for riveting stories full of shocking revelations. The plot of sensation novels hinged on a limited set of narrative functions and plot developments that the reader could easily grow accustomed to: despite the variations of each specific title and the interpolations deriving from a mix of genres such as the sensational-*bildungsroman* of *Bound to John Company*, most narratives repeated a successful formula. I am deriving the term narrative functions from Vladimir Propp's formalist analysis of oral history and Russian folklore. With this formalized view I do not mean to diminish the contribution that each individual author gave to the genre with their choice of subject and specific stylistic features. I only want to note that sensation novels, like many forms of popular literature, tended toward a standardization of narrative and character development. Riveting scenes and heart-wrenching conflicts migrated from one novel to the other and constituted a sort of *koinè*, a common language, of late Victorian sensationalism in popular literature. These narratives, by means of their repetitive and simplified structure, could captivate a massive audience and linger in their memory until the next installment, or title, would reactivate the readers' interest in new combinations. Nineteenth-century popular fiction, therefore, counted on its recognizable generic features to become a staple with the public, in the same way in which other popular forms of art, such as the vaudeville, the pantomime, or its predecessors within the practice of *commedia dell'arte*, built their following upon stereotypical characters and settings. As the rest of the chapters in this book have shown, the commercial success of sensationalism extended to print culture at large and was not limited to novelistic narratives. The strategy of sensationalism and its tropes reappeared in other contemporary cultural products, from industrial journalism to written advertising, from scientific popular education to the construction of a national identity around the telling of history. Sensationalism was not so much a formalist residue deriving strictly from literary production, even though it was popularized through sensation novels. Sensationalism was rather a structuring matrix of the culture of modernity. Noting the formalization of sensation novels around recognizable narrative functions does not mean that these narrative devices existed independently of a historical context, which is also the point of Propp's morphology of Russian fairy tales. Propp's investigation into the historical roots of oral narratives anchors the fictional appeal of fairy tales in specific folkloric traditions that reveal the historical nature of the same narrative functions. The apparently interchangeable and limited set of events that may befall the protagonist of a sensation novel, likewise, went beyond the pleasure of escapist fiction: it spoke, as the case of Propp's analysis of fairy tales demonstrates, of a system of beliefs and practices shared by the whole community. Obviously, in the case of sensation fiction, these values were not the reemergence of long lost folkloric traditions that survived only as narrative; they had an origin more markedly rooted in contemporary culture. The anxiety associated with the plights of the protagonists of sensation novels spoke of the power of market economy to seep through established rituals of class distinction and to subvert them from within. The prolonged suspense that would captivate the reader of a sensation novel was also the result of the reconfiguration of the notion of value that industrialized cities were undertaking, in a world where appearance had replaced substance. Value per se was up for grabs; it was based more in manipulation and performance and less and less in a fixed and real factor. It comes as no surprise, then, that sensation narratives that demystified the appearance of distinction of their upper-class characters enjoyed such a success.

I pointed to several intertextual reverberations of sensationalism that can be traced in late-Victorian print culture. The intensified emotions sensation novels thrilled audiences with have often been associated to popular forms of entertainment, such as the melodrama. While keeping in mind the larger implications that sensationalism had in Victorian culture, I want in this chapter to focus on another aspect of nineteenth-century visual culture that has not been explored yet, since most works discussing the relation between the Victorian novel and the arts focus mostly on the theater, music, drawing, dancing, and architecture. I am going to focus on pre-cinematic culture, more specifically, the several practices of popular vision that preceded but were not totally replaced by the emergence of the cinematograph at the end of the nineteenth century. I intend to discuss the iconography and social history of Victorian magic lantern shows, peep-boxes, and phantasmagorias, which capitalized on the sensational since the late seventeenth century: their appeal worked both through a fragmented spectacle of unrelated images and through the use of normative narratives of moralistic and scientific instruction. My interest in these visual practices that catered to a mass audience that grew increasingly used to subjects and narrative techniques based in fragmented juxtapositions, which the early film industry later adopted, is both historical and narratological.[1] From the *historical* point of view, a study of pre-cinematic entertainment suggests that popular culture and technology, in transforming the perception and cognitive processes of the viewers, transformed also the idea of the text and their understanding of reading. The fast-paced succession of images became a more and more complete text in itself; the apparently unsystematic logic of associating diverse elements constituted a new manner of thinking through and by means of fragmentation. I want to insist on this understanding of the technologically based cognitive processes of a specific age, following, with some reserves, the influential work done by Jonathan Crary in this field.[2] I think that the cultural implications of a historically specific attention to the process of perception as it has been shaped both by scientific knowledge and popular entertainment are not limited to the specific context of late-nineteenth-century popular culture. Keeping this hidden history in mind helps illuminate the later experimentation of twentieth-century modernism through and beyond the innovations of nineteenth-century modernity. Tracing the hidden presence of pre-cinematic entertainment past the nineteenth century, for instance, can help understand the recurrent references in Walter Benjamin to nineteenth-century spectacles. This perspective offers also an insight into the visual nature of Proust's process of conceiving narrative structure through phantasmagoric epiphanies and double exposures of his perceptions over time. Considering the whole history of the optical devices that were popular forms of mass entertainment throughout the modern age allows to pre-date and complicate the paradigm shift placed by Crary at the beginning of the nineteenth century. An attention, moreover, to the largely social visual practice associated with magic lantern entertainment—as well as camera obscuras—can also highlight a history of observer*s*—in the plural—and not of the single perspective of the metaphysical subject of scientific and philosophical treatises discussed by Jonathan Crary.

From the *narratological* standpoint, a study of pre-cinematic entertainment next to the history of popular fiction can open a new understanding of the shaping of narrative techniques. I want to focus on how pre-cinema impacted the history of the novel, particularly popular sensational fiction. So far the history of the modern novel and that of pre-cinematic entertainment have proceeded on parallel lines with occasional tangential points when, for instance, novels enter the repertoire of magic lantern shows or, conversely, optical devices are mentioned in the plot of nineteenth-century novels. Here, I want to underline how both media partook of a narrative strategy shaped by the forces of market economy. The shocking effect of the sensational has an optical, traumatic meaning that became a pervasive mode of entertaining (and manipulating) an audience. The same fragmented, simplified focus of emotional sensational attention punctuates a stroller's walk in the city streets, as well as fiction, theatrical melodrama as well as magic lantern entertainment and popular journalism.[3] I want to link pre-cinematic entertainment and popular fiction not to sketch a linear narrative of influence of the former versus the latter, but rather an osmotic exchange between the two that extended past the late-Victorian age into the silent film industry of the 1910s and 1920s. I shall also consider the social histories of both the magic lantern and the novel inasmuch as they can help illuminate important changes in the conceptualization of the public and the private spheres of entertainment and instruction.

THE MAGIC LANTERN (AS) JOURNAL

The cumulative sensory stimuli coming from texts and illustrations assembled through the *montage* effect characterizes both the production and the reception of Victorian serial publications and popular entertainment.[4] The way in which these fragmented stimuli of print culture are juxtaposed randomly or arranged in a narrative that gives them consecutive meaning through *montage* can easily suggest an analogy with the development, during the Victorian age, of the many pre-cinematic techniques that were devised, building upon earlier examples, to project images on a screen and set them in motion. The magic lantern holds a preeminent but not monolithic place due to its long history, its many metamorphoses, and its wide accessibility particularly since the industrial production of lanterns made it available to countless spectators and artists. The functioning idea of the magic lantern, going back in time to the studies and experimentation of the German Jesuit Athanasius Kircher and the Dutch humanist Christian Huygens, covers a wide period of history, a history of incessant improvements that ultimately transformed it into the projection machine of the modern movie theater.[5] The history of the magic lantern reflects the ongoing preoccupation inventors and producers had with realistic accuracy in representation, as well as with the creation of an effect of movement and narrative consequence. These mimetic and narrative prerogatives were shared by painters, inventors, and projectionists alike, thus requiring an interdisciplinary approach when tracing the history of nineteenth-century visual culture beyond the traditional hierarchical focus on the 'fine' arts. Magic lantern entertainment is also important because the device evolved considerably during its history and resurfaced in many periods, thus capturing the imagination of different generations. Magic lantern shows are significant for literary historians because the attraction of one of its show went beyond the visual lure constituted by projecting disparate painted glass slides on a screen: a verbal and at times musical commentary by the lanternist accompanied the images, thus making the magic lantern show an important, partially textual form of popular culture that employed coded narrative techniques.

The functioning principle of a magic lantern has often metamorphosed, allowing the representation of different spectacles: real-world images—at times in motion—were predominant as well as the sensational conjuring up, always through the magic lantern, of the spirits of famous historical figures or of terrifying fiends, particularly in the act of the phantasmagoria. The history of the magic lantern, therefore, is wide-reaching, as it involves technical aspects as well as anthropological and sociological ones. In the long nineteenth century that saw film entertainment emerge by incorporating the technology of earlier devices such as the phenakistiskope or the zoetrope, the dream of creating an alternative and lifelike reality to contemplate could never dispense with the basic and long-lasting technology of the magic lantern.[6] The magic lantern holds a pre-eminent place in popular culture in the time before the film industry supplanted its popularity without, however, dispensing completely with its operating principle. The name of the magic lantern was certainly more enthralling and more familiar to many than the scientific neologisms chosen to name newer forms of entertainment. In the second half of the nineteenth century, when the magic lantern was manufactured industrially, it became even more accessible, supplanting the original itinerant lanternists with new city-based entertainers in popular theaters, bourgeois families, and lecture halls. Camera obscuras, panoramas, magic lanterns, and other optical devices all captured the imagination of countless writers and poets: many mentioned them in their works but few merged their own creativity with the functioning of these devices to the point of innovating narrative style in unprecedented ways. I want to trace some of the recognizable traces of the poetics of the magic lantern and pre-cinematic entertainment in popular periodical fiction. Before doing that, I want to further expand on the popularity of the magic lantern, which was the only device, among pre-cinematic devices, that has enjoyed both a literary life through innumerable appearances and metaphors, and a lasting life in linguistic usage. Understood metaphorically, the magic lantern alludes to a new psychological reality, the registering of motley stimuli that characterize the experience of modernity in the urban, industrialized environment. Publishers quickly understood the viability of the magic lantern spectacle as a catchy metaphor that helped to refashion established literary genres such as the memoir or the satirical sketch book with a blink to modern forms of entertainment. In the nineteenth-century French press in particular, the magic lantern becomes a chosen title for launching new periodicals, thus making officially recognizable a similarity between the experience of reading unrelated news, articles, and images and that of perceiving magic lantern slides in a show. Both magic lantern shows and periodicals are miscellaneous compositions that juxtapose informative articles on history and science, fictional narratives, articles on exotic locations, illustrations of poems, and caricatures inspired by contemporary history. The link between magic lantern shows and the periodical press is not limited to the acknowledged similarity in presenting episodic news, narrative installments, or disjoined newspaper articles as part of a somewhat coherent fragmentary genre. An iconographic continuum between the two artifacts can be documented: many magic lantern slides originated in illustrations from the periodical press; illustrators, moreover, worked for both industries, as the case of the *Belgravia* illustration I shall refer to later shows.[7] The periodical press, therefore, competed with magic lantern entertainment in captivating readers by capitalizing on the same visual lure of images accompanied by an explanatory text that would make the success of a magic lantern show. The press, by choosing sensational matter as a bait to attract a wider public, targeted readers and buyers in the same way in which a sensation novelist or a theatrical entrepreneur would do.

The London audience in the Victorian age had grown accustomed to a variety of optical projections such as dioramas, panoramas, and magic lantern shows, at least since the end of the eighteenth century.[8] The London urban space had specific permanent sites, which were threatened by devastating fires that periodically destroyed them. Magic lantern spectacles had an earlier itinerant history through the work of Savoyards who would set up their shows in rural squares, inns or, by invitation, in bourgeois homes.[9] The presence of the cry of the itinerant lanternists on the road often followed the calendar of seasonal fairs and annual festivities. Some of the popular attractions for the London crowds had a permanent home: the panoramic Colosseum was set up in Regent's Park in 1812, the Kineorama in Pall Mall, the Kalorama on Bond Street. The newly redesigned artery of Regent's Street along the north-south axis of town,[10] following the Roman camp's urban structure, was a popular destination for it boasted both the Cosmorama and the Royal Polytechnic Institution where magic lantern lectures attracted huge crowds. Leicester Square was already the center of block-busting entertainment as it is now, housing both the Royal Panopticon of Science and Art and the Great Globe.[11] Projecting light effects on a screen was what made these spectacles possible. In the phantasmagoria, light effects were invisible to the audience and came from behind the screen, like in the technology of the panorama and diorama, thus inspiring an awe that the magic lantern technology, being placed in front of the screen and at times in the midst of a seated audience, would dispel. In the phantasmagoria, the light effects and projections coming from the unknown recess behind the screen did not sensationalize natural phenomena such as sunsets, volcano eruptions, and storms but the superstitious beliefs associated with magical thinking. The subjects of magic lantern projections, by contrast, were more diverse and as miscellaneous as the content of a periodical. The images included geographical locations of travel, devotion, or, following the imperial expansion in the colonies of Africa and Asia, colonial rule, coupled with an interest in the population that inhabited those lands.[12] The sequences of images with a historical topic cover events from the past, such as *The Story of the Mayflower*, *The Accession of Edward VII*, or *The French Revolution of 1789*, and contemporary history, such as coronation ceremonies. All major events of British history, particularly wars, such as *The Tale of the Great Mutiny*, *Transwaal War part 1–6,* and *The World War*, appear to have been documented with an increasing frequency starting in the second half of the nineteenth century through photographic magic lantern images. Some slides detailed a day in the life of a big city like London or adopted the perspective of the *flanêur*, like the series entitled *Street Life, or, People We Meet.* Others had a more direct colonial angle to them, like *Our West African Settlements* or the conspicuous series *Our Colonies: Canada*, *South Africa*, *Australia*, *India*, *New Zealand*. Literary adaptations were popular with narratives inspired by *Aesop Fables*, *Paul and Virginia*, *The Adventures of Don Quixote*, *Bunyam's Pilgrim's Progress*, *Robinson Crusoe*, major fairy tales, and the more sensational *Visions of Hell by Dante Alighieri*, which in some cases was made from the Gustave Doré illustrations that had appeared in book form. Religious themes were quite common, too, with passion plays, lives of martyrs, adaptations from the Old Testament and the Gospels. Temperance stories pertained to the lives of working-class characters on their path to repentance or sobriety, such as *Father Come Home*, *Shadowed by Sin*, and *The Way to Heaven for a Sixpence.* All of the genres mentioned earlier could easily migrate to silent film and their popularity in term of content did indeed continue in the silent age of the cinematograph. The practice of scientific lectures accompanied by magic lantern images constituted a sub-genre specific to the slide show of magic lantern entertainment; it survived past the monopolistic domain of the projected image reached by silent film in the genre of the scholarly lecture. The *Natural History* series could focus on specific classes of birds, reptiles, or other animals; some other series illustrated the stages of the history of human locomotion or the possible experiments that could be done, for instance, with glass.

I now turn to the impact of this visual language on popular literature, keeping in mind that the migration of genres and forms from nineteenth-century magic lantern entertainment to silent film did not happen without a textual mediation represented by popular fiction and the periodical press. There is a link, which has been so far overlooked, between magic lantern shows, silent film, *and* popular nineteenth-century fiction that can illuminate how the wide popularity of cheap novels, which were structured in very simplistic and visual terms, contributed to shaping narrative structures and motifs of the silent film industry.

The Iconic Quality of Sensational Narrative Functions

Sensationalism has been a constant thematic and narrative feature throughout the whole history of the optical devices I consider here. Disturbing content informed both projected images and dazzling light effects in panoramas, dioramas, and peep-boxes. In phantasmagorias the shocking value was in the surprise and fear generated by an increasingly enlarged image of a ghost or devilish figure that would materialize in front of a frightened audience immersed in darkness.[13] Peep-boxes offered a daylight image on print of a specific location, such as Frankfurt, the Bay of Naples, or New York, which glowed with night lights, fires, or natural catastrophes when lighted from inside the box. The effect made possible a temporal transition to a nocturnal view of fireworks, like in the Frankfurt scene celebrating the emperor Joseph II, or to a more dramatic and brightly lit scene of a volcanic eruption, an earthquake, or a devastating fire, like in the *vue d'optique* of Naples, the Messina earthquake, or the 1776 New York Fire from the collection of the Museo Nazionale del Cinema of Torino and the Museum of Pre-Cinema, Minici Zotti Collection in Padua.[14] These examples of sensationalism might have the same thrilling effect on the audience as later forms of visual and literary sensationalism had for more lucrative purposes. I think that despite the shared success phantasmagorias and peep-boxes entertained, the genealogy of their iconography, however, was starkly different: phantasmagorias seem more indebted to the folkloric tradition of the rural gathering of "witches" and Pan-like devils marking the calendar of peasant's life. Some of these ghostly apparitions were expected in association with specific times of the year, like the darkest days of winter and fall that would cyclically renew the anxieties produced by the apparent death of the natural world. These disembodied figures in the popular imagination would take the form of creatures brightly emerging from a dark environment to visit the living.[15] Peep-boxes, on the other hand, are more indebted to the tradition of Edmund Burke's philosophy that classified the aesthetic sensation of the sublime by ascribing it not only to unmanageable extensions of darkness but to phenomena of light: the latter was classified as sublime when it was either too dazzling, or sudden, like in the case of lightning or the fireworks darting from a peep-box at the turn of a switch. Magic lantern entertainment, while adopting some of the stock images of peep-boxes and *diableries*, offered, particularly after 1850 when photographic slides were introduced, an idea of realism and narrative complexity more in tune with contemporary reality. The sensational appeal of these sequences, like in popular fiction, relied on the shocking excitement produced by catastrophic events taking place in contemporary reality. I want to refer here to the common series of sensational slides depicting a rescue from a building on fire that belongs to the collection of David Francis and Laura Minici Zotti.[16] The example reproduced here, from the Minici Zotti collection, provided the almost exact iconography as in the illustration of Braddon's novel *Fenton's Quest*, which was serialized in *Belgravia* in 1870–71 (figures 5.1 and 5.2). This subject matter illustrates how the popular industry capitalized on scenes and narratives of realist inspiration that transformed the space of the home in a locus of sensational entertainment that was thrilling as well as educational. The manipulation of the readers by means of strong emotions partakes, I believe, of the logic of sensationalism that is typical of sensation fiction and specifically of Braddon's editorial run of the *Belgravia* magazine. The presence of danger in the home is, in the case of magic lantern slides and in the novel *Fenton's Quest*, a reminder of the risks associated with living in a crowded urban environment. Both the catastrophic slides and the revelations of the sensational kind are a shocking call to reality that breaks with the escapist nature of both kinds of entertainment.

The quick occurrence of sensational turns in Braddon's fiction applies the narrative technique of magic lanterns shows to periodical literature: the novel installment shares with the projected images of the magic lantern a direct, immediate appeal that relies on a simplified, fast paced sequence of events. Sensational turns, in order to captivate the audience, needed to be recognizable at a glance, simplified of any surplus informational quality that would distract the viewer-reader, or fail to catch their attention. In book installments sensationalism needed to acquire an iconic quality, the ability to strike the optic nerve with a quick and strong impression that a magic lantern slide would have achieved immediately. The quality of sensationalism that marked the years in which Mary Elizabeth Braddon edited her magazine *Belgravia* is similar to the shockingly stunning sort of sensationalism common in pre-cinematic visual entertainment. The category of the "sensation" novel has often been used too broadly, both by the Victorian publishing industry that promoted its products with easy catchwords and by scholars working on Victorian fiction. The fact that many authors were branded as sensation novelists may be

Figure 5.1 Firemen to the rescue. Magic lantern slide. Museo del Precinema of Padua. Collezione Minici Zotti.

Figure 5.2 Louis Huard, *The Rescue,* illustration for Mary Elizabeth Braddon's *Fenton's Quest. Belgravia* magazine, 1871.

an indication of the subject matter but oftentimes "sensation novel" became a comprehensive term that applied to different styles of sensation fiction as well as to different genres that were grafted onto the popular tradition of sensation fiction, as the Vizetelly series of "French sensation fiction" that I shall discuss in chapter six attests. Only the language of advertisement or the marketing strategy of the publishing industry would happily present sensation authors as a uniform product by referring to them with one memorable word. As I argued in chapter two, other sensation novelists, such as Mrs. Ellen Wood and Wilkie Collins, structured their narratives according to a different economy of the emotional response. The melodramatic quality of the scenes in Mrs. Wood's *East Lynne* is most compelling when the progress of the action is halted in a *tableau vivant* of intense feelings that envelopes the reader for a number of pages. Wilkie Collin's *Woman in White*, to name just the most successful title that inspired Mary Elizabeth Braddon to write her *Lady Audley's Secret*, chooses another strategy to capture the reader. His story creates an all-pervasive ominous atmosphere around the characters that only the slow unraveling of the investigative plot can dispel, thus easing the tension generated by the mystery. Wilkie Collins novels reproduce and sustain the same atmosphere at each installment until the plot finds its teleological closure. Mary Elizabeth Braddon differs from any of the other sensation novelists in basing her stories on a constant shocking effect that punctuates each installment with some extraordinary event. Contemporary reviewers, Henry James *in primis*, noted that Braddon's novels were novels in which the narrator's technique privileged actions over psychological analysis and detailed description. Many of the most thrilling passages in her novels use at their best the habitual settings of modern life and the newest forms of communication that are based on quick impressions. Characters share their knowledge of the current stage of the investigation by sending telegraphs, which may or may not reach their destination, exciting even more the anxious involvement of the reader who knows more than some of the characters in the plot. Some mysteries are solved with a railway timetable at hand to track the movements of a character, or when finally the definitive revelation comes from an easily recognizable commodity, like the japanned case in *Bound to John Company* that I discussed in chapter four. The demise of the villains, or the suspected villains, can be illuminated by the burning glow of a fire that condemns them to their (apparent) death. All these instances of sensational surprise have a visual quality to them common to magic lantern entertainment. The thrilling effect can be achieved in a simple and direct way that refrains from any useless description or digressive aside. It is the immediate appearance of the events narrated that stands out and gives the narrative a focus and a form of visual consistency that was common to other popular types of visual entertainment. The case of the rescue of a maid from a building on fire in *Fenton's Quest* can best illustrate this link between quick, realistic thrills of urban magic lantern spectacles and Braddon's sensation novels, which were often inspired by contemporary conditions of living. In the novel installment appearing in the March 1871 issue of *Belgravia*, Mrs. Ellen Whitelaw smells smoke in her home, does not find her husband Robert in the parlor (he had retired upstairs), and walks into the corridor to find the house on fire! She goes and wakes up the servants in the upper rooms by ringing the alarm bell. They all run to the kitchen as the noise and the smoke increase, then they make it together to the yard as the fire gains ground. While Ellen's husband recovers in the fresh air, a look at the house reveals that the west wing has been surrounded by flames and the access is blocked! Someone has been kept locked there, "a poor relation of Stephen's perhaps—a helpless mindless creature, whose infirmities had been thus hidden from the world. Such things have been too cruelly common in our fair free country" (p. 115). The spasmodic suspense reaches a cathartic climax when the firemen arrive and liberate the woman imprisoned in the building on fire. The narrative formula of the rescue from a building on fire features as a realist urban scenario that journalism, periodical literature, and pre-cinematic entertainment had capitalized on through sensational accounts. The narrative formula soon migrated from Victorian print culture to the early film industry, for instance, in Edwin S. Porter's 1903 *The Life of an American Fireman* and in other similar stories involving a woman threatened in the quiet respectability of her own home.

The Private Economy of the Spectacle

Before turning to the reemergence of sensationalism in silent film, I want to compare two different histories, namely the social history of a nineteenth-century object, the magic lantern, and the history of the novel in order to retrace the actual place entertainment holds in these histories, both explicitly, as the site where entertainment is consumed, and implicitly, in reference to the sites represented in these forms of popular culture. Both the history of the magic lantern and of the novel attest that the site of entertainment became increasingly detached from the public, open space of their respective earlier history, thus engendering a consequent "privatization" and normalization of the scope and aims of popular entertainment. The early history of the modern novel, in its "omnivorous" capability to encompass the whole experience of human life, has often depicted public spectacles, in a competitive attempt to mimic and somehow surpass other forms of entertainment. Some examples, among many, may be the puppet show in *Tom Jones* by Henry Fielding, the walks in Vauxhall to see the fireworks in *Evelina* by Fanny Burney, the court entertainment in *La Princess de Clèves* by Madame de La Fayette, the street scenes with jesters, clowns, and peep-boxes in William Wordsworth's *Prelude*, not strictly a novel but still an influential narrative poem dubbed "an autobiography of the poet's mind."[17] The shows mentioned in these narratives take place in the shared, public sphere of an institutional space, the city or the court, and not in the drawing room or in the toys room of a bourgeois home where both the magic lantern and the domestic novel will eventually end up. These examples from seventeenth- and eighteenth-century fiction, probably following previous ones in the picaresque tradition, like the episode of the puppet show in *Don Quixote*, feature characters belonging to all classes who are allowed to see one another in the public place where the entertainment takes place; social status is therefore performed according to naturalized conventions and understood in reciprocal recognition with the other members of society (see figure 5.3).

The later history of the novel presents a different scenario: entertainment, as represented in several genres of nineteenth-century fiction, becomes an increasingly privatized pastime. Thackeray's *Vanity Fair* does depict the wonders of acting and the intrigues of the social scene of the nineteenth-century London bourgeoisie but does not limit the excitement of public entertainment to the institutional space of the theater. The function of theatrical performance has entered the private space of the bourgeois home and has become, with the social game of the charade, or the *tableaux vivants*, a pervasive function that breaks down the barriers between stage and audience. As far as other nineteenth-century novels go, singing, too, appears to be taking place in the drawing room of a home and not necessarily in the by then established locus for the consumption of classical music, the concert hall.[18] The Cremorne gardens, the pleasure garden that supplanted Vauxhall in terms of popularity and high attendance rates since its opening in Chelsea, do not feature prominently in canonical novels. If we shift focus from the actual locus of entertainment

Figure 5.3 Pinelli, *La Lanterna Magica* (in fact, a *mondo niovo/* peep-box). Museo del Precinema of Padua. Collezione Minici Zotti.

to the mental image that novels evoke through the setting of their stories the tendency to an increasingly privatized space is even more remarkable as the century progresses. In domestic fiction and sensation novels, for instance, the trajectories of their protagonists inevitably revolve around the walled-in space of the home and, thus, seem to fit in the same category of a privatized space for entertainment. The astute marketing machine behind the sensational craze follows the same pattern: it sells an addictive thrill that entices the reader until the closure of the novel brings all conflict to a resolution within the reinstated values of the dominant class represented by the Victorian home. The space of the Victorian home is often opposed to heterotopic locations such as the mental institution or the cemetery to which the sensational female character is relegated to make possible the "happy ending" of the novel. In both domestic fiction and the sensation novel, therefore, the private space of the home is a coded feature in the narrative economy of the novel that reinstates the values of the dominant class and stresses the separation of the private and public spheres by ascribing a normative standard to the heroines that accept their roles as limited to the accepted conventions of lady-like behavior confined within the private sphere. That the interest of the public could be somehow manipulated by strong and often traumatic impressions and led to a type of normative control masked as fictional escapism is not unique to nineteenth-century culture. The dazzling logic of *maraviglia* in the baroque age is a poetics of sheer visuality that is not separate from a political interest in distracting the intended public, even when sharing a public space, as the example of Versailles demonstrates. Sensationalism in the private sphere becomes a coded narrative form that extends to other genres of popular entertainment. The narratives of early cinema, for instance, present topical characters and settings that captivate the audience with sensational narratives, like the stories of a woman who is home alone and is threatened by an ill-intentioned intruder. Films such as the Pathé productions *Terrible Angoisse* (Terrible Anxiety, 1906) by Lucien Nonguet and *Le Médicin du Château* (The Palace's Doctor, 1908), as well as D.W. Griffith's *The Lonely Villa* (Biograph, 1909) used sensational topics to thrill and awe the audiences gathered to see the films in the public space of the theater. Capitalizing on the fears centered on what may happen to women when their husbands were not home, these films instilled in the audience a normative code of passivity for female behavior in the private space of the home, while reiterating the addictive thrill associated to the experience of going to the cinema.

The magic lantern follows a path similar to the one I have underlined in the history of the modern novel. After being for centuries an itinerant spectacle that gathered its public in city squares or countryside yards, occasionally visiting more prosperous homes, in the nineteenth century the magic lantern becomes a gadget to be owned and used within the private space of the middle-class home.[19] In its confined space, the lantern becomes a signifier for a domestic form of entertainment detached from public spaces. The employment of magic lantern projections for the large audiences attending scientific and historical lectures or magic lantern shows in theatrical venues seems at first to contradict this trend. When considering the equally normative power that such narratives have in shaping a popular knowledge of race, colonial history, and even military industry, this particular use of the magic lantern resembles more a form of normative entertainment within a somewhat privatized space than an eighteenth-century or earlier example of a popular public culture.[20] Public entertainment, which pre-dates the inception of the modern novel and the practices of the baroque age, has often taken place within the public space of city squares or allotted areas. Many of the early forms of popular entertainment fell within the sphere of the sacred; when these spectacles included the performance of literary works, the narrative structures, myths, and symbolic undercurrents were bound to the dominant religious systems, as both the dionysian festivals at Athens and the medieval plays and fabliaux can attest. The presence of a comic inspiration in some of these performances does not question the solid intellectual foundation of the collective ritualized experience that attending these festivals meant. The comic elements in the medieval fabliaux—as well as its carnivalesque traits—featuring also in the Greek old comedy and in tragedies are examples of a liberating, albeit strictly coded, manifestation of the sensational overturning of the logic usually recognized in accepted social roles. The logic of reversal of the carnivalesque, however, differs from the logic of sensationalism in that the carnivalesque functions as an irresistibly funny and disturbing inversion of social hierarchy along a more determined line than the unexpected break with accepted social norms of the sensation novel. The narrative functions of sensation novels are not driven by any ritualized exchange of identities across the opposite polarities of class, when the poor can become a king only for a day and viceversa, like in the carnival; sensation novels, moreover, usually do not introduce any liberating license from logic like in the culture of the carnivalesque. The sensational turn breaks the assumed notions of propriety and questions the essential qualities of the dominant classes by insinuating the idea that what is believed to be a naturally given quality, female propriety in the private sphere or male and female social standing, is actually a carefully constructed performance. The stress on performativity is not a ritualized and liberating folkloric practice, like the carnival, which a whole community gleefully took part in, albeit temporarily. Sensational literature does reverse expectations on social codes of behavior; the reversal these novels enact, however, is never a shared practice that a community understands through the normative value of the ritual, but rather a challenge to conformity that entails the immediate social ostracism of the sensational figure, when discovered. The apparently subversive revelations in a popular novel that invert social structures produce only anxiety and fear of an imminent retaliation, which define the repeated formula of this type of escapism. I would not describe the repeated appearance of the intense peaks of spasmodic emotion typical of sensationalism "ritualistic," despite their coded frequency, but rather mechanized, since they are industrially produced thrills for a paying public. The place where the sensational narrative is set is also different from the traditional places of folkloric traditions: sensation fiction focuses its demystifying aim primarily on the space of the private home and indirectly on the purported universal values of the bourgeosie that are associated to it. Sensation fiction, therefore, represents in the history of popular entertainment a move away from the public dimension of art, as well as from the sphere of ritualized folklore following a religious calendar. In a similar manner, the history of magic lantern shows points to a limitation of the political sphere, in the sense of "pertaining to the civic dimension," which was originally present in the earlier forms of public entertainment. The privatized nature of most lantern shows also demystifies the terrifying images summoned by the fantasmagoria: the home use reduces them to mechanized projections in the private space of home entertainment. The magic lantern, in the earlier stages of its history before massive industrial production of lantern kits, was an itinerant spectacle that had the cadence of random encounters with the unfamiliar, even the exotic. Its practitioners, the "savoyards," had no fixed dwelling; they were *colporteurs* who traveled with the lantern on their back and were able to create a festive atmosphere at any corner, fair, or inn.[21] As the iconography of the magic lantern in prints and paintings can illustrate, the use of magic lanterns and other pre-cinematic devices changes later in history. Lantern shows go from being an itinerant spectacle for the entertainment of the general public (or those who could afford a show to amuse their guests) to a simple commodity that targets the general public in a theater or in a bourgeois home that bought their own device.[22] The late nineteenth century uses, therefore, dispense with the thrilling magic of the foreign represented by the appearance in a familiar setting of the society of the savoyards; these uses also abandon an overt association with rituals of rural folklore. The compelling charm cast by the magic lantern, like other devices employing the projection of light on a screen, can still be viewed in an anthropological sense as a product of the fascination with the powerful symbols associated with light present in several cultural traditions. This fascination, particularly in the form of the phantasmagoria, appears to be in part an uncanny resurgence of folkloric beliefs associated with magic in the urban, bourgeois environment, which has repressed them, only to be haunted again by them both in the horror of the phantasmagoria and in gothic tales of *revenants*. Magic lantern shows, in becoming more and more a private practice, exemplify a detachment of public entertainment from its traditional roots in popular folklore and in the public space, while instilling new values and beliefs that substituted the old ones. The riveting effects that the variety of magic lantern slides could have was soon discovered to be a means of instructing and at the same time manipulating the viewers, just like the wondrous surprises of the baroque age served the purpose, for instance, at Versailles, to keep in check the nobility. The history of late-nineteenth-century magic lantern entertainment, which combined shows with an educational purpose and shows of an apparently dominant escapist nature, had a normative value in shaping the knowledge and consciousness of the public. As scholarship on the magic lantern has made clear, magic lantern shows were not always a random selection of isolated slides or of visual tricks. Many series of slides illustrated a moralistic narrative aimed at normalizing the reactions of the popular public, like the temperance stories meant to police practices of unrestrained consumption of alcohol usually among the working classes. This educational turn is particularly evident in the latter part of the nineteenth century with the industrialized production of slides. Even the apparent fragmentation suggested by the appearance of countless images from all over the world was never a random exercise. These images would indirectly hint at the expansion of European colonial power and at the proximity of renowned destinations for the upper-class leisure tourist. Shows were organized thematically and often presented articulated narratives. The selective scope of the narrative of magic lantern series carries, therefore, the same ideological implications of any other narrative. The ideological construct of any of the many magic lantern narrative genres is even more evident when considering that the popularity of the lantern shows was soon co-opted by the commercial sector. The concern of nineteenth-century producers extended beyond narrative per se to target specific audiences that were considered most impressionable and weak, and thus in need of instruction: children, the working class and women. It is not surprising that children constituted at the end of the century and into the twentieth one of the most lucrative markets for magic lantern producers and entertainers, if one considers that the audience of other popular forms, such as the novel, was similarly singled out and thus policed. The consumption and production of novels had often been categorized as a practice pertaining one group, the public of women readers and authors.[23] That the novel was often considered a gendered form explains the pervasive fear sensation novels caused among conservative critics as to what effects popular entertainment might have on female readership. Both the sensation novel and the industrially reproduced magic lantern targeted a market of individual private users that were encouraged to indulge in their pleasure in a setting that would keep them away from the public spaces of the street or of the politically charged square.[24] The normative power implicit in instructive lectures at institutional locations such as the Royal Polytechnic would likewise envision the audience as a manageable entity. Both magic lantern shows and novels were part of a "culture industry" that, by the end of the nineteenth century, multiplied occasions for consumption while giving a normative spin to its contents. It is true that sensation novels may have had a more subversive effect, particularly in their serial publication; the context of the magazine in which so many of them appeared, however, mitigated it, as well as the sheer teleological conclusion of the narrative plot that often punished—at least in the British context—their transgressive heroines *á la* Thelma and Louise.

The trope of sensationalism appearing in pre-cinematic entertainment, popular fiction, and print culture was not limited to one period, the late-Victorian age. The osmotic exchange between visual entertainment and popular fiction had ramifications extending into the silent age of the early-twentieth-century film industry. An aspect that has not been adequately considered by scholars is the role of sensational literature, particularly popular, periodical literature, in shaping the narrative structures of silent film.[25] Literary sensationalism, while being extremely popular as early silent film adaptations can attest, has not received due consideration by silent film scholarship so far. The existing records of the immense and largely perishable production of silent film lists, for instance, two film adaptations of Braddon's *Lady Audley's Secret*. Two cinematic adaptations of *East Lynne* were produced in 1908 and in 1916. Wilkie Collins' *The Moonstone* was made into a film twice in a decade: in 1909 and 1915. *The Woman in White* was distributed in 1917 by Pathé Exchange, the American branch of the French company. The 1908 adaptation of *Lady Audley's Secret* no longer survives, while the 1915 version still exists. Braddon was invited to the opening screening but did not comment on it in her diaries.[26] Her silence, one can imagine, might as well have been out of an act of quiet recognition of a lifetime commitment first to the stage and then to the editing of the scattered and disparate contents of Victorian society through sensationalism. The early film industry had made accessible to wider audiences the same genres of fiction and non-fiction of a Victorian periodical; its formal structure, moreover, relied on the psychological process of reading separate images in rapid succession or connecting related scenes through editing, which became a dominant narrative technique. This new psychology of reading, as my previous chapters have shown, had been shaped by the periodical press through the same process of juxtaposing events and structuring them into a larger ideological narrative. In order to start reevaluating the role of literary sensationalism in silent-film studies I am focusing here on the depiction of a female sensational character in silent film through the example of a silent film serial drama, Louis Feuillade's *Les Vampires* (1915–16). Scholarship on silent film has written widely on the suffering female characters in melodramatic films but not so much on the hidden track represented by the fortune of sensation narrative forms depicting a different female character. I will discuss the character of Irma Vep in particular, which is more akin to Mary Elizabeth Braddon's brand of sensational women and, to some extent, to the foreign *femme fatale* from French periodical sensational fiction of the 1870s and 1880s, which Braddon contributed to with her own feuilletons. I do not mean with this parallel to essentialize a given personality trait and imagine that its presence in literature and popular art might be an unaltered common thread across the ages. Rather, I am interested in distinguishing how the construction of femininity varies at different times and reflects, in this particular case, different stages in the development of industrial capitalism.

SENSATIONAL REALISM: FEIULLIADE'S *LES VAMPIRES*

Conventions that are largely historically specific have defined throughout the ages the category of realism. The "realism" associated with the genre of the novel was an ideological rendition of relations of gender, class, and race according to the dominant views of a middle-class golden standard. To have a sense of how paradoxical the recognition of a mimetic quality in novel writing is, one may consider the question of linguistic realism. The ability of a narrator to speak through many jargons and inflections, and thus be perceived as true to life contradicts the nineteenth-century novel's pretense to realism. A contrapunctual auditory effect in fiction, made possible by a variety of linguistic styles, appears to be inversely proportional to the development of the British novel. The plurilinguistic audacity of the eighteenth-century satirical imagination was reduced by the second half of the nineteenth century to a monolingual voice of uniform characterization.[27] Sensationalism, while showing the same form of linguistic standardization as many other works from the period, uses narrative structures and characters to break the mold of other standardized practices of mimetic recognition, the social rituals of the upper class: by doing so, sensationalism indirectly questions the boundaries of the real. Accepted and recognizable behavior is exposed as a selective construction of standardized manners exclusive of contradictions and paradoxes. The realism that shocked and attracted contemporary readers broke down the barriers of class distinction and female propriety by suggesting that the social reality of accepted norm that was so stubbornly believed in was an illusion. Mary Elizabeth Braddon's sensation novels fall within the tradition of realism that has shaped the French and British novel throughout the first half of the nineteenth century. Her admiration for French novelists goes as far as recognizing the genius of Zola, at least privately, as the correspondence quoted in chapter three can attest.[28] Mary Elizabeth Braddon's sensationalism, therefore, can be seen a new form of literary realism, not necessarily an opposition to it.[29]

Sensational narratives dispensed with the traditional definition of upper-class morality based in a private decorum that matched public recognition of one's status by insinuating the doubt that any of the two aspects of one's persona, the private and the public, could be founded on a mystification. The female protagonists of sensation fiction negotiated their position along the demarcation of private female virtue and public male authority by adapting the resources of the public male persona to the private sphere of action they were allowed: the respectability of the bourgeois home. The paradoxical definition of realism throughout different ages and media allows to trace the complex construction of identity at the intersection of several discursive formations constantly reshaping the boundaries of the public and the private. Following this premise, I shall examine the sensational female characters of Braddon's fiction and of Feuillade's silent film serial drama *Les Vampires* (Gaumont, 1915–16). My choice of silent film is not dictated by content only or by an interest in the many histories of mass culture and popular spectatorship. The technique of capturing and reproducing movement by means of a sequence of consecutive images is deeply rooted in the culture of sensationalism that I charted. The mechanism of the cinematograph grows out of the perception and study of visual fragmentation, as well as out of the juxtaposition of visual stimuli that made the experience of nineteenth-century print and visual culture a motley inscription of visual, intellectual, and verbal stimuli. The poetics of silent film, like novelistic fiction or editorial practices, is a compromise between an omnivorous curiosity toward the myriad fragments of the seen world and the careful selection of the narrative elements on which to inscribe cohesive and thus normative meaning. I am mainly interested in the serial drama by Feuillade as the depiction of a female character such as Irma Vep can help illuminate to what extent sensational characters survived in popular culture by reaching the silent age through their constant presence in print culture and periodical fiction.[30] I shall also discuss how sensation narratives could question and expand the perceived boundaries of what constituted a "realist" depiction. I want to examine how the latter notion, realism, was shaped and redefined by the development of the capitalist mode of production.

Produced between August 1915 and March 1916, the ten-episode series *Les Vampires* was Gaumont's French response to the periodical silent film drama *Les Mytères de New York* that the American-based Pathé-Exchange had launched in a European market of silent film that had been heavily damaged by the war and the competition of American distribution companies.[31] The idea of the film-novel allowed a title to be shown for ten weeks in movie theaters capitalizing on the word-of-mouth and newspaper advertisement coming from printed novelistic installments of the same title. The characters and settings that appeared in both film and newspaper were made ever more familiar by periodical consumption, thus making a serial drama more of a household trademark than a unique work of art. The narratives of a weekly episode fit a generic form that could thrive by introducing in each film episode new variations to the main plot and to the settings that were the backdrop to the adventures of the same characters.[32] This serial formula was a guarantee for success, if one considers that 331 films that were distributed in France between 1916 and 1929 were serial dramas.[33] The narrative structure of a silent film serial obviously differs from a novel published in installments as each episode of the former is a self-contained, miniaturized version of an entire novel. The silent film serial may be closer to the endless number of novels that constitute popular French periodical series such as the adventures of Rocambole by Ponson du Terrail, or titles such as *Les Habits Noirs* by Paul Féval where the same characters reappeared in different scenarios. A serialized publication, however, required a run of several weeks, if published in a daily paper, or of several months, if published in a monthly magazine, to reach a conclusion. The silent film industry compressed canonical forms of entertainment—and the time it took to experience them—and made them more readily accessible to wider audiences. The pilot episode of the serial drama *Les Vampires* introduces the main character, Philippe Guerande, a reporter for the paper *Le Mondial* who is investigating the death of inspector Durtal. His dossier on the band of the Vampires that is the prime suspect for the crime is stolen from his home. Despite this intimidation, he pursues his quest at the castle owned by a friend of his father's, Doctor Nox, in whose residence the corpse of the inspector Durtal had been discovered. More mysterious events follow: the inspector finds in the pocket of his pajamas a note, signed by the Vampires, with the injunction to abandon his investigations. Later, the stolen cigarette case of another guest, the American Mrs. Simpson who is interested in buying the property, reappears in Philippe's hands, thus casting doubts on his morality. The setting of the whole episode is a realist representation of contemporary life: Philippe walks the streets of Paris and passes by posters advertising contemporary cabaret shows. The realist inspiration of the setting, however, is constantly contradicted by a mysterious parallel world of hidden passages, communicating rooms, and surprising encounters. What astounds the spectator most is the inability to recognize the relations between the characters appearing in the narrative, as a family friend may turn out to be the main suspect of a crime, and a new maid might turn out to be a spy sent by the invisible enemy. The inexplicable discoveries of notes or the momentary loss of precious items are often explained to the public as the workings of an unnamed and unrecognizable character belonging to the band of the Vampires. It appears on the screen as a black silhouette that easily moves in darkness and is able to access different spaces without being caught by anyone. The secret connections between the different classes and professions involved in the plots of the band are not left to the understandable paranoid suspicions of the protagonist who cannot immediately sort them out. These secret societies are explained to the audience through the use of an uncanny shadow, a blind spot on the screen that operates at night and dissolves in the surrounding darkness.

In the third episode, a recovering Philippe who had escaped in the previous episode a kidnapping by a band of hooded criminals guided by a masked master, Dr. Nox, quits his job at the paper and takes some time off, while being closely and invisibly watched by the Vampires. His maid's forced absence to take care of a dying relative forces him to temporarily hire a new maid, sent by the Employment Office. She turns out to be one of the Vampires, Irma Vep (the anagram Irma Vep—Vampire—is indicated at one point in the film by a dance of letters on a poster), who impersonates the agile black silhouette, which, when the mission is accomplished or when in peril of being caught, escapes through the window and comfortably finds its way out on the roofs of Paris. Played by the actress Musidora, Irma Vep is one of the reasons of the popularity of the serial. She reappears in each episode as the unsuspected secretary, neighbor, or maid with a pivotal role in the transactions of capital that the secret society of the Vampires pursues. In one of the posters advertising the serial, she features as the sensuous female shadow sitting comfortably in a living-room armchair while being watched by the frightened face of a man peeking from a little corner on the upper right. Her place in the domestic space of a bourgeoise home is not identified with any of the social functions associated with the female gender: she is both an insider who knows her way around and a disturbingly malleable signifier that can take all shapes and meanings. Unlike magic lantern shows and phantasmagorias that captivated countless viewers with visible projections of light and suggestions of magic and necromancy, Feuillade's visionary talent found an unprecedented use of darkness, both sublime and human, to signify the mysterious relations between people that revolved around the production and accumulation of capital. The figures involved in the wide network of crime woven by the Vampires are beyond any suspect: noblemen, bankers, real estate tycoons lead a respectable existence surrounded by the luxurious trappings of the leisure class. Their specialized and respectable trades would cast them worlds apart were they not secretly connected through other members of the criminal band that occupy less conspicuous places in the system. The outcome of their plots is in the hands of other members of the gang, the professionals of crime that do the dirty work and, if necessary, gain access to any recess through the protean figure of Irma Vep. The sway a character like Irma Vep held on the audience was certainly due, as mentioned earlier, to the uncommon role she plays in the narratives, defying traditional expectations of middle-class female propriety. Like Aurra Floyd and Lady Audley, Irma Vep does not hesitate to recur to any means to accomplish her ends, risking her life and leaving a trail of bewildered victims behind her. Like Lady Audley, she can change her identity and perform any role that might help her and her accomplices survive: she can be a clerk assistant and a maid, thus gaining access to the respectability of both private homes and professional offices. She is also shown to have an athletic agility and a bodily strength that never fails Lady Audley and Aurora Floyd. Irma Vep can be seen as a symbol of the protean nature of social conventions that can be worn as a robe defying any ossified perception of reality. She is also an elemental force of pure potentiality: her dark suit makes her undetectable as she infiltrates private homes and offices in search of binding documents to protect her accomplices. In both cases the female gender appears to be a screen onto which the projections of a specific system of economic production shape a compatible identity. The two characters operate within different social structures: Lady Audley, on the one hand, works solely within the boundaries of the bourgeois space of the private home. She ascends the rungs of the private hierarchy of the domestic economy of Victorian Britain in going from the humble and submissive role as a maid to that of the childlike, spellbinding lady of the house. She seems to acquire the skills of an unscrupulous businessman and apply them to her life within the private sphere to which she is confined. The space of action allowed to female characters is still limited to the private world of the family and when not compliant, to the yet more confining space of the mental hospital. Irma Vep and her accomplices, by contrast, live in a more complex society where what is at stake is not just the role of women in the private sphere. In each episode of the serial the relations between people in the Parisian world of the high functionaries of industrial capitalism is mysterious and mystifying. The members of competing interest groups congregate in secret societies whose membership is unknown to many, including the viewer, until the final sensational revelation of their identity shows them to be involved in the criminal plots of the Vampires.[34] They navigate easily both in the world of finance and in the functions of everyday life that fall within the private sphere. The narrative of the film editing presents them as isolated characters devoted to their business in their offices or absolving their social obligations at parties, concerts, and in their family life. The juxtaposition of the settings they live in and the separate activities they invisibly conduct follows a logic that is alien to the viewer's. An understanding of the larger network that links them is left to the narrative deployment or to the viewer's inference. The network of relations between the characters points to the increasingly alienated nature of human relations introduced by the fully developed capitalist system of production in which the relation between people is obfuscated. What replaces a human, non-alienated interaction is an inexplicable juxtaposition that the condensed narrative of cinematic editing makes even more evident than a literary narrative would: the separate environments, which the editing juxtaposes, communicate only through a secret understanding of things that is an elitist vantage point belonging to few. The protean silhouette moving in darkness and through the walls that separate private and public, personal and professional, metaphorically represents the sensational revelation on the secret criminal operations of prominent figures in modern society that is kept hidden from the audience. In its infinite potentiality, this figure defying categorization also signifies the ever-changing modulations of malleable identities that can be made to serve the purpose of the system, in this case through the depiction of the sensational female character of Irma Vep.

My analysis has focused on sensational characters from nineteenth-century fiction and silent film serials in an attempt to examine their space of action and, by doing so, define their agency within their respective environments. I showed how both their characterization and the narrative structures employed by different authors appear as categories of an evolving history that posits the construction of gender within the discursive practices that constantly negotiate the scope of the private and public spheres. I meant to underline not only the ideological construction of gender but to examine gender relations in the context of an ongoing history that does not end in the Victorian age or in its surrogates. I believe it to be a most viable form of analysis, following the example of what Miriam Hansen has produced in the field of film history, for it helps to reevaluate the political role that mass culture has at different times and locations. Comparative in approach, the study of two epochs and two distinct forms of popular entertainment takes my scope of analysis away from a purely historically specific, albeit necessary, point of view that informed the rest of my work. In this perspective, the insistence that scholarship on the Victorian age has at times shown on time-specific formulations of gender can be avoided when it runs the risk of essentializing not only female identity but paradoxically the structures of power it was relegated to. Even a non-canonical author such as Mary Elizabeth Braddon can become an example of the cultural practices of canonization. Her works, like *Lady Audley's Secret*, that stirred more controversy and were immensely popular can definitely help define the ideological implications of the sensation novel. Mary Elizabeth Braddon's whole literary career, however, offers also examples of novelistic plots that undermine the very narrative structures of the most celebrated sensation novels. In her feuilleton novel *La Chanteuse des rues*, which appeared in the *Rappel* in Paris in 1873, the sensation pattern of victimizing the lady with a (secret) past takes an unexpected turn. Jenny, the protagonist, escapes the abuses she suffered in her life as a street singer, marries into abundant wealth until her past comes back to haunt her through her former "protector." As a result of that, she is unjustly turned away from her new home, but she refuses to give in to her persecutor: she moves to London, hires a detective, and neutralizes the forces of evil plotting against her. No mention of the feuilleton is made in *Sensational Victorian*, the exhaustive biography by Robert Lee Wolff. I shall discuss the novel in the next chapter that examines the fortune of the sensational formula across the Channel, more specifically in the French periodical literature of the 1870s and 1880s.

Chapter 6

Mary Elizabeth Braddon in Paris: The Cross-Chunnel Relations of Periodical Sensational Literature in the 1870s–1880s

The setting: "the quietest road" in the Marais quarter in Paris—rue St Gilles, "where gossip flourishes as rankly as the grass between the paving-stones." The time: a Saturday evening, April 27, 1872. A man of thirty is noticed in the area as he wanders from door to door seeking information about the house of M. Vincent Favoral, supposedly for a cousin of his who is considering a job offer as a cook in the mansion of M. Favoral, at number 38 of rue St Gilles, "an old type of house, not so common anymore, that the housing market values at 1200 francs per square meter." M. Favoral is chief cashier and one of the principal shareholders at Mutual Credit Bank, an institution that, "sprung up with the Second Empire, won heavily on the bourse the day the Coup d'État was played on the street." While he sits at dinner entertaining his guests for the evening, he is interrupted by M. de Thaller, an elegant baron, who takes him to another room for an animated conversation. All money in the bank is lost, the police wait outside of the house to arrest him for forgery and embezzlement.

End of chapter one.

In few pages we find, almost condensed to a mechanical prototype, all the ingredients that make the successful narrative formula of the sensation novel's plot:

1. A specific location with the description of a wealthy residence.
2. A quiet bourgeois interior with scenes of domestic life.
3. A visitor who breaks into the secluded peace of the family, posing, with the information he carries, a major threat to the reputation and the economic stability of the family.
4. A suspenseful ending that closes the chapter.

While the incidents setting in motion the narrative are quite elementarily clear and, in their direct simplicity, guarantee the aroused curiosity of the reader, some other elements in the picture seem less relevant, at first sight. The introductory remarks lead inevitably to the major, memorable incident in the plot, which is revealed at the end of the chapter. In following the main, most riveting elements in the narrative, the reader may not register all the details in the plot equally. One of them, for instance, is the man inquiring about the house of M. Favoral. He plays the equally stereotypical role of the seemingly unrelated character who ends up bringing to a resolution the other conflicts that the subplots present. He is actually, the reader will later find out, conducting his own private investigation to help another character, the love interest of the daughter of M. Favoral, reclaim his right to an inheritance he has been swindled out of by an associate of the (fake) baron. The plot unfolds in the years immediately following the Paris Commune, when many archival records were not available, having been destroyed by the war. Identities that the surveilling institutions of the modern state could define and keep track of were not easily ascertained anymore, unless in person or through direct testimony. No matter how closely knit a neighborhood like the one of rue St Gilles might seem, the village-like quality of its daily activities that the opening of the novel suggests is enmeshed in larger criminal plots.

The Vizetelly Catalogue

The novel in question, Émile Gaboriau's *L'Argent des Autres*, was published posthumously in France by the publishing house Dentu in 1873, with a dedication to Gaboriau's mentor Paul Féval, journalist and popular author of periodical literature, by the Gaboriau widow. The British edition, *Other People's Money*, appeared in 1885, as the third novel by Gaboriau in a series of "sensation novels" that the London-based publisher Vizetelly had dedicated to the French author, whom the catalogue calls "the favorite reading of prince Bismark."[1] Throughout the 1880s Vizetelly published a considerable amount of sensation fiction imported from France in series such as "French Sensation Fiction," "The Gaboriau & Du Boisgobey Sensation Novels," or simply "Popular French Novels." At the cost of one shilling, in pocket-size book format typed in small print and manufactured in Scotland and Ireland, Vizetelly made the English readers acquainted with more than one title by authors such as Aléxis Bouvier, while other novelists appear with one title only, like William Busnach, Henri Chabrillat, Alberic Second, Jules Mary, and Georges Grison. French fiction and, to a lesser degree, Russian literature feature prominently in the catalogue of the publisher, with a series of several "Powerful Realist" works by Zola, which included *Nana*, *The Assommoir*, and *Germinal*, translated from, respectively, the 127th, 97th, and 47th French edition. No matter which genre of fiction the series "French Popular Fiction" would include, the quotes from the reviewers reproduced in the catalogue insist that the novels move at an exciting tempo, that the plot is "highly ingenious" (*London Illustrated News*), the narrative "thrilling," "absorbing till the very end" (*Dublin Evening Mail*), structured with "marvellous dramatic skill" (*Sheffield Independent*), or that "the interest of the reader is secured from the opening chapter to the last page" (*Brighton Guardian*). The bits of reviews quoted in the catalogue focus not so much on the artistic quality of the work but on its effect on the reader, and show a frequent concern for the moral implications that the content may have, particularly for women: the one and only quote used to advertise the whole "Popular French Novels" series states that the volumes "may be safely lying where the ladies of the families can pick them" (*Sheffield Independent*). The insistence on the word "sensation" in promoting titles that reached at times a circulation of thirty thousand copies, while a sure bait for readers, requires cautious disclaimers such as "of a slightful sensational kind not hurtful either mentally or morally" (*Dumbarton Herald*).

Vizetelly promoted his titles differently depending on the established popularity of the authors translated into English. For Zola, for instance, the catalogue reprints large chunks of review articles by equally established authors such as Edmondo De Amicis and Henry James, who describes Zola as a "novelist with a system, a passionate conviction, a great plan not easily found in England or the US" and continues his comparison between French- and English-language fiction by calling "our English system" "a good thing for virgins and boys, and a bad thing for the novel itself." By contrast, when promoting the more popular fiction by unknown authors, the London publisher based in Henrietta Street, Covent Garden, employed a marketing strategy that sought to secure a review or some space in provincial and lesser known papers, at times no longer than three lines, in a column dedicated to recent publications. Again, the quotes culled from reviews have an immediate promotional value. For *Bewitching Iza* by Aléxis Bouvier the quote from the *The Whitehall Review* simply says: "We strongly recommend it." *The Meudon Mystery* by Jules Mary is for *The Sheffield Telegraph* "a sensation gem of the first water." The publicity from provincial papers would ideally accompany the appearance of these titles in the bookseller's market of the capital and hopefully bolster their sales with the build-up of a success that started somewhere else. In the daily *Brighton Guardian*, a "Fashionable Chronicle" for the Sussex and Southern County established in 1827, reviews of books by Vizetelly appear regularly in the summer of 1888. The frequency is quite high: once or even twice a week. The reviews of the *Brighton Guardian* highlight, among the publications issued by other publishers, a Vizetelly edition of classical plays, a novel by the Goncourt brothers, and three sensation novels in less than a month. The sensation novels are reviewed at weekly intervals toward the end of the 1888 summer season. *Dominique Panterne* by Godfrey Barchett is praised for the "tragic excitement" of the material, which is artfully condensed in one hundred large print pages, and is "sufficient for a three volume of the long-drawn-out Braddon type." The review of *A Convict's Marriage* by Aléxis Bouvier, belonging to the "French Sensation Novel Series," before summarizing its plot, calls it a "truly dramatic and sensational novel." Again, the reactions of the reader are what matters: "the interest of the reader is always maintained at high pressure," concludes the review.

In the *Sheffield Daily Telegraph* from the same year, another source of critical appraisals used by Vizetelly in promoting the series of French novels, reviews of sensation fiction are quite frequent. The October 11 issue, in the period when news of the Whitechapel murder appear in the paper with the frequency and sensational titles of a serialized novel, has a review of *Solved Mysteries, or Revelations of a City Detective* (the title appears in capital letters) by James Mc Govan, a volume of stories that, the review claims, "no one can put down without finishing [each] story." The October 22 issue reviews another thrilling kind of narrative, adventurous traveling, with an illustrated edition of "Stories of Sensational Baloon Ascents." Sensationalism had spilled over other kinds of journalistic writing, a tendency that *Belgravia* anticipates since the 1860s. The evening edition of the *Sheffield Daily Telegraph* of the same day offers another example of sensational journalistic narrative with a story entitled "Man Attacked by Bears/Exciting Scene." The story occupies approximately forty lines of a column, while the coming strike, which featured in the morning edition, is reduced to a reference of three lines among other advertisements.

The publishing industry of the 1880s, therefore, still feeds on the narrative strategies of sensationalism and on the certainty of commercial success that the sensational formula would guarantee. Vizetelly tries and associates with the tag "sensation novel" different genres of French fiction his house had in stock. Mary Elizabeth Braddon features in provincial reviews as a canonical figure, maybe too much so, for she seems to have become a stereotype. The sense of "movement" that sensational plots had evoked among the first critics such as E.S. Dallas has by now, it seems, been surpassed in the tastes of critics by a newer, even faster narrative technique which, in the French examples, does not "drag" like Braddon's.

Choosing to focus on the catalogue of a publisher, as I did, is important not only to reconstruct the fortune of a literary genre. Publishers catalogues, which are quite rare to find as sheets of advertisements are in the bound editions of 1860s and 1870s British magazines, are important also because they can help revive literary history by expanding the boundaries of existing periodization. They also pose a challenge because they place the canonical choices, which literary history builds upon, in the larger context of an uncharted and magmatic literary production. The books in a catalogue expose the limits and at times the biases in canonical choices that have traditionally defined our understanding of a period. I call the contribution to literary history (and to cultural history) that catalogues offer reviving because they reveal that the development of the novel unfolds through a myriad of genres that are all intertwined in the textual fabric of mass culture. Detective novels in France are perceived as sensation novels in Britain, a much broader category than detective fiction. Both "judiciary novels" (that's the category used at the time in France) and sensation novels, however, are indebted to melodramas from earlier in the century, at times to historical novels and to realist fiction at large. Sensation novels in the pages of *Belgravia* do exemplify the hybridity of the genre of "popular" fiction, since the domestic-sensation novel coexists with the *bildungsroman*-historical novel à la *Bound to John Company*, and even influenced other forms of journalistic writing. Accessing the actual market of books through a catalogue, therefore, allows to enhance, complement, and even correct literary history if the latter employs generic categories that do not grow out of a thorough excavation in the field.

The Gaboriau Case

All too often literary history tends to inherit the canonical choices of previous historical narratives, particularly when discussing a specific genre, or the most representative works by one author. This reduction of the examples supporting literary history narratives tends to create gray areas in the study of literature that limit the complexity of the market of books as well as the path of an author's career. Émile Gaboriau is a case in point, for his works, like *Other People's Money*, that do not fit in the generic definition of "detective novel," and in most cases do not receive the critical attention due, except in a monographic work dedicated to him.[2] I shall here explore the intersection of industrial production of popular literature, compartmentalized critical categories, and marketing labels that often create paradoxical fault lines in the landscape of literary history. Pitching strategies by publishers who create marketing labels often end up summoning the intended critical responses by journalists and critics. In such cases advertising and critical responses coincide: the commercial interests of the publisher seeks to single out an item in the market of books, while the interest of critics and historians often aims at managing the massive output of books with simple categories for the annals of literature. I mean to underline the paradoxes that simplifying cultural complexity can entail, particularly when dealing with the omnivorous form of the nineteenth-century popular novel. I shall refer here primarily to the authors of "French sensation novels" in the Vizetelly catalogue because they help identify the perception of what was sensational, scandalous, and thrilling on the two sides of the Chunnel in the 1870s and 1880s.

The novels of Émile Gaboriau are associated in mid-twentieth-century literary histories with the genre of detective fiction. In light of this inclusion, his work features prominently in all histories of detective fiction, where he plays a specific, albeit simplistic, role in the teleological development of the genre from Edgar Allan Poe to Conan Doyle and beyond. When literary history simply refers to his work as "popular fiction," however, the tone of the discussion becomes dismissive. If his name features, even to take the blame for the decay in the standards of literary production, other master weavers of thrilling narratives such as Georges Grison, William Busnach, and Henri Chabrillat do not, or make only a fugitive appearance, like Alberic Second, Alexis Bouvier, author of a thrilling series a title of which, *Bewitching Iza*, appears in the Vizetelly catalogue translated from the eightieth French edition, or Juels Mary, who is usually mentioned for his other works.[3] Within the long career of Gaboriau works such as *Other People's Money* seem less interesting because the novels in question retrospectively do not contribute to the evolution of detective fiction and thus do not help a discussion of the twentieth-century masters of the genre. Why would a novel set in the Paris of the immediate aftermath of the Commune, when governmental forms of surveillance through data collection fall apart due to the massive loss of documents caused by the war, thus multiplying detective investigations, be overlooked? The plot weaves a thick mystery, involving the reckless works of speculators that speed up the national crisis. Investigative characters do abound, exposing not so much the easily demonized figure of the low class criminal, but the questionable workings of financial institutions, like other popular novels earlier in the century had done.[4] What seems to be the master trope of sensation fiction, the association of bourgeois propriety and "improper" or criminal behavior, while certainly inducing pangs of anxious suspense in the readers, does not feature in many literary histories as the classical narrative of detective fiction. The "sensational" master trope was, however, very present at the time as a set of narrative functions available to the author of periodical fiction. Sensation fiction and, more generally, periodical literature had indeed inspired many writers who incorporated the multiple suggestions and narrative common places typical of popular fiction. Periodical literature from the second half of the nineteenth century is not alien to this form of incorporation, despite the eventual development of a crystallized form for crime fiction. Many books dedicated to the history of the detective novel have a teleological progression that simplifies the discussion of popular fiction in the nineteenth century by dealing only with select examples. Gaboriau features more as a pioneering figure than an *auctoritas* (an authority) in the genre.[5] Wilkie Collins has a similar fate to that of Gaboriau in this history, especially for his "extravagant" titles that are indicated as not being exactly "detective novels." While *The Moonstone* is always mentioned as a turning point in the history of crime fiction, *The Woman in White* is not.[6] Mary Elizabeth Braddon, not surprisingly, rarely features in most works on detective fiction, even though the recent, specific studies of the genre of sensation fiction do acknowledge, and discuss, the contribution to the genre of the narrative function of the "detective in the house."[7]

The history of detective fiction is often not only teleological, but proceeds desultorily by jumping from one canonical author to the next, at times at an interval of twenty–thirty years: after a treatment of Poe what follows is a jump cut to Gaboriau with his "many flaws" until we reach Doyle and the much awaited contemporaries of the critics writing around the mid- or second half of the twentieth century. This approach comes inevitably with a distortion in which the scarce reprints of nineteenth-century literature by twentieth-century publishers play a significant role. The choice of representative texts by one author is limited to very few examples, so that popular fiction appears in isolated cases that may reinstate the idea of the "original" or "unique" work. Canonicity here helps to easily identify the commodity of the "crime novel" and keeps the literary history of the genre easily memorable through few examples. The current trend of digitizing the most prominent titles by one author in the collections of public libraries contributes to the simplification of history that the digitalization of print artifacts in its current stage entails. One needs remember that once digitized, or even reproduced in microfilm, the original works are not easily accessible to the scholarly reader, and the reading process of the interface—not to mention of the microfilm—complicates and at times hinders a study of the material history of the book.

Nineteenth-century popular fiction, like the history of the press, is a much more complex reality than what a thematic reading—of the press or of detective fiction—might give account of. The press cannot be studied only through some thematic samplings; detective fiction, likewise, is not the only fiction that has a structural theme in it, that is, the presence of a professional detective or other narrative functions associated to the genre. The complexity of periodical literature reflects the expanding market of print products in an industrial age that seeks no limitation to its lucrative enterprises. The exponential issue of titles in the culture industry of the second half of the nineteenth century had only to cater to the standardized and malleable demands of the readers, particularly in England, whereas in France the market had also to navigate the limited agency imposed on authors and publishers by strict control by governmental institutions. This massive and not yet fully charted production should certainly not, however, be confined to the premises of a limited historical perspective. The modern novel's inherent feature and the mark of its modernity is its formal freedom and its restless innovations: born far from the ossified conventions of courtly canonical genres on the roads of the picaresque, the "voracious" modern novel has in the course of its history woven many genres into its fabric. Periodical fiction had a similar freedom to mix melodrama, the gothic, historical novel, newspaper narratives, *causes celèbres*, as the example of sensation fiction can attest. It may not be purely a commercial calculation if the Vizetelly catalogue calls sensation novels what an enumerative taxonomy of literature calls "detective fiction." The study of the vast field of periodical fiction, which seems still unexplored, would benefit from acknowledging the limits of traditional generic definitions and from privileging a thorough and synchronic study of the vast archive of popular fiction available. In order to avoid the implicit pitfalls in the use of canonical categories, I propose that the literary historian of the popular periodical novel introduce a hyphenated form to describe novel writing. Only when hyphenated, generic definitions of periodical fiction in the nineteenth century, a century in which the popular novel was a relatively new and unrecognized form, may give a sense of how multifaceted the construction of the novelistic plot was, proceeding as it did by appropriation and incorporation. The references to the hybridity of the sensation plot in scholarly literature should be applied to the equally hybrid demarcations of popular literature at large. It is not only the sensation novel that can be seen as a "generic hybrid—formally, thematically and idoeologically— . . . ," popular culture is as omnivorous, due to the commercial nature of its entrepreneurial production.[8]

Sensationalism Across the Chunnel

The Vizetelly catalogue reveals that sensationalism, and thus periodical literature, was not only an open category but had a cross-chunnel dimension to its popularity that most scholars, trained in the professional discipline of national literary history, have not explored.[9] Further elaborating on the historical relevance of the Vizetelly catalogue of "French Sensation Novels," I want now to discuss the relations between French and British popular literature, since the sensational formula was commercially viable on both sides of the Channel. If the genres of popular periodical literature should be hyphenated, to stress the intertextual nature of their inspiration, the category of a "national" identity to describe popular literature should be equally questioned. A constant presence of French works in England and English works in France, not necessarily in translation, should help to catch a glimpse of the *lingua franca* in which popular literature speaks. If sensationalism, in its simplest manifestation, is the attention-gripping strategy employed by market economy in its persuasive expansion through narratives of all sorts, existential as well as fictional, there is no question that a primary national origin of the phenomenon cannot be ascertained with certainty, nor should it. The focus here on two national neighboring industries, among others, can show that the sensation novel simply adapted and translated into a literary form an ultimately commercial strategy, that is, pitching commodities through intensified stimuli calling the attention of buyers and readers. The genre did so by constantly incorporating, on both sides of the Channel, suggestions coming from novelists in the neighboring country. Mary Elizabeth Braddon is one of the prominent authors in the market of books in both France and England in the second half of the nineteenth century. Mary Elizabeth Braddon is not only present in French booksellers catalogues but in French feuilleton editions of her own work, as I shall show, in the years in which Émile Gaboriau, and his mentor Paul Féval, were popular authors, too. Far from ascribing the works of many different authors and their narrative styles solely to the imperative of market economy, I shall also discuss the cultural specificity of each author and of each national production, in order to define how the shock of sensationalism was articulated in each context and how sensationalism resonated with different contemporary discursive formations. Finally, I want to return to the intramediatic aspect of reading sensational fiction in monthly and in daily installments to clarify, from the standpoint of a material history of reading, the different meanings that the experiences of reading fiction in daily or monthly formats suggest.

The commercial flow of English and French translations of popular literature from across the Channel continued throughout the nineteenth century. Imports of novels from France were as conspicuous as exports of British novels into France. British and American literature had been a crucial point of reference for nineteenth-century French novelists in the development of the relatively new genre of the novel: this is particularly true of the French popular novel. The works of Walter Scott had been widely read and imitated in the first part of the nineteenth century, one may think of Balzac's *Les Chouans.* Eugène Sue acknowledges in the preface to his immensely popular *Les Mystères de Paris* that Fenimore Cooper was his inspiration. Sue meant to find in the modern city of Paris the "savages among us," as marginalized as the ones depicted by Cooper: he found them in the Parisian underworld. Edgar Allan Poe was famously discovered and made popular by Baudelaire. Magazines such as *La Revue des Deux Mondes* featured in each issue a section where reviews of contemporary British novels appeared. In 1863, the year of Mary Elizabeth Braddon's breakthrough in the Parisian market of books, Hyppolite Taine published the first volume of his five-volume edition of *L'Histoire de la Littérature Anglaise.* In that same year, 1863, the same publishing house, Hachette, issued three novels by Braddon: *Le Secret de lady Audley, Aurora Floyd*, and *Le Capitaine du "Vautour."* Braddon herself contributed to the translation of *Aurora Floyd*, which was by Charles-Bernard Derosne, while Judith Bernard Derosne was credited as the translator of the first edition of *Le Secret de Lady Audley.* Editions of Braddon's works kept on appearing in France throughout the 1860s, 1870s, and 1880s, the years I consider here, and continued past the 1880s. The work of Mary Elizabeth Braddon also appeared in feuilleton editions in Paris, not only in the *Figaro* in the 1880s, as Robert Lee Wolff informs us,[10] but also in *Le Rappel* in 1873, the year in which a fourth edition of *Le Secret de Lady Audley*, a second of *Le Triomphe d'Eléanor* and a third of *La Femme du Docteur*, also appeared.

Braddon's sensation fiction, like the French forms of popular fiction translated by Vizetelly, had an omnivorous inspiration that incorporated the models of melodrama, historical novel, realist fiction, popular entertainment, and the more recent newspaper chronicles of *causes celèbres.* The frightening thrills the fiction offered did not recreate the dread of the gothic or of romantic fiction, which were often relegated to an exotic Southern European setting; contemporary life became the source of extreme emotions. The realist inspiration applies to Braddon's novels as well as to Gaboriau's "judiciary novels," and to Gaboriau's titles closer to the sensational-melodramatic formula. My approach does not mean to use analogy to level out the differences between French and British authors. Braddon and Gaboriau, in fact, employ very different narrative techniques. Mary Elizabeth Braddon juxtaposes from the very beginning of her novels completely unrelated social scenarios that the rest of the plot intertwines until the many parallel story lines are woven into one. Braddon organizes her narrative primarily with a technique that may proleptically give the impression of a cinematic "parallel editing" made of prolonged intercut chunks of narrative. Gaboriau's style differs from Braddon's in that he tends to interrupt his linear narratives with flashbacks that extend over several chapters until the motives of each character in the opening of the plot are made clear enough for the reader to be caught into the suspense of the final action, a technique used also by Balzac in many of his novels. Braddon breaks more frequently the

Aristotelian unity of place, Gaboriau the unity of time. The fiction of both has an intertextual dimension to it that reveals the incorporation of several generic conventions, belonging to both the literary tradition and contemporary journalistic writing.

The popularity of sensation fiction in England and France is not new. Novels driven by a mystery—of personal identity or of criminal agency—were widely popular throughout the nineteenth century in England, France, and in the rest of Europe where they were sold. Suspicions of wrong doing and—at times—acts of criminal behavior abound in Balzac's *Comédie Humaine*: the personal histories of the main characters and the narrator's observations on their personal motivations make this clear. The wide reach of Balzac's social observation includes members of all classes, which the author describes with a self-proclaimed distant, objective impartiality that he supposedly shares with a scientist. Stepping outside of the standard morality, however, is never a matter of thrilled surprise, nor does the narrative usually indulge in breaking the expectations of respectability that usually come with status. In the opening pages of *Ursule Mirouët* (1841), for instance, the narrative voice presents the middle-class characters in the circle of the old Minoret's family circle as greedy and envious of the young niece that seems destined to inherit the old man's fortune. The ordeal to which she is subjected later, involving stealing the man's will and tampering with legal documents—the secret fear around which the last scenes of *Bound to John Company* revolve—comes as a direct consequence of the premise set out in the opening and not as a sudden reversal of an impression of respectability as in the British sensation novel. In several occasions Balzac, loyal to "the throne and the altar," casts the new order of French history signaled by the post-revolutionary bourgeois affirmation as the widespread triumph of selfish material concerns, which appear in most characters within the several subdivisions of the *Comédie Humaine.* The frequent and disdainful references to "British gold" in many novels, moreover, underline not so much the high quality of the British products, which was trumpeted in the *Belgravia* magazine, as the wide-reaching power of the nineteenth-century British economic standards to triumph and corrupt.

The stories, characters, and narrative functions of popular periodical "sensation" fiction of the 1860s–1880s on two sides of the Channel make an interesting case as they respond in different ways to the anxiety associated with the question of social mobility that these novels present. I want to discuss how sensationalism in England and France circulated specific discursive formations that resonated in different ways among the many groups that constituted the popular audiences. Just like "popular fiction" has proven to be too abstract a category, any reference to the "people" in the nineteenth century can be misleading for the modern reader. "The people" traditionally represented the social force opposed to the aristocracy; it was a new force and a new political agent that gained more prominence in the aftermath of the 1789 Revolution in France and throughout the slow fight to gain political recognition and more economic stability in England. In nineteenth-century studies "people" and the adjective "popular" often refer with one word to the two different forces that gained more visibility in the century of industrialization, that is, the working classes and the middle classes, which were allies often fighting for the same political goals. The term "people" in this meaning, however, does not account for the shift in power and in political agency that happened whenever the middle class reached a political success, typically to the detriment of the former ally. As a result of the reconfiguration of the powers at play after a democratic innovation, the lower rungs of the social scale were usually repressed, often violently, whenever they made further demands. This is true of both France and Great Britain. How "popular," then, was literature at the time? French scholarship has often grouped the authors of popular fiction by calling them either "left" or "right" wing. I want to shift focus from the identity of the author to the textual fabric of the works they wrote, in order to outline the main and not necessarily univocal discursive formations that emerge from the narrative development. I also want to discuss more in depth what Umberto Eco calls the "codes" of the "destinataire," the social and political implications that the reading of periodical literature had for the two political groups that constituted the "popular" classes of readers: the middle, upwardly mobile class and the so-called lower class.[11]

French fiction presents a realistic representation of the lower classes, which the literature following academic standards had rarely offered. Popular fiction, therefore, has the lure of a discovery; it is a thrilling exploration of invisible social strata. The popular class of some characters, however, is only a masquerade: by the end of the plot the same characters reveal a highborn origin, like in Raymond in Eugène Sue's *Les Mystères de Paris.*[12] This ultimate recognition, present in many popular novels following Sue's model, immediately clears the characters reputation of any commixture with crime or with the lower rungs of the social ladder they were temporarily relegated to. The recognition of their status, coming at the end of the elaborate peripateia of many of these characters, reminds us of the narrative patterns so dominant in Greek novels and in Shakespearean comedies. Unlike the classical model, however, in which the protagonists are unaware of their high-class pedigree till the end, when an object they carried from birth, or, the words of their adoptive parents clarify their status, in many examples of French popular fiction like the novels of Ėmile Gaboriau, Aléxis Bouvier, and Georges Grison, the protagonist is a post-edenic character who, not blissfully ignorant of his or her pedigree, lives in a state marred by the notion of decay, associated with a (often unjust) fall. This temporary exile into the lower strata of society, which are often engaged in criminal schemes at the expense of the same middle-class protagonists, essentializes the nexus between (im)morality and (lower) class status. The main characters' fall, however, is never eternal; it awaits redressing of the wrongs suffered, through the agency of the forces of good that intervene to reaffirm not only their human dignity after having suffered unjustly, but also their social status.

French sensation novels by Gaboriau, Grison, and Bouvier revolve less around a mystery of identity, since the readers know who the main characters really are from the beginning, or from the first flashback that halts the course of narrative progression. The *cause* of the main characters' misfortune is what is shrouded in mystery: the downfall, the reader finds, is caused by unexpected financial upturns and evil schemes orchestrated by tenacious villains. At the opening of Gaboriau's *La Degringolade*, published by Vizetelly in 1885 as *The Catastrophe*, Raymond Delord is found fainted on the street outside a café, the victim of a brutal attack. He is the son of a general who made his fortunes in the colonies but fell from grace upon his return to Paris where he died in strange circumstances around the time of the coup d'état by Napoleon III that he opposed. In *Other People's Money* from the same series, the flight of the banker Favoral accused of embezzlement is only the premise to the main plot lines involving his children: the love interest of his daughter Gilberte is Marius de Trégars, whose father was swindled out of his fortunes by, it turns out, the same gang of schemers who are putting pressure on the banker to claim responsibility for the crack of his bank. *The Gilded Clique*, published by Vizetelly in 1885, too, opens with the attempted suicide of M.lle Henriette, who now lives in the fifth floor garrets of a prim building, but is actually Henriette de la Ville-Haudry, the daughter of a widowed noblemen whose new wife maneuvered to have Henriette removed from her home and from any claim to her family fortune. In a variation to the ruined-scion-of-a-noble-family pattern Aléxis Bouvier's *Bewitching Iza* (Vizetelly,1888) introduces a female protagonist, Cécile Tussaud, who is the daughter of a ruined bronze founder. Her inter-classist love interest is one of her father's workmen, Maurice Ferrand, but she ends up marrying the wealthy André Houdard, the party her father would opt for, to avenge her mother who has been seduced and threatened by the same André. George Grison's *Dispatch and Secrecy* (Vizetelly, 1888) presents the pattern only at a later stage in the narrative, after the investigations of the protagonist, Count Horace de Prigny, lead him to that discovery. The protagonist is a nobleman who hires a private detective, ironically named M. Loyal Francœur, to check the reputation of his friend's fiancee, M.lle Jeannne de Rieumes, only to be drawn into a wide-reaching intrigue woven by the same detective who fabricates compromising information and sells it at a high price.

The consequences of the schemes ordained by the villains and their allies against the bourgeois victimized protagonists aggravate their misfortune. Some end up incarcerated, like Maurice, the bronze worker in Bouvier's *Bewitching Iza* who is accused of the murder of a neighbor, a coquette who had unwisely entrusted her bonds to André, the husband of his boss's daughter, Cécile, whom he secretly marries. M.lle Jeanne de Reumie in Grison's *Dispatch and Secrecy* is kidnapped and imprisoned in a summer residence off-season by the gang led by the fake detective M. Loyal Francœur in order to prove an elopement that would compromise her and allow the detective to spill more money from the baron that hired him to investigate her past. Jeanne eventually escapes and, after walking long distances barefoot trying to regain the fauboug St Germain, she falls unconscious and is rescued by a ragpicker who brings her to the welcoming community of the ragpickers living on the outskirts of Paris.

The way out of the injustice is an arduous one, for the victimized protagonists are surrounded by corrupt members of all classes with strong links to powerful political figures. The detective Boyard in *Bewitching Iza*, a former convict who joined the secret police, like Vidoq and Balzac's Vautrin, steals shares from a dying relative and, when caught selling them in Belgium, convinces the police that he was going to donate the proceedings of the sale to the Society for the Moral Redemption of Prisoners. The latter philanthropic society is run by the Abbé Dutilleul, a defrocked priest who has not abandoned his social persona to better go on with his illicit businesses. Among the political opponents of Raymond, the son of the murdered captain in *The Catastrophe*, are recent members of the Legion of Honor who quickly moved up in their ranks thanks to the protection of friends of the prince-president after the coup d'état. The architect who, hoping to secure commissions for the grand plans Napoleon III has for the city of Paris, falsifies permissions to build mansions that benefit the intimate circle of the president, splits the revenues of his illicit deals with the lawyer who was hired by the killed general to represent his interests.

The forces of evil are generally greedy *parvenus*, or corrupt professionals gravitating around the highest spheres of power, who find allies in crime among all classes only to ruthlessly eliminate them when no longer needed or in possession of compromising information. The workings of crime, like in Feuillade's *Les Vampires*, involve an elaborate social network that the plot of the novels exposes. At the highest levels of these secret societies, besides the members of the new ruling class of the Second Empire and its allies, are foreign-born *femmes fatales*, sensational women that the novels cast against the more moral example of the French woman. The "bewitching Iza" of Bouvier's novel is a Moldavian woman who lived with the *Zingarij*: before coming to Paris she married a Swiss financer who ruined himself for her and died in an asylum. Dolores Wilson, the mastermind behind the abduction of Jeanne in *Dispatch and Secrecy*, is the daughter of a Spanish father and of a gypsy mother. Sarah Brandon, the nightmare of Henriette in *The Gilded Clique*, is American, the daughter of a rich banker who died when one of the oil pits he invested in caught fire.[13] By contrast, French women show a stoic endurance and a practical resourcefulness, which they resort to only as a survival strategy and never to accomplish a criminal plot. Jeanne in *Dispatch and Secrecy* escapes her captors and walks miles in an effort to reach home in the fauburg St Germain. Cécile in *Bewitching Iza*, when forced to marry André, wears her (presumed) dead lover's ring on her wedding ceremony and calls herself a widow, threatening her new husband with a knife. M.me Delorge, the widow of the mysteriously deceased captain in *The Catastrophe*, crosses paths with the cortege of Napoleon III the day after the coup d'état. "As I am a Parisian by birth"—she says—"a revolution does not alarm me." While the cosmopolitan *femmes fatales* show no particular allegiance to any nation and make opportunist choices without following any political ideal, M.me Delorge, by contrast, is outspoken in her willingness to oppose the new government founded on the crime of December 2, the day of the coup, and endures the consequences of her political beliefs. While the foreign *femme fatal* sees no end to her greed, M.me Delorge, who lost her husband's income and lives off of her own, promises an annuity to the widow of one of the key witnesses of her husband's murder, who is prematurely killed. The good and innocent

French young victims, at any rate, are victorious in the end against the forces of evil. The novels, by sensationalizing the role of foreign rich women that animate the high spheres of the criminal circles they belong to, offer a nationalist angle that casts doubts on the foreign, itinerant forms of capital that feed the evildoers tied to the circle of Neapoleon III.[14] The secret societies in these novels loose the legendary association with the secret gatherings of free-masons and other utopian societies whose activities featured in literary works from the earlier part of the nineteenth century. These groups no longer perpetrate the lore of the allegiance to a hierarchical secret structure of power. The characters involved in the criminal schemes are individuals from very recognizable contemporary professions. The narrative exposes the "secret" of their evil alliances quite early: the villains are easily identifiable, whereas their tentacular reach affecting the life of the protagonists prolongs the suspense of the reader until the criminals, among whom are the many foreign-born *femmes fatales* I mentioned earlier, are punished.

Even though some of Gaboriau's novels published by Vizetelly are categorized by literary historians as detective novels, the characters of the detectives that pursue the crimes narrated in them are not crystallized into a stereotype that would confirm the expectations of a strictly taxonomic historian of the detective novel. Many characters become improvised detectives, in the tradition of British sensation novels, when forced by the adversary circumstances they find themselves in. Other ones are common citizens who obsess about the mystery surrounding another character and invest all their intellectual and physical energies in discovering the causal link of events that may explain their puzzled curiosity. The novels have sometimes up to three different detectives follow their own investigations independently. The detective Loyal Francœur from Grison's *Dispatch and Secrecy* has almost a meta-literary authorial function because he holds the threads of the whole narrative action of the novel. Count Horace de Prigny seeks his help not because he needs it but because he decides, out of a whim, to respond to one of the advertisements he regularly receives in the mail regarding his business of discovering mysteries. All the information that the detective promises upon payment of high fees is fabricated by the detective himself, with the help of his lover, who lives in the same building, and his accomplices, who are ready to follow any criminal direction imparted by him. Loyal Francœur represents the authorial function of narrative whereas the count represents the reader's function; the count is an outsider who enters the world of detection and crime to satisfy his own curiosity about a woman, without realizing the implications for his own safety and peace. As a matter of fact, very soon after visiting the detective, the count's whole life will depend on the resolution of the (fake) mystery the detective is able to spin. He is asked to pay for every new installment in the fabricated plot that destroys the reputations of the main characters until the happy ending resolves all the conflicts. Oscar de Verchement, the investigative magistrate in *Bewitching Iza*, is also an unusual detective; he has the case set against André but falls madly in love with the foreign-born Iza, who prevents him from accusing her *protegé* André. She convinces the magistrate to part with important documents that she proceeds to falsify in favor of André. Oscar, in the midst of a crucial interrogation, falls on his knees and confesses his love for Iza. "You are bewitching Iza." "No"—Iza replies—"Iza the Ruinous." Their relationship, which makes the scenes in which they both appear worthy of an *operetta*, ends with their escape to Belgium, from which they will return in the following novel from the series. Iza represents an interesting metaliterary perspective into the intertextual inspiration behind popular periodical fiction of the sensational kind. She confesses that she is an avid reader of the "celebrated cases in the evening news" for the emotions they stir in her, which are similar to those that "witnessing a melodrama" would cause. The genre looks both at the stylized forms of popular theater and at the contemporary narratives created by journalistic reports from the courts, which often adopted the same sensational narrative strategies. The presence of the character of the detective, therefore, so crucial to a twentieth-century definition of detective fiction, proves to be a shifting category in the early history of the genre; this confirms the open-ended and intertextual nature of periodical fiction.

The examples of French periodical popular novels included in the Vizetelly catalogue sensationalize the discovery of the illicit profits that benefited the social adventurers of the Second Empire and their aristocratic allies. Their engagement in reckless investment schemes and dubious money transactions has, therefore, a specifically historical implication. Evil in these novels is not a universal feature of dramatic action; it is enmeshed in the structures of power behind the coup d'état of Neapoleon III.[15] The victimized bourgeois protagonists, in order to defend themselves, expose the schemes of the new privileged classes. These sensational revelations implicitly denounce the new economic powers that fall outside of the bourgeois ethos of respectability and honesty that accompanied the rise of the middle classes throughout the first part of the nineteenth century. In Balzac's 1844 *Modeste Mignon*, which appeared in *Le Journal Des Debats*, the father of the protagonist, a banker hit by the economic crisis of 1826, does not simply run away like the banker in Gaboriau's *Other People's Money.* "Citizen Mignon," who is actually of noble origin, buys a space in the local paper to give specific directions to his clients on how to be compensated for the losses in assets, investments, and savings, which he finances by selling his properties and seeking a new economic venture overseas. The protagonist of *César Birotteau* (1837), a perfume monger who goes bankrupt, by the end of the novel reestablishes his reputation with creditors and the public after years of savings and hard work, only to die at the party thrown in his honor.[16]

The bourgeois ethos in these novels from the second half of the nineteenth century is still the moral standard in comparison to which the actions of both the lower classes and the aristocratic classes are measured. The lower-class characters should model their upwardly mobile itinerary on the same middle-class values that the suffering protagonists strive to maintain. The aristocratic characters are reprimanded for the greed that adulterates their noble disinterestedness and contradicts the bourgeois ethos. Villains ignore this ethos; their system of accumulation of wealth tramples upon the ideals of propriety and of industrious laboring that are a badge of honor of the bourgeoisie. The Second Empire features in these novels as a watershed moment signaling a transition to a new phase of capitalist expansion. The inspiration of the sensational French novels, therefore, is realistic for several reasons: it exposes the hidden links in the perpetration of injustices under the Second Empire; it identifies the agents of evil within a specific ruling class, and it condemns in other social contexts the behaviors that fall outside of the bourgeois standard of morality.

The detective novels where the culprits are not upper-class characters but middle- and lower-class characters are a subdivision within the same genre of sensational novels. The cases that the investigations bring to light are often motivated by a more private greed that incenses the actions of a limited number of characters, when compared to the social networks involved in the criminal plots of the novels with upper-class villains. In *The Meudon Mystery* by Jules Mary (Vizetelly, 1888) the prime suspect of the horrendous murder of the butcher's shop assistant is the butcher himself, who was in love with her. The investigation reveals that the culprit is actually his mother, who in her youth had suffered a humiliation from the family of the shop-assistant. In Gaboriau's novella *The Old Man of Batignolles*, whose third edition was published in 1884 by Vizetelly under the name of J.B. Casmir Godeuil, the *nom de plume* Gaboriau had used for a sensational marketing launch, the man in the title is found dead on the floor of his living room, where in his last moments of life he wrote with his blood the name of his nephew. The detective assigned to the case notes an unusual circumstance: the name had been written with the dead man's left hand, not with his right hand that he would customarily use to write. The preface warns the readers that "Punishment can be deferred but it always comes at last." At the end of the novel the real culprit, the wife of the dead man and her lover are brought to justice. While the French novels closer to the sensation formula make their realistic inspiration clear by referring to precise historical figures, the realistic inspiration of some of these novels is made apparent by the asides of the narrator. Jules Mary, the author of *Le Bucher de Meudon* remarks that

> this drama is not an imaginary one. We have changed the names both of persons and places to avoid recalling painful memories to those who were mixed up in the affair, but we have drawn the characters exactly as they were, and no doubt many will recognize them for Denise, Lauriot, Charlotte and the old peasant woman who stood out in strong relief in this recent and touching case of which we are only the faithful narrator. (P. 65)

Despite the elaborate and often incredible plots that the narrators create, the realistic references coming from history or from contemporary life constantly step the reader outside of a purely escapist appreciation of fiction. Georges Grison introduces the new setting of the community of ragpickers with an introduction that may feature in a journalistic article or a governmental report: "60,000 ragpickers [live] in the city of Paris, pushed out from the old quarters like 'Little Poland' which are replaced by palaces, but still present in plebeian nooks in the 13th, 15th, near the fortifications, at Montmartre, Belleville, La Villette, Passage du Nord, Sud, Clichy, Saint-Ouen, Gentilly." The narrative voice in Gaboriau's *Other People's Money* hardly believes the numbers of hopeful investors who entrusted their money to reckless speculators:

> It is sufficient to open from time to time the "Gazette des Tribunaux" to read some trial of the ex-managing director of the "Company for the Drainage and Improvement of the Swamps of the Department of the Orne" to which many subscribers gave their money up to 60,000 francs each, for a total of 600,000 for swamps that did not exist, under the promise of 10%... Despite the trial being published in the gazette, Tiffla Mines, Bretonêche Lands, forests of Formanoir still find supporters!

The changes to urban living caused by speculators dominating the housing market and the stock-exchange are very visible: "But as landlords now only built palaces, divided into immense apartments, people with limited resources did not know where to live, for they could not expend the sixth of their revenue on rent."

The authors of these novels are aware that the narrative strategies they use are only a convention that allows to speak of contemporary life. Reality breaks the fictional conventions that novels are based on. The distinction between fiction and fact is not always so clear cut: real life scenarios in which the scammers operate are so complex that they could be narrative stuff worthy of inclusion in a popular novel. When the repented former secretary of Loyal Francœur, who started collaborating with the police, escapes the den where his boss locks him after kidnapping him he starts his account by saying to the police: "You have no idea what happened to me." "It is a novel, a regular novel." In Grison's *Dispatch and Secrecy* there is a further intertextual reference to contemporary popular fiction, that is, to the endless series of the adventures of Rocambole by Ponson du Terrail, which started appearing in 1857 on the conservative paper *La Patrie* and continued even after the death of the author in 1871. The commissary in Grison's novel, confronted with one of the many astute disguises under which Loyal Francœur appears, remarks: "That man is Rocambulus in person!" Loyal Francœur, however, is not a towering character like Rocambole, who escaped from prison to fight his arch-enemy Sir Williams and to establish his popularity in countless adventures. Rocambole is a super-hero with a charismatic appeal that grants him the submission of his admiring subordinates and the equally awed devotion of readers. Rocambole is a hero—the narrator notes—whose charm no one could resist, and who could never die in his fight against the evil plots of a British villain.[17] The middle-class characters in the novels here discussed, by contrast, are mostly left to their own resourcefulness in defending themselves from their oppressors. Rocambole is nonetheless interesting in the history of French popular periodical literature because, like the characters in earlier popular novels, he, too, blurs the distinction between lower-class and upper-class identity. The former convict's beauty is "aristocratic"; his impeccable choices in clothing equal him to a "gentleman"; his whole figure emanates a sense of distinction. Both lower- and upper-class readers could identify with him, while leaving to his legendary heroism the solution to the conflicts in the plot that the readers follow as passive observers. Popular periodical novels, therefore, build their narrative credibility by explicitly pointing to the intertextual inspiration behind them, which connects fiction, journalistic writing, melodrama, popular fiction, and real life.

British sensation novels, while still revolving around the anxieties connected to the transmission and the accumulation of wealth in the industrial age, dramatize again and again the feared and unexpected clog in the mechanism of structured upper-class social relations that the sensational turn represents. Two forces are at play in the social fabric of the society depicted in sensation fiction: first, a proud sense of belonging to a class, requiring blind acceptance of its ethos, together with the sense of privilege that comes from ignoring any other reality, including one's own previous life, in the quiet living described at the opening of the novel. The second social force is the entitlement to guard with all means this peace against intruders. The freedom these characters enact is the self-granted right to exclude others not befitting their order. Sensation narratives revolve around the feared breach of decorum by the discovery that upper-class distinction comes with an assumption of moral superiority that does not exclude but rather hides or coats immorality. The more successful the performance of social distinction is, the more able the protagonist is to pass among upper-class characters. Decorum seems unadulterated due to the convincing pose that each character plays in the social system. The sensation plot casts doubts on the very essence of a class that self-proclaims its superior morality: it insinuates, at least in the most common development of the sensation plot, that prestige may be founded on crime. The success of the genres on both sides of the Channel implies that the thrill that galvanized the reader is based on the deeply set knowledge of the vagaries of social value and social distinction in the industrial age. The narrative development of sensation fiction, while exposing criminal behavior in the upper classes, casts doubts on the very notion of social mobility by focusing on failed forms of passing. In France, despite the more frequent social upheavals that shook the establishment through three major democratic revolutions in a century, the fiction popular with readers that subscribe to relatively expensive journals to read Sue, or that, later in the century, buy the much cheaper individual issue of the daily paper containing a feuilleton, reinstates in an often surprisingly determinist fashion the bourgeois standard of morality that is threatened from both above and from below. The notion of moral superiority of the bourgeoisie is reaffirmed in a determinist fashion in the very popular *L'Affaire Lerouge* by Gaboriau: exposing the culprit means automatically casting aside a character that, even when appearing as refined and noble, actually turns out to be of lower-class origin. Despite the more critical novels that expose the injustices perpetrated by the adventurers of the Second Empire the very popular title *L'Affaire Lerouge* still makes a tendentious association in the narrator's mind between the lower classes and crime. Gaboriau's *L'Affaire Lerouge*, published first in 1863 and then interestingly reissued to great acclaim in 1865, signaled a major shift in the novelist's career. The editorial history of the novel enjoyed a fortune in the twentieth century that many of Gaboriau's other, equally successful and more sensational novels did not. The canonicity of the title is also due to the novel's inclusion in the diachronic temporality of the histories of crime fiction that seeks precursors and innovators and does not investigate the synchronic development of popular narrative forms. The plot of the novel, so important in revealing its ideological implications and the reasons for its success, has a seemingly upper-class character found guilty of murder. The unraveling of the plot, however, reveals that the nobleman had been changed at birth with another baby who, unlike him, really belonged to a wealthy family and grew up in a poor household. The recognition, at the end of the novel, of the "false noble" as the only culprit reinstates a stereotypical view of the "dangerous classes" that essentializes their proclivity to crime. Large swaths of the bourgeois public that gained some political clout with the July monarchy and sought, after the coup d'état, an alliance with the new structures of power identifies with a narrative that casts aside as guilty or as undesirable the lower fringes of society. This may indirectly explain the great popularity of the title. The assumption that casts the lower classes as criminal extends from fiction to history, for, even when the power of the bourgeoisie is unchallenged by imperial intrusions or coups d'état, like after the Republic of 1848, the political demands of the lowers rungs of the social scale are repressed, at best brushed aside or, more insinuatingly, fed popular literature that instills in them a sense of hope. In having upper-class characters temporarily in disguise among the poor and later reinstated in their class, many popular novels offer an upwardly mobile fiction of redemption. Popular fiction enacts a collective drama of partial confrontation with the low life, for the upper-class character wears the persona of a low life character only temporarily. The drama that ends, inevitably, with the rescue of the upper-class character from what is perceived as the horror of real working-class life culminates in the discovery of the actual social class to which one of its fallen angels belongs to, like in the widely popular *L'Affaire Lerouge*, or, more commonly, with the return of the fallen bourgeois heroes to their former status. While many of Braddon's novels likewise dramatize the anxieties connected with social mobility, they do not preclude it if performed properly and if any "improper" or criminal behavior is well hidden. There are stories of social mobility by Braddon that, while questioning the very notion of social mobility through the sensational turn that reveals criminal acts behind a wealthy facade, have a happy ending that does not require any illicit behavior. In the feuilleton edition that appeared in the French paper *Le Rappel*, for instance, the typical sensational woman who marries, like lady Audley, a rich, older man after a life of suffering must confront her former oppressors who blackmail her. Unlike Lady Audley, however, she does not succumb to the discrediting charges used to push her out of her new privileged life: Honoria, formerly the street singer Jenny exploited by her "protector," refuses to pay her former oppressor and, when maligned in her circle, she moves to London, hires a detective, and pursues the villains.

The bourgeoisie of the Second Empire in France is riveted to narratives that, in their formulaic predictability, reaffirm the bourgeois ethos that triumphs in the happy ending. The claim to propriety and moral respectability prevails; the characters who appear to be evil are not so much the noble and lower classes per se, but the corrupt ones that fall outside of the productive and honest ethos of traditional middle-class values of early-nineteenth-century liberal ideology. The final redemption that saves the upper-class character temporarily fallen from grace certainly had a universal appeal that went beyond one class. Large swaths of the middle and lower classes read these narratives. Readership, however, cannot be mistakenly identified with the abstraction of "the people." The consumption of this genre of industrial literature has different driving forces among each class of readers that grow addicted to the novel over several weeks of publication. Even if the subscription to a magazine serializing a popular novel was too expensive, the less economically stable readers would share the cost of a subscription or read a novel at the library, or, earlier, in a cabinet of reading where books were rented by the hour.[18] After the rotative press was implemented, thus allowing readers to buy individual issues of a daily paper at a cheap price, readership becomes less easily distinguished in terms of income. At this time, the distinction among readers comes not in terms of the actual numbers of readers owning a copy but in terms of the reverberations that this fiction has among them. The overall sense of redemption that most narratives instilled attracts a wide audience because the reaffirmation of the upper-class identity of many characters is not seen in terms of exclusion from privilege, which is what happens at the closing of the sensation novel where the "improper" woman is committed to an institution or excluded. The universal sense of redemption that many French novels inspired may have been so successful even among lower classes because the lower classes may have felt a mystified identification with the dream of social mobility impersonated by the nobler character: the upper bourgeois character in disguise in a poor setting *becomes* "one of us" for the reader. The final success of the upper bourgeois character temporarily disempowered is a matter-of-fact realization for the bourgeois reader, who eases one's anxieties and reaffirms its confidence. For the struggling class the same ending is less a realistic realization than a dream projected into the future; this reader still awaits a redemptive turn in the narrative of both personal life and of social history. In the case of the more economically secure reader, the nightmare protracted over many installments ends with a sense of relief. This ending also eases any lingering anxiety about the return of the repressed that may bring back the danger of a fall from grace due to economic overturns. In the case of the less economically stable reader who is also shut off from artistic representation, the lure of narcissistic identification is so strong when a character seems "one of us" that, as a member of an unrepresented or misrepresented class, the reader overlooks the ideological constructs of the narrative.

The discursive formations that I outlined in discussing some examples of French fiction intertwine invisible and at times contradictory ideological cues, which can hardly fit the definition "right" or "left wing." Very tangible social and political pressures, however, impinged upon the narrative development of French periodical literature and the profession of journalism at large. Censorship had targeted feuilletons since the time of the Second Republic. Trials against prominent writers such as Flaubert and Baudelaire were not isolated cases, even though in other instances a warning, or the confiscation of a paper, was enough to shut down an unwelcome voice. The incarceration of journalists in the prison of St Pélagie was routine under the Second Empire, so much so that a *Journal de St Pélagie* appeared, handwritten. Jokes circulated among journalists, like "It's the only place where I can do some serious work."[19] The killing in 1869 of a twenty-one-year-old journalist Victor Noir by a cousin of Napoleon III caused quite a stir, also because Prince Bonaparte was soon after acquitted. Despite the fact that censorship was a form of white noise that ran through the daily practice of writing periodical fiction, Gaboriau's sensation novels do not shy away from the ethical inspiration behind sensational journalistic reporting. In many of his novels Gaboriau typically ties fictional plots of private misfortune with very specific historical events that help explain the suffering of the honest bourgeois protagonists and at times provide a solution to the mysteries that haunt their lives. Gaboriau's novels published after the end of the Second Empire make very explicit accusations against the illiberal regime that ruled for two decades. In the novel *La Degringolade*, for instance, the main narrative line leads to the funerals of the murdered journalist Victor Noir in Neuilly, where an immense crowd gathered, in the midst of which are the pamphleteer Rochefort from the daily paper *La Marseillaise* and Delescluze, future leader of the Paris Commune. The protagonist, Raymond Delorge, the son of a general who fell out of grace and was killed mysteriously when he opposed the machinations that were to lead to the *putsch* of 1851, recognizes in the arrogance that accompanied the cover-up of the murder of the journalist the same murderous insensitivity that attempts to put his quest for justice to an end. Published in *The Petit Journal* during the last years of the author's life, *La Degringolade*, which Vizetelly issued in 1885, is an indignant accusation against the upper-bourgeosie that supported the rise to power of Napoleon III and found an institutional protection for its rampant corruption under his regime. Sensationalism here serves the purpose of revealing a truth that the triumphant rule of injustice had eclipsed for too long. The sensational narrative revolves not exclusively around the social distinction that upper-middle class characters strive to keep in their circles, like in the British examples, but in a social class that feels invested with a civic responsibility, which, in the broader context of French politics, may also be a cover for equally selfish motivations.

Periodical Literature: An Automatic Form of Writing?

The discursive formations of British sensation fiction and French popular literature that I described in this chapter exemplify different ideological implications contained in the plots of each novel. I consider the novels in question from afar, as a complete narrative unit whose narrative progression is a critical point in assessing the "moral lesson" contained in them, which is not a univocal expression of the author's beliefs but a more complex system of intertwined discursive formations. I shall now reflect on the authorial function in periodical literature in reference to the daily publication of novelistic installments. I want to discuss not the individual monthly installment of a sensation novel in relation to the rest of the magazine, as I did for the shocking effect of sensation fiction in the month-long interval between one issue of *Belgravia* and another, but rather the publication of periodical literature in daily papers. I intend to clarify, from the standpoint of a material history of reading, the different meanings that the experiences of reading fiction in daily or monthly formats suggest.

The cross-channel popularity of periodical literature is evidence of a transnational, indeed global development of industrial literature that I limited in my discussion only to the examples of sensational periodical literature in England and France in the 1860s to 1880s. *Belgravia,* as my archival research shows, was widely distributed beyond the confines of the national market or of the ones of an easily reachable bordering country. Many booksellers in Europe and the rest of the world contributed to popularize Braddon's brand of sensation fiction, through her magazine and her books. Galignani, for instance, distributed the *Belgravia* magazine in Paris, as did other booksellers all over the world.[20] Braddon's novels, likewise, were a more transnational phenomenon. In Leipzig, Germany, for instance, where Alphons Duerr distributed *Belgravia,* the publisher Tauchnitz issued, in collaboration with the French publisher Reinwald, an English version edition of *Rupert Godwin* in 1867, volume 917 in the "Collection of British Authors," which included several titles by Braddon, as well as by Collins, Reade, and Mrs. Wood. While the book format exemplifies the ultimate inclusion of periodical fiction in the realm of literature, and hence the alternating fortunes of its canonicity among literary critics, the ephemeral periodical origin of many titles sheds light on an interesting aspect of literature: the changing, increasingly automated writing function represented by the authors of periodical fiction. Some novelists developed and wrote the installments for up to four novels simultaneously. The periodicity of the publication, however, changes considerably the perception of the literary artifact. Mary Elizabeth Braddon wrote the installments of her novels that were to be published monthly in the magazine that she directed; by contrast, some French authors produced installments on a daily basis. Prolific authors such as Ponson du Terrail contributed new episodes of five *different* titles for five different daily papers.[21] The only feuilleton novel by Braddon mentioned by Robert Lee Wolf, *Le Pasteur de Marston*, appeared on the *Figaro* daily paper consecutively from November 26 to December 5, 1881. While the publication on a monthly periodical like *Belgravia* still preserves the separate typographical and intellectual identity of the work of fiction, a publication in a daily paper, particularly in the lower section of a page, makes the work of fiction less distinguishable from the other stimuli present on the page of a daily paper. The dialogue between fact and fiction becomes closer and the separations among the two more porous. Periodical literature published daily, given the amount of pages produced in few days, appears as a massive, almost "spontaneous," form of automatic writing. The writing of this fiction is like an unchecked flow of ideas, recurrent characters, topical plot lines from many other forms of popular fiction. Periodical literature of this sort is a form of automatic production because it reveals the undercurrents of the society, mixing suggestions of all sorts. Despite the immediacy of the daily publication, the temporality of literary writing, while simplifying its structure due to the accelerated rhythm of publication, creates a stable point of reference for the reader. A novel published in daily installments in a paper allows room for a live commentary on contemporary society by fictional characters whose ideas, direct words, and personal concerns are not always explicitly featured in the impersonal coverage of contemporary news within the paper. Periodical daily fiction appears to be an interface, a mediated access to contemporary life in the midst of its chaotic, fragmented, and simultaneous happening that the daily paper reflects. Fictionalizing contemporary stories in a feuilleton-novel that was religiously read on a daily basis offers the certainty of a stable narrative voice and a moral judgment that the single article may not have provided. In this sense, daily publications of stereotypical sensation or crime novels, unlike monthly issues of the same material, play the role of integrating into a conventional form the nonlinear and noncentered vagaries of modern city life. Since the stories of crime often feature corrupt aristocrats and upper-middle-class characters or noble ones masqueraded as members of the lower class, the middle-class reader is not directly involved; this reader is more a bystander in the workings of crime and illicit behavior. The popular novel in daily format, therefore, reconstructs the bourgeois system of moral values navigating and policing the thrilling trips to the underworld that crime fiction guaranteed. Periodical literature appearing in daily installments has a more cohesive nature: it mirrors events from contemporary life making sure that the laborious and self-righteous ethos of the middle class is not shaken. Crime fiction with fake aristocrats and adventurers as protagonists allows the middle-class reader to walk the fine line between the upper-class status it strives to reach and the lower, sometimes "improper" behavior of the lower classes it seeks to forget or to demonize as being too uncanny, or *(un)heimliche*. Periodical sensational literature of this sort, in presenting the same characters and the same narrative patterns, may be seen as a form of automatic writing that expresses the deep structures of middle-class ideology by mechanically reproducing them through interchangeable characters and authors that help, with their narratives, to give meaning to the many topics and events that the paper covers.

Periodical literature of the sensational sort, by the end of the century, has become a language in itself, a *langue*, a common repository of forms and communication strategies that critics should not approach expecting to find the authorial *parole* of formalist analysis that is expected to reinvent literary language with the subjective turn of the artist. Periodical literature incorporates the direct communication strategies of what formalist critics may call a colloquial language, or standardized *langue.* Literary critics trained in the formalist study of the language of poetry expect the popular novel to be able to speak a *parole* when the genre speaks only a *langue.* The motley collection of canonical episodes from city life, with the constant references to city addresses, daily practices, and common existential paths of life, contains in condensed form all the dominant elements of urban modernity as viewed through the lens of bourgeois ideology. Periodical daily literature of the sensational sort, tied to the rhythms of publication of the press, takes cues from the press' chronicle of contemporary events: literature condenses these suggestions through the time-honored tradition of a consistent linear narrative. The literature published daily and read consecutively inevitably preserves traditional modes of narrative that the episodic nature of city life and journalistic writing challenge. Periodical literature, while dismissed by literary historians as a form of "mediocre" literature—lesser and lesser so now that the study of the periodical press has established itself—becomes of utmost importance for the cultural historian and the sociologist of literature interested in the history of reading.[22] Periodical novel-reading increased literacy rates; it also exposed a wider public to literature both individually and through forms of social reading in public and private spaces of gathering where the novels could be read aloud. Less obviously, periodical literature exemplifies how to actively *read* contemporary life in the midst of the scattered representation of daily life that a daily paper offers. Periodical daily literature was a literary exercise following the standardized rules of a variety of genres it incorporates. Periodical popular literature, however, created also a daily language of narrative consistency that structured the reactions of the readers when processing the facts of modern life. Literature gives a narrative development and an interpretation to modern life, which readers would otherwise experience in a more dispersive manner. The reflection in reader's minds that reading novels daily would generate is a mediated and structured form of reading modern life. While sensation fiction published in the monthly magazine creates shocking interruptions in the inveterate expectations that readers have about how life is represented in novels, the case of the publication of sensation fiction in a daily paper changes the meaning and the role that fiction has in relation to the rest of the publication. The juxtaposition of fiction and fact in two different forms of periodical publication shifts the prominent role that fiction may have over reality or that reality may have over fiction. In the case of the sensational magazine edited by Mary Elizabeth Braddon fiction functions as a breach in the screen upon which readers would project their preconceived notions of acceptable social behavior. The rest of the magazine reconstructs unity through the presence of recurrent narrative patterns and discursive formations dispersed in the articles that accompanied the fiction as well as, indirectly, the reader, until the next installment a month later. The study of the material history of reading sensational fiction in a daily paper reveals a different pattern: the stories the paper reported on, in presenting new and unpredictable outcomes, could not be understood by the reader who cannot, given the scarcity of knowledge available on facts unfolding in real time easily identify agents, facts, and thus establish meaning. Literary representation in a feuilleton daily edition of the same stories, by contrast, reduces the fragmentation of history to manageable narrative units. The installments create an experiential and intellectual continuum that shapes the way readers process the information from day to day. The dispersive nature of news coverage offers an unmediated reality that traditional forms of linear narratives, like the novel, could give meaning to over the course of the narrative published periodically. No matter how sensational and shocking the novel may be, fiction incorporates its revelations in a narrative pattern that builds excitement but also progresses in predictable terms, for the genre uses a variety of strategies already employed for decades by authors of popular fiction. The white noise of the ideological formations in the back of these narratives give unity and shape to the new exercise of reading modern life. This daily exercise engaged the reader in interpreting the whole page of the daily paper: the top of the page, where contemporary life features in fragmented forms, and the bottom, where novelists condense in literary narrative a mediated view of modern life. This form of popular literature is written expressly for the daily paper and can make its commercial fortune. Novels by established authors who did not write them expressly for the daily publication but simply issued them in daily installments were oftentimes not successful with the readers. The publication of daily periodical fiction written for that purpose generates a hermeneutic circle in which writing, publishing, and interpreting happen almost simultaneously. The publication in feuilleton functions as a footnote to the contemporary facts reported in the newspaper. This form of commentary can reorient the reader while at the same time maintaining the power of fiction intact.

Appendix

Index to *Belgravia* 1866–1876

Belgravia/A London Magazine/conducted by/Mary Elizabeth Braddon/Author of "Lady Audley's Secret," "Aurora Floyd," etc./ office:/Warwick House, Paternoster Row, London, E.C.

November 1866

Birds of Prey/by the author of "Lady Audley's Secret"
Swells
African Martyrology/by W. Winwood Reade
An Adventurous Investigation
In the Schools Quad. An Oxford Study
Belgravian Prose Ballads.1. The Chaperon
An Indictment [poem] Evelyn Forest
A Fireside Story. Told by the Poker
Market Street, Manchester/by George Augustus Sala
Feast of St. Partridge at Park Hall
Slain at Sadowa [poem]
The Iron Casket. A Tale of the Travaux Forcés
Love in November [poem] Mortimer Collins

December 1866

Birds of Prey/by the author of "Lady Audley's Secret"
Ten and Twenty. A Drawing-room Reverie [illustrated poem] J. Ash by Sterry
Hill Scandals/by Sidney L. Blanchard

Jacob Snider, Inventor. J. Scoffern, M.B. Lond
Faust-Dramatic and Legendary. John Oxenford
University Union Societies
The Death-Walk. William Duthie [illustrated poem]
Stage Jewels/by Dutton Cook
Through Cornwall. Mortimer Collins
On Balls. Percy Fitzgerald
Belgravian Prose Ballads. 2. The Friendly Chop
The Iron Casket. Part the Second
A Sunset Idyll. [poem] Quallon

JANUARY 1867

Birds of Prey/by the author of "Lady Audley's Secret"
Lyrics of the Months. January. A.T. [illustrated poem]
Enough at Christmas. W. Blanchard Jerrold
My Love Amy. A New Year's Gift by Francis Derrick
Snowflake. J. Ashby Sterry [illustrated poem]
How I Won Polly and a Postmastership/by Tom Hood
Actors in the Great Play. Joseph Hatten
At Daggers Drawn/by Babington White
New Year's Day. Octave Delepierre, LL.D.
A Christmas Vision [illustrated poem]
Eveline's Visitant. A Ghost Story by the editor
Dykwynkyn at Work. T.W. Robertson
The Iron Casket. Part the Third
A Christmas Carol [poem] Mortimer Collins

FEBRUARY 1867

Birds of Prey/by the author of "Lady Audley's Secret"
Lyrics of the Months. February. Gathering Snowdrops [illustrated poem] J. Ashby Sterry
Gavarni
The Pitman's Perils
Sackville-Street, Dublin by George Augustus Sala
Private Theatricals. Percy Fitzgerald
Vacillating Characters
On Brighton Pier. W. [illustrated poem]
Belgravian Prose Ballads. 3. Honeymoonshine
The Four Suits. Astley H. Baldwin
How I Heard My Own Will Read

The Basilisk. J.S.
Rachel's Folly
A Girl-A Horse-A Tree. [poem] Martimer Collins

March 1867

Birds of Prey/by the author of "Lady Audley's Secret"
Lyrics of the Months. March [illustrated poem] A.T.
New Courts-of-Justice Designs
My Friend's Villa/by Walter Thornbury
Decline of Drama. J. Francis Hitchman
In the Wind [illustrated poem] Astley H. Baldwin
From St. Paul's to Piccadilly W.S. Gilbert
Gustave Doré A.T.
Stone's Love Affair
A Red-Indian Legend/by Rev. H.S. Fagan
Married for Money [illustrated poem] J. Ashby Sterry
Vivisection/by Dr. Scoffern
Belgravian Prose Ballads. 4. Behind the Scenes
Circe/Or Three Acts in the Life of an Artist/by Babington White

April 1867

Birds of Prey/by the author of "Lady Audley's Secret"
Lyrics of the Months. April [illustrated poem] A.T.
Paris Universal Exhibition
Valerian's Honeymoon
Dean Swift's Cathedral
How My Debts Were Paid/by the author of "Lady Flavia," etc.
The Wrong Side of the Stream. [illustrated poem] J. Ashby Sterry
Amusements of Paris
Bric-a-Brac Hunting/by Major H. Byng Hall
Vivisection/by Dr. Scoffern
"Sweet Violets" [illustrated poem] M.
Literary Criticism. J. Campbell Smith
Circe/Or Three Acts in the Life of an Artist/by Babington White

May 1867

Birds of Prey/by the author of "Lady Audley's Secret"
Lyrics of the Months. May [illustrated poem] M.
English Pictures and Picture Dealers. B. Folkestone Williams

Letters from Lilliput/Being Essays on the Extremely Little/by George Augustus Sala
Episodes in the Life of Miss Tabitha Trenoodle/by the author of "Mildred's Wedding," etc.
At Last [illustrated poem] H. Savile Clarke
Literary Honours
London Squares/by Walter Thornbury
Verse de Société. J. Francis Hitchman
The Late Dowager Countess of Jersey. J. Frances Scoffern
The Route [illustrated poem] T.S.S.
The Wizard of the Edge
On a Clifton Pebble. Joseph Hatton
Circe/Or Three Acts in the Life of an Artist/by Babington White

June 1867

Birds of Prey/by the author of "Lady Audley's Secret"
Lyrics of the Months. June [illustrated poem] M.
Bric-a-Brac Hunting/by Major H. Byng Hall
Letters from Lilliput/Being Essays on the Extremely Little/by George Augustus Sala
The Physiology of Picnics
The Paris Exhibition
Zoological Memories [illustrated poem] J. Ashby Sterry
An Awkward Mistake/by the author of "Lady Flavia"
Carpenters' Scenes
London Squares/by Walter Thornbury
Held in Play (A Fragment of a Young Lady's Letter)
Summer Term at Oxford. T.H.S. Escott
Circe/Or Three Acts in the Life of an Artist/by Babington White
The Trinity of Art [poem] Mortimer Collins

July 1867

Birds of Prey/by the author of "Lady Audley's Secret"
The Giant Sword [illustrated poem] Charles H. Waring
London Squares/by Walter Thornbury
How I Wronged My Friend
Inhabited Planets. T.L. Phipson, Ph.D. F.C.S.
Lyrics of the Months. July [illustrated poem] C.S.C.
Letters from Lilliput/Being Essays on the Extremely Little/by George Augustus Sala

French Novels M.
A Little Music. Percy Fitzgerald
Before the Mirror. Georgiana. C. Clark
Summer Time [illustrated poem] H
Periodical Literature
Circe/Or Three Acts in the Life of an Artist/by Babington White

August 1867

Dead-Sea Fruit/A Novel/by the author of "Lady Audley's Secret," etc.
Ceyx and Halcyone [illustrated poem]
London Squares/by Walter Thornbury
The Friend of Talleyrand. Dutton Cook
Salamanders. J. Scoffern, M.B.
Periodical Literature
Birds of Prey/by the author of "Lady Audley's Secret"
Life in an Oasis. R. Arthur Arnold
Lyrics of the Months. August [illustrated poem] J. Ashby Sterry
Outside the World/by the author of "Bitter Sweet," "The Tallants of Barton," etc.
The Gorilla, as I Found Him/by W. Winwood Reade, F.R.G.S.
Circe/Or Three Acts in the Life of an Artist/by Babington White

September 1867

Dead-Sea Fruit/A Novel/by the author of "Lady Audley's Secret," etc.
London Parks/by Walter Thornbury
Lyrics of the Months. September [illustrated poem] M.
Circe/Or Three Acts in the Life of an Artist/by Babington White
Forbidden Fruit [illustrated poem] T.S.S.
A Ride From Bude to Boss by Two Oxford Men
Camp Life at Wimbledon
Away at the Sea [illustrated poem] Charles H. Waring
A Norman Watering-Place
Sessio Mirabilis
Birds of Prey/by the author of "Lady Audley's Secret"

October 1867

Dead-Sea Fruit/A Novel/by the author of "Lady Audley's Secret," etc.
Lyrics of the Month. October [illustrated poem] C.S.C.
London Parks/by Walter Thornbury

Michael Faraday. J. Scoffern, M.B.
The Paris Fashions/by George Augustus Sala
Lusignan [poem]
Birds of Prey/by the author of "Lady Audley's Secret"
Deloraine's Holiday. Mortimer Collins A Lancashire-Coast Adventure. J.A.D.
Off and Away [illustrated poem] J. Ashby Sterry
Diana Gay/A Novel/by the author of "Bella Donna," "Never Forgotten," etc.

November 1867

Dead-Sea Fruit/A Novel/by the author of "Lady Audley's Secret," etc.
Horse-Shoes on Church Doors
Lyrics of the Months. November [illustrated poem] C.S.C.
The Romans at Home. J.D.B.
The Cant of Modern Criticism/by George Augustus Sala
My Aunt's Pearl Ring/by Ada Buisson, author of "Put to the Test," etc.
Happy Tidings [illustrated poem] T.H.S.E.
London Parks/by Walter Thornbury
A Remonstrance by Captain Shandon to the Editor of the "Pall-Mall Gazzette"
A Fortnight in Corsica. T. Ansted F.R.S.
Netting [illustrated poem]
Bric-a-Brac Hunting/by Major H. Byng Hall
Diana Gay/A Novel/by the author of "Bella Donna," "Never Forgotten," etc.

December 1867

Dead-Sea Fruit/A Novel/by the author of "Lady Audley's Secret," etc.
A Round of Operas P.F.
Letters From Lilliput/Being Essays on the Extremely Little/by George Augustus Sala
Moonshine in Paris [illustrated poem]
County Newspapers. J. Francis Hitchman
Lost Sight Of. A Tale of Corsica/by Astely H. Baldwin
Cosmetics. J. Scoffern M.B.
Studies in Tennyson. W.S.

Lyrics of the Months. December [illustrated poem]
The Blameless Aethiopians. James Hutton
Diana Gay/A Novel/by the author of "Bella Donna," "Never Forgotten," etc.

JANUARY 1868

Dead-Sea Fruit/A Novel/by the author of "Lady Audley's Secret," etc.
A Great Ball and a Great Bear. A Story of Two Birthdays/by Babington White/author of "Circe," "At Daggers Drawn," etc.
He Stoops to Conquer. H. Savile Clarke
London Parks/by Walter Thornbury
On Marriage Settlements
"Le Roi Est Mort, Vive le Roi!" A.H.B.
The Grand Duchess/or the Cupidity of Monsieur Quibosch/by George Augustus Sala
The Queen of the Realm of a Million Delights/A Christmas Story/by Charles Smith Cheltnam
Two Christmas Eves. The First
Lost Sight Of/A Tale of Corsica/by Astely H. Baldwin
Christmas in the Olden Time [poem] William Sawyer
The Ghost's Summons/by Ada Buisson
Diana Gay/A Novel/by the author of "Bella Donna," "Never Forgotten," etc.
Music and Memory [poem] Mortimer Collins

FEBRUARY 1868

Dead-Sea Fruit/A Novel/by the author of "Lady Audley's Secret," etc.
Communicative Persons. T.H.S. Escott
Lying in Wait [illustrated poem]
Recollections of Her Majesty's Theatre/by Noel d'Arcy, A.B.
The Portrait's Warning/by H. Savile Clarke
Living Upon Paper. S.N.E.
The Last Days of Pompeii [illustrated poem] W.T.
On the "Sensational" in Literature and Art/by George Augustus Sala
Bric-a-Brac Hunting/by Major H. Byng Hall
London Palaces/by Walter Thornbury
The Last of the Wreck [illustrated poem] H. Savile Clarke

Nitro-Glycerine and Other Explosives. J. Scoffern, M.B.
Diana Gay/A Novel/by the author of "Bella Donna," "Never Forgotten," etc.
After the Battle [poem] M.E. Braddon

March 1868

Dead-Sea Fruit/A Novel/by the author of "Lady Audley's Secret," etc.
London Palaces/by Walter Thornbury
The Mudie Classics/by Babington White/author of "Circe," etc.
Saint May. A Civic Lyric [illustrated poem] J. Ashby Sterry
Letters From Lilliput Being Essays on the Extremely Little by George Augustus Sala
Nice Girls. William Sawyer
In the Firelight. A Dream [illustrated poem] W.T.
Paragon Paris. Edward R. Russell
The Hawking Party [poem] M.E. Braddon
Manchester Men
Technical Education. J. Scoffern, M.B.
Bric-a-Brac Hunting/by Major Byng Hall
A Bit of Scandal [illustrated poem] W.S.
David Garrick
Diana Gay/A Novel/by the author of "Bella Donna," "Never Forgotten," etc.

April 1868

Dead-Sea Fruit/A Novel/by the author of "Lady Audley's Secret," etc.
Glimpses at Foreign Literature. George Sand. M.
The Dawn of Truth [illustrated poem]
The Mudie Classic/by Babington White/author of "Circe," etc.
Paletteville/A Pilgrimage to the Country of "Art for Art"/by George Augustus Sala
London Palaces/by Walter Thornbury
Ill Tidings [illustrated poem] T.H.S.E.
Léon Faucher, Statesman and Journalist
Diana Gay/A Novel/by the author of "Bella Donna," "Never Forgotten," etc.
Land in Sight! Home at last! [illustrated poem] W.T.
"Beautiful For Ever." J. Scoffern, M.B.
Jane Eyre's School

Charlotte's Inheritance/by the author of "Lady Audley's Secret," etc.

MAY 1868

Dead-Sea Fruit/A Novel/by the author of "Lady Audley's Secret," etc.
Disagreeable People. William Sawyer
The Strange Harper. A New Version [illustrated poem] William Stigand
London Palaces/by Walter Thornbury
On Leave/by the author of "Lady Flavia" "Lord Lynn's Wife," etc.
An Old Venetian sketch [illustrated poem] J. Ashby Sterry
Literature in Purple. Edward R. Russell
Diana Gay/A Novel/by the author of "Bella Donna," "Never Forgotten," etc.
By the River [illustrated poem] H. Savile Clarke
Cosmetics for the Hair. J. Scoffern, M.B.
A Million a Minute
The Mountain of Michelet
Vagueness. T.H.S. Escott
Pairing [poem] Astley H. Baldwin
Charlotte's Inheritance/by the author of "Lady Audley's Secret," etc.

JUNE 1868

Dead-Sea Fruit/A Novel/by the author of "Lady Audley's Secret," etc.
University Men in Town
London Palaces/by Walter Thornbury
Tyro [illustrated poem]
Another Episode in the Life of Miss Tabitha Trenoodle/by the author of "Kiddle-a-Wink," "Mildred's Wedding," etc.
Literature of the Line. Sidney L. Blanchard
Fallen Among Flunkeys/A Recollection of the Arabian Nights/by George Augustus Sala
Diana Gay/A Novel/by the author of "Bella Donna," "Never Forgotten," etc.
Death Upon the Mountains [illustrated poem] H. Savile Clarke
French Etiquette
Sensationalism in Science: Our Coal Fields. R.H. Patterson

The Story of St. Thomas's Hospital. E.M. Dermott
The Aloe [illustrated poem] R. Hogarth
Charlotte's Inheritance/by the author of "Lady Audley's Secret," etc.
Insurance and Assurance/An Essay/by Goerge Augustus Sala

July 1868

Bound to John Company/or the Adventures and Misadventures of Robert Ainsleigh
London Clubs/by Walter Thornbury
Bracelets. M.G. Watkins
Missing, a Householder/by Francis Jacox
Awaiting the Conqueror [illustrated poem] H. Savile Clarke
Diana Gay/A Novel/by the author of "Bella Donna," "Never Forgotten," etc.
Sensationalism in Science: Is the Sun Dying? R.H. Patterson
The Lady of the Land/Adapted from Sir John Mandeville [illustrated poem] M.E. Braddon
A Sketch from the Far West/by George Augustus Sala
On the Teeth. J. Scoffern, M.B.
Dead-Sea Fruit/A Novel/by the author of "Lady Audley's Secret," etc.
Flourishing. W.S.
Father Prout in Paris. Blanchard Jerrold
A Summer-Noon in Town
Charlotte's Inheritance/by the author of "Lady Audley's Secret," etc.

August 1868

Bound to John Company/or the Adventures and Misadventures of Robert Ainsleigh
Letters from Lilliput/Being Essays on the Extremely Little/by George Augustus Sala
Personalities of a Scotch Tour. T.H.S. Escott
Habet [illustrated poem] William Stigand
London Clubs/by Walter Thornbury
A Summer Day-Dream. J. Campbell Smith
Diana Gay/A Novel/by the author of "Bella Donna," "Never Forgotten," etc.
Sensationalism in Science/by R.H. Patterson

Morning Dreams [illustrated poem]
The Whitebait Mystery. J.G. Bertram
Dead-Sea Fruit/A Novel/by the author of "Lady Audley's Secret," etc.
The Trooper's Story [illustrated poem] William Sawyer
Marriage Versus Celibacy
Horace in Pall Mall. Walter Thornbury
Pins
Charlotte's Inheritance/by the author of "Lady Audley's Secret," etc.
Under the Limes [poem] Mortimer Collins

SEPTEMBER 1868

Bound to John Company/or the Adventures and Misadventures of Robert Ainsleigh
In the Common Room/an Oxford Sketch
The Mummy. W. Stigand
Out of the Stream [illustrated poem] Henry S. Leigh
London Clubs/by Walter Thornbury
Dead-Sea Fruit/A Novel/by the author of "Lady Audley's Secret," etc.
Will-O'-The Wisp. T.L. Phipson, Ph.D., F.C.S.
In Carnival Time [illustrated poem] W.S.
The Great Kermesse of Antwerp/by the author of "Hester Kirton." "Wild as a Hank," etc.
Diana Gay/A Novel/by the author of "Bella Donna," "Never Forgotten," etc.
Landing [illustrated poem] T.H.S.E.
How Should We Dine—If We Could/An Essay on Cookery/by George Augustus Sala
Charlotte's Inheritance/by the author of "Lady Audley's Secret," etc.
"All For Nothing" [poem] Evelyn Forest

OCTOBER 1868

Bound to John Company/or the Adventures and Misadventures of Robert Ainsleigh
Playing at Pleasure. William Sawyer
Cavalier-Hunting [illustrated poem] W.S.
London Clubs/by Walter Thornbury

Sensationalism in Science: Are There More Worlds Than One? R.H. Patterson
How to Get Married
Singularity. George Stott
The Avalanche [illustrated poem] J. Ashby Sterry
Diana Gay/A Novel/by the author of "Bella Donna," "Never Forgotten," etc.
The Great Circumbendibus/A journal of Travel on a Loop-line/by George Augustus Sala
La Première Jeunesse [illustrated poem] T.H.S.E.
The Conjurer at Home. Desmond Ryan
Charlotte's Inheritance/by the author of "Lady Audley's Secret," etc.
Death and the Seasons [poem] Godfrey Turner

November 1868

My Enemy's Daughter/by Justin Mc Carthy, author of "Paul Massie," "The Waterdale Neighbours," etc.
In the Temple/Marie Antoiniette's Reverie [poem] F. Cashel Hoey
Simona [illustrated poem]
"Thorough" in Criticism. Edward R. Russell
London Clubs/by Walter Thornbury
Women and Men. H.L.
A Day in Ancient Rome. James Hutton
Bound to John Company/or the Adventures and Misadventures of Robert Ainsleigh
Letters From Lilliput/Being Essays on the Extremely Little/by George Augustus Sala
Artists in Love and Poison. W. Stigand
Jeffrey de Mettray [illustrated poem] William Sawyer
Sensationalism in Science. Autocracy of the Sun. R.H. Patterson
Novelists Law. W.S.
Charlotte's Inheritance/by the author of "Lady Audley's Secret," etc.
Reputation/(Adapted from the Hungarian Ráday) R. Reece

December 1868

My Enemy's Daughter/by Justin Mc Carthy, author of "Paul Massie," "The Waterdale Neighbours," etc.
The Costlines of Age. William Sawyer

The Omen [illustrated poem] by H. Savile Clarke
Behind the Scenes/by George Augustus Sala
The Flight to Varennes. W. Stigand
Euthanasia. John Scoffern, M.B.
Bound to John Company/or the Adventures and Misadventures of Robert Ainsleigh
Women of Fashion in Ancient Rome. J. Hutton
The Dedication of the Cathedral/Temp. 1370 [poem] Walter Thornbury
Bob Kennedy's Canvass
Conquest [illustrated poem] T.H.S.E.
King Alfred as Poet and Man/by John A. Heraud
Charlotte's Inheritance/by the author of "Lady Audley's Secret," etc.

JANUARY 1869

My Enemy's Daughter/by Justin Mc Carthy, author of "Paul Massie," "The Waterdale Neighbours," etc.
Letters from Lilliput/Being Essays on the Extremely Little/by George Augustus Sala
The Lady and the Lobster/by Alfred Thompson
The Mystery of the Seasons. R.H. Patterson
Ivo de Talboy's Picnic [poem] by Mortimer Collins
London Theatres and London Actors/by Walter Thornbury
In the Firelight [poem] B.
Links in a Chain/A Tale. William Sawyer
A Christmas Soirée/by F.W. Robinson, author of "Grandmother's Money," etc.
A Lady Faust [poem] Astley H. Baldwin
Bound to John Company/or the Adventures and Misadventures of Robert Ainsleigh
The Case of a Pipe/by Albany de Fonblanque
The Lorelei [illustrated poem] W.S.
Charlotte's Inheritance/by the author of "Lady Audley's Secret," etc.
Country-House Life. Percy Fitzgerald
The Holly's Teaching [poem] William Sawyer

FEBRUARY 1869

My Enemy's Daughter/by Justin Mc Carthy, author of "Paul Massie," "The Waterdale Neighbours," etc.
Sensationalism in Science. Photospheres. R.H. Patterson

Le Bal de l' Opéra [illustrated poem] Zeta
Byron and the Countess Guiccioli. William Stigand
Bound to John Company/or the Adventures and Misadventures of Robert Ainsleigh
Prosecutions of a Country Clergyman. G.S.
The Suffolk Witches. John Scoffern, M.B.
At Bay [illustrated poem] W.S.
London Theatres and London Actors/by Walter Thornbury
Fragments of and Old File/by Joseph Hatton, author of "The Tallants of Barton," etc.
The Prude/A Warning to Young Ladies in General, and Engaged Ones in Particular/by George Augustus Sala
Charlotte's Inheritance/by the author of "Lady Audley's Secret," etc.
Intellectual solace. T.H.S. Escott
Anacreon's Fourth Ode/ΕΙΣ ΕΡΟΤΑ [poem] John Scoffern, M.B.

MARCH 1869

My Enemy's Daughter/by Justin Mc Carthy, author of "Paul Massie," "The Waterdale Neighbours," etc.
The Central-Asian Question. James Hutton
In Request Rather.
The Myths of London. William Sawyer
The Brown Lady/by Mrs. Castel Hoey/author of "A House of Cards," "The iron Casket," etc.
London Theatres and London Actors/by Walter Thornbury
A New Game for Ladies. W.W. Tulloch, M.A.
The Eve of St Bartholomew [illustrated poem] William Sawyer
Fire and Snow. Walter Thornbury
On Stage Costume/With Some Reflections on my Lord Sydney's Rescript/by George Augustus Sala
Bound to John Company/or the Adventures and Misadventures of Robert Ainsleigh
Grooves. George Stott
White Gunpowder. John Scoffern, M.B.

APRIL 1869

My Enemy's Daughter/by Justin Mc Carthy, author of "Paul Massie," "The Waterdale Neighbours," etc.
Taking Things Easy. George Stott
Spring [illustrated poem] William Stigand

Serpents and Venomous Snakes. N.A. Woods
The Brown Lady/by Mrs. Castel Hoey/author of "A House of Cards," "The Iron Casket," etc.
The Human Finger and Thumb. Andrew Steinmetz
London Theatres and London Actors/by Walter Thornbury
Beetroot-Sugar in France. John Scoffern, M.B.
Told by a Table. An Oxford Sketch
The Madman's Prayer. C.B.J.
Bound to John Company/or the Adventures and Misadventures of Robert Ainsleigh
Letters from Lilliput/Being Essays on the Extremely Little/by George Augustus Sala
Noctambulism. Francis Jacox
The Voice of Grief [poem] George Smith

May 1869

My Enemy's Daughter/by Justin Mc Carthy, author of "Paul Massie," "The Waterdale Neighbours," etc.
Gold
The Dreaming Sea [illustrated poem] Catherine Wilton
Serpents and Venomous Snakes II. N.A. Woods
On Certain Passage in "Vanity Fair."/An Essay Suggested by a Picture in the Royal Academy/by George Augustus Sala
Beyond [poem] William Stigand
Glamour/by the Countess Von Bothmer
Fragments of an Old File
Concerning M. or N. William Sawyer
London Theatres and London Actors/by Walter Thornbury
Bound to John Company/or the Adventures and Misadventures of Robert Ainsleigh
The Cycles of the Worlds. R.H. Patterson
The Honeymoons/An Autumn Adventure/by Sidney Blanchard

June 1869

My Enemy's Daughter/by Justin Mc Carthy, author of "Paul Massie," "The Waterdale Neighbours," etc.
The Return of Bear-Hunters [illustrated poem] W.T.
The Late Prince Consort as a Composer
Underground Gods. William Stigand
The Beggar of Vernon. Robert Harrison

First Down in the Morning [illustrated poem] William Sawyer
Bound to John Company/or the Adventures and Misadventures of Robert Ainsleigh
Changing the Venue
Sunday Labour. William Duthie
Political Immorality. Frederick Thomas Monro
Letters from Lilliput/Being Essays on the Extremely Little/by George Augustus Sala
Glamour/by the Countess Von Bothmer
A 'Feast of Flowers." Llewellynn Jewitt, F.S.A.
Writing for Money. G.H. Guest
Lovers' Vows/A Song for Music. William Mitchell, K.T.

JULY 1869

Stern Necessity/by the author of "Poor Humanity," "No Church," "Mattie, a Stray," etc.
Ostend Gaieties. Peter Fitzgerald
My Namesake and I
A Victim of Patents. William Sawyer
Fairy Blossoms [poem] William Stigand
A Very Charming Hostess/A Study from Art and Nature. John Baker Hopkins
Cartridges/by Dr. Scoffern author of "Projectile Weapons and Explosive Compounds"
My Enemy's Daughter/by Justin Mc Carthy, author of "Paul Massie," "The Waterdale Neighbours," etc.
Strangers in Paris/by George Augustus Sala
Horace in Pall Mall. Walter Thornbury
Truth Is Stranger Than Fiction. Frederick T. Monro
Tame Lunatics. W.H. Lewis
The Elopement-Door [illustrated poem]
The Ghosts of Glenlussa/by Cuthbert Bede, author of "Verdant Green," etc.
Intellect and Cruelty. George Stott
Bound to John Company/or the Adventures and Misadventures of Robert Ainsleigh

AUGUST 1869

Stern Necessity/by the author of "Poor Humanity," "No Church," "Mattie, a Stray," etc.
The Forest [illustrated poem] William Stigand

A Regatta-Day. Percy Fitzgerald
Giovanni Baptista Piranesi
The Moon and the Maiden [poem] Mortimer Collins
A Night With King Pharaoh/by the Baron Schlippenback, K.S.L.
Whose Fault Is It? M.E. Braddon
Summer in Normandy/by Henry Blackburn, author of "Travelling in Spain," etc.
In the Season [illustrated poem]
My Enemy's Daughter/by Justin Mc Carthy, author of "Paul Massie," "The Waterdale Neighbours," etc.
Mute of Malice. Francis Jacox
Torrentcraig Castle [illustrated poem] M.C.
Strangers in Paris/by George Augustus Sala
Bound to John Company/or the Adventures and Misadventures of Robert Ainsleigh

SEPTEMBER 1869

Stern Necessity/by the author of "Poor Humanity," "No Church," "Mattie, a Stray," etc.
A Day in the Telegraph Office. C.W.
The Ring of Polycrates [illustrated poem] William Duthie
France Adrift
Gatherings in Brittany/by the author of "Mildred's Wedding," "Olive Varcoe," etc.
British Pearls. A.C. Blackstone
Nereids of Wire [poem] Mortimer Collins
The Baron's Coffin/by Ada Buisson, author of "Put to the Test," etc.
Letters from Lilliput/Being Essays on the Extremely Little/by George Augustus Sala
My Enemy's Daughter/by Justin Mc Carthy, author of "Paul Massie," "The Waterdale Neighbours," etc.
Experiences of a Gentleman in a Red Coat. Sidney L. Blanchard
Bound to John Company/or the Adventures and Misadventures of Robert Ainsleigh

OCTOBER 1869

Stern Necessity/by the author of "Poor Humanity," "No Church," "Mattie, a Stray," etc.
Ghosts of the Season. T.H.S. Escott
Maledictum [illustrated poem]
London Theatres and London Actors/by Walter Thornbury

My Enemy's Daughter/by Justin Mc Carthy, author of "Paul Massie," "The Waterdale Neighbours," etc.
In the Valleys [illustrated poem] T.H.S.E.
In the Heart of the Ardennes/by Florence Marryat (Mrs. Ross Church)
Bric-a-Brac Hunting, Abroad and at Home/by Major H. Byng Hall
"In My Mind's Eye, Horatio!"
An East-End Entertainment. F.W. Robinson
At a Masquerade [illustrated poem] William Sawyer
Gatherings in Brittany/by the author of "Mildred's Wedding," "Olive Varcoe," etc.
Bound to John Company/or the Adventures and Misadventures of Robert Ainsleigh
Fatal Jewels/by Albany de Fonblanque
A Lover's Legacy. L. St. B.

NOVEMBER 1869

Stern Necessity/by the author of "Poor Humanity," "No Church," "Mattie, a Stray," etc.
Does the Earth Grow Sick? R.H. Patterson
On the Origin of Story-Telling. Octave Delepierre, LL.D.
"Do You Know This?" [illustrated poem] T.H.S. Escott
Parliamentary Representatives. Frederick T. Monro
Little Ones at Limehouse F.W. Robinson
Curious Reflections. Francis Jacox
Saint Francis of Assisi. William Stigand
My Unlucky Friend
The Maories. John Scoffern, M.B.
London Theatres and London Actors/by Walter Thornbury
The Ambuscade [illustrated poem] William Sawyer
The Perfect Man/by George Augustus Sala
Thodore of Corsica/the Story of a Real Adventurer/by Percy Fitzgerald, M.A., author of "Diana Gay," "Bella Donna," etc.

DECEMBER 1869

Stern Necessity/by the author of "Poor Humanity," "No Church," "Mattie, a Stray," etc.
Brighton in November
The Incumbent of Bagshot

The Siren. [poem] William Stigand
A Very Narrow Escape
Mad Folk [from] *A memoir of John Conolly M.D., D.C.L.* by Sir James Clark
Our Nice Servant/A Domestic Drama/Communicated to George Augustus Sala
Jack Layford's Friend/With an Account of How He Laid the Ghost. L.N.
London Theatres and Actors/by Walter Thornbury
Summer Reminiscences [illustrated poem] William Sawyer
Thodore of Corsica/the Story of a Real Adventurer/by Percy Fitzgerald, M.A., author of "Diana Gay," "Bella Donna," etc.
Youth's Farewell. [poem] C.A. Ward

January 1870

Stern Necessity/by the author of "Poor Humanity," "No Church," "Mattie, a Stray," etc.
Christmas in Scotland. Edmund S. Roscoe
The Diamond Bullet /by William Sawyer
Levinson's Victim
Princess Cancrin's Revenge/by George Augustus Sala
A Costermongers' Club
Christmas in Canada
The Missing Beronet/A Strange Trial of the Last Century/by Walter Thornbury
Two Christmas Seasons at Oxford. H. Vincent Watson
The Sailors' Home. C.F.F. Woods
Franklin's Confession/by Amelia Thomas
Thodore of Corsica/the Story of a Real Adventurer/by Percy Fitzgerald, M.A., author of "Diana Gay," "Bella Donna," etc.

February 1870

Stern Necessity/by the author of "Poor Humanity," "No Church," "Mattie, a Stray," etc.
The Natural History of Bicycles. Pollington
Mr. and Mrs. De Fontenoy
Gold and Glitter. William Duthie
Insanity and Its Treatment
My Sister Caroline/A Novelette/Edited by M.E. Braddon

The Lily. William Stigand
National Obsequies. C.F.F. Woods
The Lost [illustrated poem] William Sawyer
London Theatres and Actors/by Walter Thornbury
The Loves of Famous Men/by Percy Fitzgerald, M.A., author of "Bella Donna," "Diana Gay," etc.
Lend Me a Florin/A Tale of Hambourg/by Lady Jackson
Who is Mr. Rochefort? J. Redding Warre

March 1870

The Splendid Stranger/by the author of "Lady Audley's Secret," etc.
The Carnival of Madrid/by George Augustus Sala
Physic. John Scoffern, M.E.
Stern Necessity/by the author of "Poor Humanity," "No Church," "Mattie, a Stray," etc.
Man's Destructive Agency. W.E. Hall
Poets' Wives. William J. Tate
The Golden Furrows [poem] Godfrey Turner
The Loves of Famous Men/by Percy Fitzgerald, M.A., author of "Bella Donna," "Diana Gay," etc.
My Sister Caroline/A Novelette edited by M.E. Braddon
The Rose [poem] William Stigand

April 1870

Fenton's Quest/by the author of "Lady Audley's Secret," etc.
Antipathies. W.E. Hall
Ride Away, Gay Gentleman! [illustrated poem] Charles. S. Cheltnam
Pantomime and Pandemonium/Two Nights in the New Cut/by George Augustus Sala
How They Welcome Easter in Rome. W.W. Tulloch
Under the Lilies/by Ada Buisson, author of "Put to the Test," etc.
Barren Vows [illustrated poem] James Mew
Russia and Nicholas I. William Stigand
Star-Heat. J. Carpenter F.R.A.S.
The Loves of Famous Men/by Percy Fitzgerald, M.A., author of "Bella Donna," "Diana Gay," etc.
The Spring in the Wood [illustrated poem] William Sawyer
Stern Necessity/by the author of "Poor Humanity," "No Church," "Mattie, a Stray," etc.
Violets [poem] Babington White

May 1870

Fenton's Quest/by the author of "Lady Audley's Secret," etc.
Sor Teresa [illustrated poem] Charles S. Cheltnam
On Soothing People "Down"/An Essay Suggested by a Recent Trial at Tours/by George Augustus Sala
The Loves of Famous Men/by Percy Fitzgerald, M.A., author of "Bella Donna," "Diana Gay," etc.
May-Day in Springdale. W.W. Tulloch
Captain's Newton's Diary/by Florence Marryat (Mrs. Ross Church), author of "Véronique," "Nelly Brooke," etc.
Confessions of an Eminent Swell-Mobsman/by Walter Thornbury
Broken Tryst [illustrated poem] James Mew
An Epistle in the History of the Hapsburgs/by Lady Alicia Hay
Stern Necessity/by the author of "Poor Humanity," "No Church," "Mattie, a Stray," etc.

June 1870

Fenton's Quest/by the author of "Lady Audley's Secret," etc.
Waldeck's Last Draught [illustrated poem] Charles Cheltman
Miserable Dogs/by George Augustus Sala
'Neath the June Leaves [poem] Astley H. Baldwin
The Loves of Famous Men/by Percy Fitzgerald, M.A., author of "Bella Donna," "Diana Gay," etc.
A Month With the Militia. Sydney L. Blanchard
Captain's Norton's Diary/by Florence Marryat (Mrs. Ross Church), author of "Veronique," "Nelly Brooke," etc.
The Army and the War Office. G. Forbes Crawford
Up for the Seasons. T.H.S. Escott
A Dream of the Sea [illustrated poem] William Sawyer
Stern Necessity/by the author of "Poor Humanity," "No Church," "Mattie, a Stray," etc.

July 1870

Fenton's Quest/by the author of "Lady Audley's Secret," etc.
The Pickwick Papers
The Nameless Dead [illustrated poem] Tom Hood
Arab Hospitality. William Stigand
The Politic Wax-Chandler/a Legend of Mexico/by George Augustus Sala

Whitehall to Somerset House. Frederick T. Monro
The Haunted Baronet/by J.S. Le Fanu, author of "Uncle Silas," etc.
Limoncina [poem] Mortimer Collins
New York in 1870
Horace: ode XXVIII lib I. C.A. Ward
The Flight for Life [illustrated poem] William Sawyer
Bob Kennedy's Widow-Hunt/by T.H.S. Escott, author of "Bob Kennedy's Canvass," etc.
Under the German Ocean/by J.E. Taylor, author of "Norfolk Broads," etc.
Captain's Norton's Diary/by Florence Marryat (Mrs. Ross Church), author of "Veronique," "Nelly Brook," etc.

AUGUST 1870

Fenton's Quest/by the author of "Lady Audley's Secret," etc.
A Historical Mystery of the XVIII Century/by Lady Alicia Hay
To Julia Swinging [illustrated poem] Tom Hodd
The Portrait of Mr. Pickwick/by George Augustus Sala
Crown Lands
Horace Ode V. Lib.I. [poem] C.A. Ward
An Old Peninsular Man. Walter Thornbury
The Tête Noire Revisited [illustrated poem] T.H.S. Escott
Coleridge's Country. Mortimer Collins
Scientific Balooning
The Ghost at Laburnum Villa
The Loves of Famous Men/by Percy Fitzgerald, M.A., author of "Bella Donna," "Diana Gay," etc.
The Haunted Baronet/by J.S. Le Fanu, author of "Uncle Silas," etc.
The Knights Templars. Frederick Thomas Monro

SEPTEMBER 1870

Fenton's Quest/by the author of "Lady Audley's Secret," etc.
Thrones for Three [illustrated poem] William Sawyer
A Back Window in Africa/by George Augustus Sala
The Roman Girl of the Period. Mortimer Collins
The County Palatine. John E. Taylor
An excursion in Japan. C.F.F. Woods
On the Brink/A Story/by the author of "Lady Audley's Secret," etc.
No Sorcerer, Only a Sage. Francis Jacox
The Haunted Baronet/by J.S. Le Fanu, author of "Uncle Silas," etc.

Medieval Art of Travel. Walter Besant
Years Ago, or Yesterday? [poem] R.W. Braddeley

OCTOBER 1870

Fenton's Quest/by the author of "Lady Audley's Secret," etc.
War [illustrated poem] Minnie Von Bothmer
The Loves of Famous Men/by Percy Fitzgerald, M.A., author of "Bella Donna," "Diana Gay," etc.
Young Oxford in 1870
Praed's Country. Mortimer Collins
The Haunted Baronet by J.S. Le Fanu, author of "Uncle Silas," etc.
Awake and Thinking/A Retrospect. W.F. Peacock
The Sins of the Fathers/A Tale/by the author of "Lady Audley's Secret," etc.
On Young Ladies' Schools/by George Augustus Sala
The Requiem of the Fires [poem] W.S.

NOVEMBER 1870

Milly Darrell/A Story by the author of "Lady Audley's Secret," etc.
Carlo Ponti, the Music Seller of Habana/by George Augustus Sala
Hylas [illustrated poem] James Mew
Count Bismark at Home. M. Von B.
Sun Spots. James Carpenter, F.R.A.S.
The Last Night in Babylon/by George Augustus Sala
Fenton's Quest/by the author of "Lady Audley's Secret," etc.
A Morning Call on France. Robert C. Bacon
The Grub and the Butterflies [illustrated poem] T.H.S. Escott
The Haunted Baronet/by J.S. Le Fanu, author of "Uncle Silas" etc
Matches. J. Scoffern, M.B.
Matrimony Among the Bombshells. Archibald Forbes

DECEMBER 1870

Milly Darrell/by the author of "Lady Audley's Secret," etc.
Ships on the Sea [poem] T. Hood
Mrs. Harris. Mortimer Collins
The Rhine [illustrated poem] Minnie von Bothmer
On the Prowl. A London Adventure/by Goerge Augustus Sala
Monsiuer Anatole/by Godfrey Turner
A Lady's Pet by George Manville Fenn

Fenton's Quest/by the author of "Lady Audley's Secret," etc.
South-Africa in Diamonds. G.F. Harris
My Lady's Secret [poem] William Sawyer
A Court Scandal/by the author of "Strong Hands and Steadfast Hearts," etc.
Twenty-Four Hours of Peril in Rajpootana. S.J. Mackenna
The Loves of Famous Men/by Percy Fitzgerald, M.A., author of "Bella Donna," "Diana Gay"

JANUARY 1871

Milly Darrell/A Story by the author of "Lady Audley's Secret," etc.
The Hospital Mistletoe/by Joseph Hatton, author of "The Tallants of Barton," etc.
Cymon [illustrated poem]
A Carnival at King's Cross/by F.W. Robinson
A Christmas Peal/by Astley H. Baldwin
Condiments. John Scoffern, M.B.
The Haunted Rock/by Charles F.F. Woods
A Dinner With the "Jolly Old Boy." T.H.S. Escott
Dying by Poison/by George Manville Fenn
Year One of the Republic/[Forwarded per Balloon Post]/by F.M. Whitehurst/late Paris Correspondent for the "Daily Telegraph"]
A Song of a Song [poem] Blomfield Jackson
Fenton's Quest/by the author of "Lady Audley's Secret," etc.
Thoughts in War-Time [poem] Edmund Ollier

FEBRUARY 1871

The Lovels of Arden/by the author of "Lady Audley's Secret," etc.
Poetry and Prose [poem] E.
The Prussians in Paris/A Memory of What Was in 1815, and May Be in 1871/by George Augustus Sala
Imposts and Burdens
Landor's County
Candles. John Scoffern, M.B.
Honoria's Vengeance [poem] William Sawyer
All Round Saint Paul's/by Walter Thornbury, author of "Haunted London," "Old Stories Retold," etc.
What a Ghost-Story Did
Under the Plough. John E. Taylor
Fenton's Quest/by the author of "Lady Audley's Secret," etc.
Literary Bagmanship

March 1871

The Lovels of Arden/by the author of "Lady Audley's Secret," etc.
Forget-Me-Not [illustrated poem] James Mew
Bell's Life in Rome by George Augustus Sala
Chubb Jackson. Alan Strayler
Furs. Archibald Forbes
Brother at Arms [poem] L.M. Fellows
All Round Saint Paul's/by Walter Thornbury, author of "Haunted London," "Old Stories Retold," etc.
"Me and My Pal"/A Tale of the Cuban Rebellion/by Captain Bacon, R.W. Fusiliers
Paris Under the Armistice. F.M.W.
Fenton's Quest/by the author of "Lady Audley's Secret," etc.
Manners and Meals in Olden Times. W.W. Tulloch
Snowdrops [poem] Astley H. Baldwin

April 1871

The Lovels of Arden/by the author of "Lady Audley's Secret," etc.
Speranda [illustrated poem] James Mew
The Loves of Famous Men/by Percy Fitzgerald, M.A., author of "Bella Donna," "Diana Gay," etc.
An Artist's Model/by Astley H. Baldwin
The Lords of Lorn. Edmund S. Roscoe
The River [illustrated poem]
All Round Saint Paul's/by Walter Thornbury, author of "Haunted London," "Old Stories Retold," etc.
Fragments of an Old File/by Joseph Hatton, author of "The Tallants of Barton," etc.
The Special Correspondent/His Life and Crimes/by George Augustus Sala
My Treasures [poem] Edmund Courtenay
Fenton's Quest/by the author of "Lady Audley's Secret," etc.
The Triumph of Baby/An Amenity of War/by George Augustus Sala
The "Varsity Boat Race." F.R.

May 1871

The Lovels of Arden/by the author of "Lady Audley's Secret," etc.
A Minerological Adventure in Derbyshire. J. E. Taylor
For a Day and for Ever [illustrated poem] Alice Horton
Pictures

Our Efforts to See the Eclipse. James Carpenter, F.R.A.S.
Our Photographer
Hidden Treasure [illustrated poem] William Sawyer
The Power of the Keys/A Story of West 14th Street/by George Augustus Sala
The Second Siege of Paris. F.W. Whitehurst
Un Mariage de Convenience
All Round Saint Paul's/by Walter Thornbury, author of "Haunted London," "Old Stories Retold," etc.
At Chrigton Abbey/A Tale
Dining Alone. Francis Jacox
May [poem] James Mew

June 1871

The Lovels of Arden/by the author of "Lady Audley's Secret," etc.
A Heather Festival in England. E.C.W.
Summer Flowers [illustrated poem] T.H.S. Escott
Mrs. Mellor's Diamonds/by George Augustus Sala
The Season. John Harwood
Sorrows of an Eldest Son
The Legend of Rhosberry Topping (Yorkshire) [illustrated poem] S.K. Phillips
The Loves of Famous Men/by Percy Fitzgerald, M.A., author of "Bella Donna," "Diana Gay," etc.
All Round Saint Paul's/by Walter Thornbury, author of "Haunted London," "Old Stories Retold," etc.
Charlie Norman/by Edmund Courtenay
An Essay on Epigrams. Mortimer Collins
June [poem] James Mew

July 1871

The Lovels of Arden/by the author of "Lady Audley's Secret," etc.
Shot and Shell. G. Forbes Crawford
Ferenda [illustrated poem] James Mew
A Pilgrimage in Quest of Pocahontas/by George Augustus Sala
Restlessness. John Harwood
Lochinvar at Salt Lake/by Justin Mc Carthy, author of "My Enemy's Daughter," etc.
A Valley Memory [illustrated poem] William Sawyer
Hobbledehoys. Nicias Foxcar

Cowes and the Amateur Fleet. James Bontein
All Round Saint Paul's/by Walter Thornbury, author of "Haunted London," "Old Stories Retold," etc.
A Month on the Persian Gulf/by Viscount Pollington, M.A., F.R.S.G.
Charlie Norman/by Edmund Courtenay
Progress in Paris A.D. 1871/by Felix M. Whitehurst
Sic Transit Gloria Mundi [poem] Charles J. Dunphie

August 1871

The Lovels of Arden/by the author of "Lady Audley's Secret," etc.
Aesacus [illustrated poem]
Old Major Curtis. E.N. Lamont
Torpedoes
Johnson and Mrs. Piozzi/by Percy Fitzgerald, M.A.,/author of "Bella Donna," "Diana Gay," etc.
One Summer Month/by Mark Hardcastle, author of "The Arrandel Motto"
A Rondeau [poem] J.M.
Cricket at Lord's/The University and School Matches
Domina Fulvia and the Lion/A Story of the Days before Van Amberg/by George Augustus Sala
Then and Now [poem] Edmund Courtenay
In Great Waters
Recent Studies Amongst Ferns. M.G. Watkins, M.A.
Parsons and Doctors Wanted. Stephen J. Mac Kenna

September 1871

The Lovels of Arden/by the author of "Lady Audley's Secret," etc.
From Memory's Tablets [illustrated poem] Alice Horton
Maubeuil/A Mystery/by George Augustus Sala
The Irish Poplin Trade
German Baths and Play Houses/by Felix M. Whitehurst
Only a Dream [illustrated poem] William Sawyer
One Summer Month/by Mark Hardcastle, author of "the Arrandel Motto"
Aristology. Mortimer Collins
Summer Life in the States. John C. Hutcheson
An Utter Impossibility/by Florence Marryat (Mrs. Ross Church), author of "Nelly Brooke," etc.

Modern Field-Guns/Or "Krupp" *v.* the Royal Gun-Factories
Concerning the Centenary of Scott. T.H.S. Escott

October 1871

Three to One/Or Some Passages Out of the Life of Amicia Lady Sweetapple/by the author of "Annals of an Eventful Life"
The Athole Gathering. Edmund Courtenay
The Old Love and the New [illustrated poem] William Sawyer
Baudelaire. William Stigand
The Shadow and the Ring [poem] James Mew
From Russell-Square to Kensal Green/by George Augustus Sala
The Interior Economy of a Regiment. C.J. Stow
Recollections of a Fox-Hunter
The Lovels of Arden/by the author of "Lady Audley's Secret," etc.
The Dead Summer-Time [poem] T.H.S. Escott

November 1871

Three to One/Or Some Passages Out of the Life of Amicia Lady Sweetapple/by the author of "Annals of an Eventful Life"
Fair Helen of Troy/A Discourse on the Supremely Beautiful in Womankind/by George Augustus Sala
The Value of Fiction. Walter Besant
Death's Choice [illustrated poem]/by George Halse, author of "Sir Guy de Guy," etc.
Recollections of a Fox Hunter
Flowering Sunday/by the author of "Flemish Interiors," etc.
Siege Poetry. H.S. Fagan, M.A.
Sic Fugit [poem] Astley H. Baldwin
Dining With a Mandarin
The Red Snow [illustrated poem] William Sawyer
The Lovels of Arden/by the author of "Lady Audley's Secret," etc.
The Sundial's Philosophy [poem] Charles J. Dunphie

December 1871

Three to One/Or Some Passages Out of the Life of Amicia Lady Sweetapple/by the author of "Annals of an Eventful Life"
The Sporting Gun. Cadwallader Waddy
Beside the Brook [illustrated poem] William Sawyer
Winter Life in New York. John C. Hutcheson

The Fair One with the Velvet Mask/A Passage in the Life of Tintoretto Bounatesta, Portrait Painter/Related by George Augustus Sala
The Breaking of a Shell/by the author of "The Winning Hazard"
Romance and Reality [illustrated poem] T.H.S. Escott
Among the War-Canoes
Another Tale of Tub
Loves of Famous Men/by Percy Fitzgerald, M.A., author of "Bella Donna," "Diana Gay," etc.
The Lovels of Arden/by the author of "Lady Audley's Secret," etc.
The Story of an Actress
Seven Years [poem] C.E.M.

JANUARY 1872

The Haunted House in Westminster/by J.S. Le Fanu, author of "Uncle Silas," etc.
Cabmen. F.W. Robinson
Three to One/Or Some Passages Out of the Life of Amicia Lady Sweetapple/by the author of "Annals of an Eventful Life"
Santa Klaus [illustrated poem] Tom Hood
Concerning Christmas. Cadwallader Waddy
Not All Tinsel/by Marian Northcott
Miserable Christmases/by George Augustus Sala
New Year in Scotland. Edmund S. Roscoe
The Lovels of Arden/by the author of "Lady Audley's Secret," etc.

FEBRUARY 1872

To the Bitter End/by the author of "Lady Audley's Secret," etc.
Popular Religion in America. John Conney Hutcheson
At Sea [illustrated poem] Rea.
Imaginary London/A Delusive Directory/by George Augustus Sala
John Collins. Mortimer Collins
Three to One/Or Some Passages Out of the Life of Amicia Lady Sweetapple/by the author of "Annals of an Eventful Life"
Pike-Fishing in Norfolk/by J.E. Taylor F.G.S.
The Lovels of Arden/by the author of "Lady Audley's Secret," etc.
The Eve of Saint Valentine [poem] Tom Hood
De Crinibus. Cadwallader Waddy
"Till Death Do Us Part"/by C. Maurice Davies, M.A.
Oscula Dulcia [poem] Charles Dunphie, A.B.

March 1872

To the Bitter End/by the author of "Lady Audley's Secret," etc.
Imaginary London/A Delusive Directory/by George Augustus Sala
Some Curious Old Customs/by Astley H. Baldwin
Forgotten [illustrated poem] W.A. Law
How the "Gadfly" Failed/A Newspaper Episode. T.H.S. Escott
Three to One/Or Some Passages Out of the Life of Amicia Lady Sweetapple/by the author of "Annals of an Eventful Life"
Est Procul Hinc Tellus [poem] T.H.D.
The Hebe of Mine Inn [illustrated poem] William Sawyer
The American Press. John C. Hutcheson
My Grandfather's Ghost-Story
Enthusiasm *v.* Impediment
Theoria [poem] Edmund Courtenay

April 1872

To the Bitter End/by the author of "Lady Audley's Secret," etc.
Nature's Jewels [poem] Astley H. Baldwin
Imaginary London/A Delusive Directory/by George Augustus Sala
A Tedious Treat. Nicias Foxcar
The Night Voyage [illustrated poem]
April Fools. James Mew
Old Wine in New Bottles/by J.E. Taylor F.G.S.
The Easter Lifting [illustrated poem] William Sawyer
Alabama Gossip. John C. Hutcheson
April [poem] J.M.
How I Got Pepper/by Assistant Commissary General Mumps (H.P.)
Three to One/Or Some Passages Out of the Life of Amicia Lady Sweetapple/by the author of "Annals of an Eventful Life"

May 1872

To the Bitter End/by the author of "Lady Audley's Secret," etc.
Church Music
How I Came to Fail in Literature
Poor James Wymper/by Albany Fonblanque, author of "The Tangled Skein," etc.
Imaginary London/A Delusive Directory/by George Augustus Sala

Milk-and-Water-Coloured Elysium. Nicas Foxcar
May-Dew Morning [illustrated poem] William Sawyer
Breech-Loaders and Their Inventors. Cadwallader Waddy
Go-a-Head Girls/A Discoursice Chapter on Translatlantic Floriculture. John C. Hutcheson
Three to One/Or Some Passages Out of the Life of Amicia Lady Sweetapple/by the author of "Annals of an Eventful Life"
The Hawthorne-Tree [poem]

June 1872

To the Bitter End/by the author of "Lady Audley's Secret," etc.
At Dinner. John Harwood
A June Memory [illustrated poem] T.H.S. Escott
Imaginary London/A Delusive Directory/by George Augustus Sala
A Fijian Newspaper. T. F. O'Donnell
Love's Castaway [poem] James Mew
Transatlantic Sports and Sporting Matters. John C. Hutcheson
My First Duel
A Few Days' Fishing. Henry Lake
Three to One/Or Some Passages Out of the Life of Amicia Lady Sweetapple/by the author of "Annals of an Eventful Life"

July 1872

To the Bitter End/by the author of "Lady Audley's Secret," etc.
Young America. John C. Hutcheson
Concerning Sport. Cadwallader Waddy
At the Stile [illustrated poem] William Sawyer
A Story of Claimant. Edmund S. Roscoe
At the Islington Horse-Show
Vincit Qui Patitur [poem] Charles J. Dunphie
Colonel Benyon's Entanglement/by the author of "Lady Audley's Secret," etc.
The Great International Dry-Goods Store, South Kensington/by George Augustus Sala
Trawls and Trawlers. A.H. Baldwin
Three to One/Or Some Passages Out of the Life of Amicia Lady Sweetapple/by the author of "Annals of an Eventful Life"
The Old Room [poem]

August 1872

To the Bitter End/by the author of "Lady Audley's Secret," etc.
Betrayed [illustrated poem] William Sawyer
Imaginary London/A Delusive Directory/by George Augustus Sala
My Uncle in Manchester/by Frederick Talbot, author of "The Winning Hazard," etc.
New Comedy and Old. Percy Fitzgerald
A Pilgrimage to the Sanctuaries of St. Francis
Colonel Benyon's Entanglement/by the author of "Lady Audley's Secret," etc.
The Harvest Moon [poem] Astley H. Baldwin
American Yachts and Yachting. John C. Hutcheson
A Visit to Scott's Gun Manufactory. Cadwallader Waddy
Three to One/Or Some Passages Out of the Life of Amicia Lady Sweetapple/by the author of "Annals of an Eventful Life"
In Harvest [poem] Astley H. Baldwin

September 1872

To the Bitter End/by the author of "Lady Audley's Secret," etc.
Imaginary London/A Delusive Directory/by George Augustus Sala
Signs and Tokens. C.F.F. Woods
A Life's Love/by the Rev. M.G. Watkins, M.A., author of "An M.D.'s Tale," "A Romantic Incident," etc.
Turkey as a Field for Emigration/by Lewis Farley, author of "Modern Turkey," etc.
Doretta [illustrated poem] William Sawyer
A Visit to the Schultze Gunpowder Manufactory. Cadwalalder Waddy
American Novelists. Keningale Cook, B.A.
Michealmas [poem] Astley H. Baldwin
Three to One/Or Some Passages Out of the Life of Amicia Lady Sweetapple/by the author of "Annals of an Eventful Life"
Tom D'Urfey. Walter Besant, M.A.

October 1872

To the Bitter End/by the author of "Lady Audley's Secret," etc.
To-Morrow [illustrated poem] James Mew
Imaginary London/A Delusive Directory/by George Augustus Sala
In a Country House. Edmund Courtenay

Coursing. Sirius
American Novelists. Keningale Cook, B.A.
Jack Pugh's Legacy/A Tale/by Frederick Talbot, author of "The Winning Hazard"
The Light of the Earth. R.H. Patterson
A Life's Love/by the Rev. M.G. Watkins, M.A., author of "An M.D.'s Tale," "A Romantic Incident," etc.
Serious Oddities
No Cross No Crown [poem] Charles J. Junphie, A.B.

NOVEMBER 1872

Strangers and Pilgrims/by the author of "Lady Audley's Secret," etc.
In a Country House. Edmund Courtenay
Disturbed Slumbers [illustrated poem]
Homburg in November 1871. James Hutton
A Drop of Good Beer. Henry Lake
The Story of Claimant
American Novelists. Keningale Cook, B.A.
Snipe and Snipe-Shooting. Cadwallader Waddy
Jack Pugh's Legacy/A Tale/by Frederick Talbot, author of "The Winning Hazard"
A Rangoon Paper-Chase
Imaginary London/A Delusive Directory/by George Augustus Sala
To the Bitter End/by the author of "Lady Audley's Secret," etc.
De Profundis/Written in the Days of the Commune. James Mew

DECEMBER 1872

His Second Inheritance/by Frederick Talbot, author of "Lottie's Fortune," "The Winning Hazard," etc.
Watchman, What of the Night? [illustrated poem] Charles J. Dunphie
Imaginary London/A Delusive Directory/by George Augustus Sala
My First Love
Benefit of Clergy
The Opening Meet. Sirius
Miss O'Neil / A Souvenir. J.H. Stocqueler
A Presidential Election. John C. Hutcheson
Shops and Shopkeepers in Paris. M. Laing Meason
To the Bitter End/by the author of "Lady Audley's Secret," etc.

January 1873

Strangers and Pilgrims/by the author of "Lady Audley's Secret," etc.
The Servant's Hall/by the author of "Lord Lynn's wife," "Lady Flavia," etc.
Ave! Et Vale!/In Memoriam Amatae. Charles J. Dunphie, A.B.
The Clerk's Daughter/by A.G.P., author of "My First Love," etc.
Christmas in Russia. R.M. Hayley
The Land of Gold [illustrated poem] Edwin Coller
A Night in Ghost-Chamber/by Maurice Davies, M.A.
A Perilous Ride/by C. Soames
A Visitor at Sea/by Astley H. Baldwin
The Lord of Misrule. Cadwallader Waddy
Christmas roses [poem] Frederic Broughton
The Handsome Housekeeper/A Story About a Will/by George Augustus Sala

February 1873

Strangers and Pilgrims/by the author of "Lady Audley's Secret," etc.
Imaginary London/A Delusive Directory/by George Augustus Sala
At St. Valentine's Eve. C. Boyle
Experiences with Detectives/by M. Laing Meson
The Third Jester [poem] William Sawyer
The Forest Chase
Good Form. Albany De G. De Fonblanque
Cutting Off the Entail. M.P.
In a Country House Edmund Courtenay
Only a Curate/by R.W. Baddely, author of "The Village of the West," "The Poet Boakes," etc.
Music and Drawing-Room Instruments. Henry Lake

March 1873

Strangers and Pilgrims/by the author of "Lady Audley's Secret," etc.
Imaginary London/A Delusive Directory/by George Augustus Sala
The Irish Court. M.P.
Not For Love. [poem] Guy Roslyn
Bessie and I [illustrated poem] Edwin Coller

College Scouts/by One of Themselves
Wintering in Egypt/by J. Lewis Farley, author of "Modern Turkey," etc.
Lord Lytton. M.E. Braddon
Sacred Animals
A Maid Forlorn/by Frederick Talbot, author of "The Winning Hazard," etc.
Aunt Duck/A Story/by L.K. Knatchbull-Huyessen
The Philosophy of Grand Hotels/by George Augustus Sala
Boarding and Day Schools/by One of the Authors of "Scala Graeca." R.W.B.

APRIL 1873

Strangers and Pilgrims/by the author of "Lady Audley's Secret," etc.
Mademoiselle de Montpensier. C.D. Yonge
Spring in Syria/by J. Lewis Farley
The King's Bull/by Sir Henry Pottinger
The Metamorphoses of Worlds. J. Carpenter, F.R.A.S.
Non Sum Qualis Eram [illustrated poem] Charles J. Dunphie, A.B.
Imaginary London/A Delusive Directory/by George Augustus Sala
American Novelists. Keningdale Cook, B.A.
Sir Poisson d'Avril. [poem] Maurice Davies. M.A.
Wild Gardens. M.G. Watkins, M.A.
A Money-Lender's Love. K.K.K.
Charles Dickens's Nomenclature. W.F. Peacock

MAY 1873

Strangers and Pilgrims/by the author of "Lady Audley's Secret," etc.
Golden Hours [illustrated poem] William Sawyer
Imaginary London/A Delusive Directory/by George Augustus Sala
The Working of the Postal Telegraph. Andrew Steinmetz
Light Literature. Edmund Yates F.M.W.
Books and Rook-Shooting. Sirius
The Red Lancer/by Albany de Fonblanque, author of "Tangled Skein," etc.
The Shah at Home in 1716. Frederick Talbot
The Broken Heart [poem] Sydney Whiting
Kate's Engagement/by M. Cecil Hay, author of "Hidden Perils," etc.
Charles Dickens's Nomenclature. W.F. Peacock
The Poet. [poem] M.G. Watkins

June 1873

Strangers and Pilgrims/by the author of "Lady Audley's Secret," etc.
Imaginary London/A Delusive Directory/by George Augustus Sala
La Belle Sauvage [illustrated poem] James Mew
In a Country House. Edmund Courtenay
Solvitur Ambulando. J.N. Willan, M.A.
From Shoreditch to Shönbrunn. D. Connellan
State Tailoring. Sidney L. Blanchard
Mountain Memories [illustrated poem] H. Savile Clarke
The Supervisor's Story
Critics and Their Prey
Debt and Credit. John Harwood
The Dumberdene/by L.K. Knatchbull-Hugessen
German Requisitions
In Memoriam [poem] M.M.

July 1873

Village Tyrants/A Dramatic Story/by Joseph Hatton
Imaginary London/A Delusive Directory/by George Augustus Sala
On Some University Sponges. Compton Reade
Boarding Out/A Reminiscence of New York Every-Day Life. John C. Hutcheson
Swift as a Flash/by Mrs. C. Reade
Shakespeare's Toad
Only a Jew [illustrated poem]
An Irish Excursion. Henry Stuart Fagan
A Dream of a Dream [poem] Guy Roslyn
Flanders by the Sea. James Hutton
Strangers and Pilgrims/by the author of "Lady Audley's Secret," etc.

August 1873

Through Fire and Water/A Tale of City Life/by Frederick Talbot, author of "The Winning Hazard," "Jack Pugh's Legacy," etc.
Across the Channell. James Hutton
How and Where to Dine in Paris. M. Laing Meason
Village Tyrants/A Dramatic Story/by Joseph Hatton
Charles Phillips. Percy Boyd, M.A.
Marriage Morn [illustrated poem] Guy Roslyn

The Pig-Tax
Flat-Fish Trawling Off the Weight. John C. Hutcheson
Strangers and Pilgrims/by the author of "Lady Audley's Secret," etc.
A Tramp Through Dartmoor. M.G. Watkins, M.A.

September 1873

Through Fire and Water/A Tale of City Life/by Frederick Talbot, author of "The Winning Hazard," "Jack Pugh's Legacy," etc.
Dining Out and at Home
Little Coo-Coo/Or the Khitmutgar's Revenge. A.S.B. {discontinued}
One Year Ago [illustrated poem] William Sawyer
Poetry and Water/by George Augustus Sala
The Poacher's Story
Jersey. N.
Our George and the Sultan/by the Town-Clerk of Ludborough
A Glimpse at Gretna Green. M.G.W.
Strangers and Pilgrims/by the author of "Lady Audley's Secret," etc.
Wild Sport on Exmoor

October 1873

Through Fire and Water/A Tale of City Life/by Frederick Talbot, author of "The Winning Hazard," "Jack Pugh's Legacy," etc.
Robur/An Essay on the Agonies of Thirst/by George Augustus Sala
On the Rhine [illustrated poem] William Sawyer
The Life of the Earth
The Caves of Adelsberg
Club Land. W. Bayne Ranken
Her Master/by Mrs. C. Reade, author of "Swift as a Flash," etc.
Curiosities of Bees. M.G.W.
An Odd Fish. F.T.
Bopeep the Great/by George Augustus Sala
Strangers and Pilgrims/by the author of "Lady Audley's Secret," etc.
A Russian Alliance
Lost Hours [poem] S.K. Phillips

November 1873

Lost for Love/by the author of "Lady Audley's Secret," etc.
Forecast Shadow of Death. Nicias Foxcar
Chalked [poem] William Sawyer

At the Bar/A Story of Rapacious Creditor/by George Augustus Sala
Irish Crime. B.
Mrs. Maycock's Keys
The Ashantee Country
Her Master by Mrs. C. Reade, author of "Swift as a Flash," etc.
"Love-Philters." Henry Sneyd
Through Fire and Water/A Tale of City Life/by Frederick Talbot, author of "The Winning Hazard," "Jack Pugh's Legacy," etc.
Doing Business in Paris. M. Laing Meason

December 1873

Lost for Love/by the author of "Lady Audley's Secret," etc.
The Carlists Forty Years Ago. F.T. Monro
A Free Lunch. A. De Fonblanque
Sal Parker's Ghost [poem] Edwin Coller
That Poor Dear Captain Lambswool/A Tale of Martyrdom of Man/ by George Augustus Sala
The Two Inquests
How I Lost the County. Frederick Talbot
Mulligan's Poteen. Nugent Robinson
Grisleda/A Study at the Princess's Theatre/by George Augustus Sala
The Major's Luncheon/An Owner True Tale. T.

January 1874

Lost for Love/by the author of "Lady Audley's Secret," etc.
Folk-lore of Far-off Lands. H.S. Fagan, M.A.
Aunt Lora's Long Ago
Extremes. J.N. Willan, M.A.
A Revelation from the Sea. F.T.
The Notch in the Blade [illustrated poem] Albert King
The Great Cuban Difficulty/An Essay Ending in Smoke/by George Augustus Sala
Single Life
Righted at Last/by Mrs. Price, author of "The Clerk's Daughter," etc.
In Queer Company. Anthony Leigh
On Some Difficulties in Nomenclature. Walter Simms
The Two Inquests
New Year's Day in the Country. Sirius
Annabel Brown

FEBRUARY 1874

Lost for Love/by the author of "Lady Audley's Secret," etc.
How Mr. Penlake Exercised a Proctor. Compton Reade, M.A.
Observations on English Domestic Architecture. W.E. Timmins
At the Fifth Act [illustrated poem] Guy Roslyn
Why That Old Gentleman Paid/A Sequel to "At the Bar"/by George Augustus Sala
Suspiria. C. Soames
Through the Breakers/by Mary Cecil Hay, author of "Victor and Vanquished," "Hidden Perils," etc.
Love-Tokens/A Chapter of Instances. Francis Jacox, M.A.
Something Like a Twelfth Night Character. T.H.S. Escott, M.A.
Shakespeare's Games
Dead Sorrow's Kin/by Mrs. C. Reade, author of "Her Master," "Swift as a Flash," etc.
Woodcock Shooting. Sirius
Ye Explanation of True Chivalerie [poem]

MARCH 1874

Lost for Love/by the author of "Lady Audley's Secret," etc.
My Recollections of Fenton Grammar School
The Three Generations [poem] T.H.S. Escott
On Dinner "Sent Out" from the Pastrycook's/A Homily/by George Augustus Sala
Proverbs
Dead Sorrow's Kin/by Mrs. C. Reade, author of "Her Master," "Swift as a Flash," etc.
Rossall
The Russian Court in the XVI Century. James Hutton
Lord Lytton as a Fabulist
"Well Done!"/by Mary Cecil Hay, author of "Victor and Vanquished," "Hidden Perils," etc.

APRIL 1874

Lost for Love/by the author of "Lady Audley's Secret," etc.
Before the Ball [poem] H. Savile Clarke
James Gillray/Policomastrix/by George Augustus Sala
A Royal Salute. F.T.
On Some Recent Biographies. J. Francis Hitchman

Very Low People Indeed/by Marian Northcott, author of "Tim Twinkleton's Twins," etc.
Where Are the Snuffers? Frederick Talbot
Dead Sorrow's Kin/by Mrs. C. Reade, author of "Her Master," "Swift as a Flash," etc.
On the Moorland [poem] S.K. Phillips
Plump for Blinker/An Election Reminiscence. T.H.S. Escott
George Lovelace's Temptation
Negro Love Letters. P.F.
Philister Versus Snob/by Cousin Fritz
Sicut Sagitta Volat Irrevocabile Verbum [poem] Charles Dunphie

MAY 1874

Lost for Love/by the author of "Lady Audley's Secret," etc.
How I Went to Court/A Proud Confession/by George Augustus Sala
All Round the Fire. F.T.
Slain at Colchester/A Modernised Version of a "Streete Rime," A.D. 1666 [illustrated poem] Edwin Coller
Summer on the Bosphorus. J. Lewis Farley
Days That Are Gone [poem] Astley H. Baldwin
Dead Sorrow's Kin/by Mrs. C. Reade, author of "Her Master," "Swift as a Flash," etc.
A German "Zoo." Edwin Legge
The Perjured Tryst [illustrated poem] T.H.S. Escott
People Whom We Miss. Percy Boyd
Music at Home. Henry Lake
Willow-Pattern Papers. Charles Malcolm
Life and Death [poem] Ethel De Grenier De Fonblanque

JUNE 1874

Lost for Love/by the author of "Lady Audley's Secret," etc.
'Twas the Wind. Frederick Talbot
Echoes from the Royal Academy by a Listener. W.W. Fenn
Under the Umbrella. F.T.
A Waterloo Festival/by Countess M. Von Bothmer
The Lady of Black Friars [illustrated poem] Guy Roslyn
The Venus de' Medici's Marriage/A Story of a Connoisseur's Craze/ by George Augustus Sala

Dead Sorrow's Kin/by Mrs. C. Reade, author of "Her Master," "Swift as a Flash," etc.
Two Evenings by the Lake [illustrated poem] T.H.S. Escott
The True Story of the Sewing-Machine. H.T. Wood
That Eventful Night/by Frederick Talbot, author of "Jack Pugh's Legacy," etc.
Courtship. Sydney H. Blanchard
Mr. Swinburne's New Poem

JULY 1874

Lost for Love/by the author of "Lady Audley's Secret," etc.
A Worcester Factory. E.M. Reade
My Dream [poem] James Mew
Musical Dinners/by George Augustus Sala
A Wholesale Emporium. F.T.
Wedded in Death/A Tale of the Late American War/by James Alexander Maitland
Ireland for Tourists/A Reminiscence of a Recent Excursion/by the editor
The Streamlet [poem] C.A. Ward
Willow-pattern papers Char Les Mal Kum
The Comic Muse in Russia. Edward Legge
That Eventful Night/by Frederick Talbot, author of "Jack Pugh's Legacy," etc.
Money-Making at Monaco. P. Fendall
"Eton and Harrow" at Lord's. R. Russell

AUGUST 1874

Lost for Love/by the author of "Lady Audley's Secret," etc.
Idiomatic Iterations/Or the Humour of Corporal Nym. Francis Jacox
Up the River [illustrated poem] Courtenay Boyle
On Coming Down in a Parachute/A Peculiarly Personal Experience/by George Augustus Sala
Ireland for Tourists/A Reminiscence of a Recent Excursion/by the editor
Camping Out. Godfrey Y. Lagden
That Eventful Night/by Frederick Talbot, author of "Jack Pugh's Legacy," etc.
Christiania. Thomas Shairp

The Home of the Present Day. F.T.
A Woodland Study [poem] T.H.S. Escott
My First Client/A Reminiscence of the North-East Circuit/by Percy Boyd
Holiday Ports. Percy Fitzgerald

SEPTEMBER 1874

Lost for Love/by the author of "Lady Audley's Secret," etc.
Concerning Gilded Youth. T.H.S. Escott
The Hours of the Day. F.T.
Cap-a-Pie. Maurice Davies
What is to Be Done With St. Paul's?/A Little Essay on a Great Subject/by George Augustus Sala
Rosaline [poem] A.H. Baldwin
The Academical History of Mr Chicken. Compton Reade, M.A.
Rien Ne Va Plus/a Reminiscence of Baden-Baden. Charles Hervey
The Night After the Fair. F.T.
Vis Comica. Frank Penthorne
"Dolly"/A Story of the London "Sans-Souci." H.L. Williams
Something like a Séance/by C. Maurice Davies, P.D.
That Eventful Night/by Frederick Talbot, author of "Jack Pugh's Legacy," etc.
Short Essays and Stray Thoughts
Pulvis et Umbra Sumus [poem] Charles J. Dunphie

OCTOBER 1874

Lost for Love/by the author of "Lady Audley's Secret," etc.
Bernardin de St. Pierre. Walter Besant
Walls Have Eyes [poem] Maurice Davies
Underground London/A Plea for People Buried Alive/by George Augustus Sala
A Friend "Up Town." F.T.
Ward or Wife? A Romance
All About Teeth. H.L.
A Cruise With Kidd. T.
An Autumnal Sketch [poem] T.H.S. Escott
People Whom We Miss/by Percy Boyd
That Eventful Night/by Frederick Talbot, author of "Jack Pugh's Legacy," etc.
After Summer [poem] C.A. Ward

November 1874

Hostages to Fortune/by the author of "Lady Audley's secret," etc.
New Directions to servants/by George Augustus Sala
Trifles Light as Air
An Autumn Evening's Dream [illustrated poem] Edwin Collier
The St. Swithin's Junior Proctor/by Compton Reade, M.A.
"So Unladylike" A.E.T. Watson
The Modern Mæcenas. T.H.S. Escott
Employment Wanted
Ward or Wife?/A Romance
The Home of the Past. F. Talbot
"Ould Ireland"
Lost for Love/by the author of "Lady Audley's Secret," etc.

December 1874

Hostages to Fortune/by the author of "Lady Audley's secret," etc.
The Future of the Bodleian Library. Compton Reade, M.A.
After the Ball [poem] H. Savile Clarke
Mr. Irving in "Hamlet." Charles Lamb Kenney
A Real School of Cookery/With Some Account of the London Cookshop Company (Limited)/by George Augustus Sala
Concerning Club Servants. T.H.S. Escott
Theatrical Scenery and Effects. Henry B. Backer
A Study in Gray/by Mrs. Charles Reade, author of "Rose and Rue," etc.
School Inspectors/A Sketch/by One of Them
Drifting [poem] Alexander Lamont
The Bryansfort Spectre/Founded on a Family Legend
Victorien Sardou. H.L. Williams
Ward or Wife?/A Romance
People Whom We Miss

January 1875

Hostages to Fortune/by the author of "Lady Audley's secret," etc.
A Shunt. Compton Reade, M.A.
My Father's Will/by Francis Talbot, author of "Jack Pugh's Legacy," "Lottie's Fortune," etc.
The Nemesis of Pantomime/by George Augustus Sala
A New Sonneteer. James Young

The Mistletoe in America [poem] Henry Morford
A Study in Gray/by Mrs. Charles Reade, author of "Rose and Rue," etc.
Christmas in Norway
After Dark in Westminster Abbey. A. Marshall, M.A.
Dean Swift's Ghost. E. Owens Blackburne
New Year and Old [poem] T. Hood
An Arab's Revenge/A True Story/by Edward Henry Vizetelly
Sir Rupert. An Essex Legend. Edwin Coller
Ward or Wife?/A Romance

February 1875

Hostages to Fortune/by the author of "Lady Audley's secret," etc.
Cobbett's Comedy/A Hint to Theatrical Managers/by George Augustus Sala
Rare Specimens
Margery's Valentine. A Legend of Devonshire [poem] Edwin Coller
Notes From a German Band/by Mary Cecil Hay, author of "Old Myddelton's Money," etc.
"Bound West". John C. Hutcheson
Ballet and Ballet-Dancers. Dutton Cook
Love's Telegraphy [illustrated poem] H. Savile Clarke
A Model Epic
My Pictures [poem] S.K. Phillips
The Gates of Hougomomt
A Study in Gray/by Mrs. Charles Reade, author of "Rose and Rue," etc.
Remember Me/Suggested by Alfred de Musset [poem] Maurice Davies

March 1875

Hostages to Fortune/by the author of "Lady Audley's Secret," etc.
Oxford Raffles. Compton Reade, M.A.
The Trades and Crafts of Shakespeare. Frederick Talbot
Love's Appeal [illustrated poem] Maurice Davies
Sport and Adventure in Hudson's Bay Country
Within Sound of Bow Bells. Jennet Humphreys
Charles Kinsley. T.H.S. Escott
"When Sparrows Build"/A Tale/by Mrs A.S. Beattie
Morning [poem] Augustine Briggs, B.A.

The Postal Telegraph, the Press and Race Meetings
A Study in Gray/by Mrs. Charles Reade, author of "Rose and Rue," etc.
Cheating in Nor' Easter
Reiter-Lied/translated from Körner [poem]/by Colonel H.R, Gall

April 1875

Hostages to Fortune/by the author of "Lady Audley's Secret," etc.
The Confessions of an English Chloral-Eater. Gordon Stables, M.D., R.N.
Marriage à la Mode in the Land of Freedom/A Chapter Concerning Connubial Concordances. John C. Hutcheson
A Drama [illustrated poem] James Mew
Dr. Figaro's Establishment for Young Gentlemen/A Retrospect by George Augustus Sala
Mrs. Marmaduke Millwyn's Sign/A Story of Dublin Life/by Nugent Robinson
The Fair Critic/An Ex-Post-Facto [illustrated poem] Maurice Davies
Cocoa Plantation in the West Indies. M.R.S. Ross
Oxford Raffles. Compton Reade, M.A.
"The First Appearance." Dutton Cook
April in Auvergne. R.W. Baddeley, B.A.
Hugh Melton/A Story/by Katherine King, author of "Our Detachment," "The Queen of the Regiment," etc.

May 1875

Hostages to Fortune/by the author of "Lady Audley's Secret," etc.
Oxford Raffles. Compton Reade, M.A.
Second Class. Frederick Talbot
At Billiards [illustrated poem] H. Savile Clarke
Thespis and Themis. T.H.S. Escott
A Rose at the Window/by Uncle Toby
Ancient Monuments. C.R.
The Awakening of Spring [poem] M.G. Watkins, M.A.
The Family Ghost. F.T.
The Duenna Outwitted [illustrated poem] Maurice Davies
Brighton Reminiscences. J.H. Eyre
The Food of Great Men. W.G. Murray
Hugh Melton/A Story/by Katherine King, author of "Our Detachment," "The Queen of the Regiment," etc.

JUNE 1875

Hostages to Fortune/by the author of "Lady Audley's Secret," etc.
Fruit and Flowers [illustrated poem] Maurice Davies
Carriage People/An Outburst of Envy/by George Augustus Sala
The Alexandra Palace. J. Ewing Ritchie
Hysteria on Parnassus. T.H.S. Escott
A Father's Story/by Mary Cecil Hay, author of "Old Myddelton's Money," etc.
Oxford Raffles. Compton Reade, M.A.
A Parson on the Stage. C. Maurice Davies D.D.
The Collapse of Wallahism
Hugh Melton/A Story/by Katherine King, author of "Our Detachment," "The Queen of the Regiment," etc.
La Gloire de l'Église [poem] Henry Pottinger

JULY 1875

Hostages to Fortune/by the author of "Lady Audley's Secret," etc.
Art in the Universities. Compton Reade
"Tommy Atkins"/by the author of "Tom Bullkley of Lissington," etc.
Telling the Legend [illustrated poem] Mary Cecil Hay
Left Behind at Sigüenza/A Melancholy Instance of the Mutability of Fortune/by George Augustus Sala
Predatory Instincts
Sea-Bank Farm/by Henry Jackson, author of "Gilbert Rugge," "Argus Fairbairn," "Hearth Ghosts," etc.
Last Homes. Frederick Talbot
Our Croquet Campaign/by A. Lockhart
Flowers [poem] M.D.A.
Hugh Melton/A Story/by Katherine King, author of "Our Detachment," "The Queen of the Regiment," etc.
Bolingbloke Grinds/by Wat Bradwood, author of "O.V.H.," "Ensemble," etc.

AUGUST 1875

Hostages to Fortune/by the author of "Lady Audley's Secret," etc.
"The Pickets Are In" [poem] S.K. Phillips
A Text for Miss Thompson/Respectfully Suggested by George Augustus Sala

Rose and Aspen [illustrated poem] Compton Reade, M.A.
A Passage from the Life of Mr A. Plassington/edited by F. Frankfort Moore
From Paddington to the Land's End/by the editor
His Second Inheritance/by Frederick Talbot, author of "Lottie's Fortune," "The Winning Hazard," etc.
On the Art of Beginning Well. E.R.
Our Home Among the Vikings. U.B.K.
The Man of Speech. William O' Brien
A Bad Black Dog F.T.
Sea-Bank Farm/by Henry Jackson, author of "Gilbert Rugge," "Argus Fairbairn," "Hearth Ghosts," etc.
One Face in the Fire [poem] James Mew

SEPTEMBER 1875

Hostages to Fortune/by the author of "Lady Audley's Secret," etc.
A Night of Mystery
Belinda's Toilette [poem] T.H.S. Escott
Wills and Bequests/Not for the "Illustrated London News"/by George Augustus Sala
Shooting Stars [poem] Ethel Gray
A Passage from the Life of Mr. A. Plassington/edited by F. Frankfort Moore
A Model Maiden [illustrated poem]
North, with a Rod. Alfred Kinnear
Some Clerical Eccentrics. Maurice Davies, D.D.
A Birthday Treat. E.R.
Warriors in Town. T.H.S. Escott
Michalmas [poem] Astley H. Baldwin
His Second Inheritance/by Frederick Talbot, author of "Lottie's Fortune," "The Winning Hazard," etc.
Herring-Town. F.T.
Upon Sticks

OCTOBER 1875

Hostages to Fortune/by the author of "Lady Audley's Secret," etc.
The Ghost of Barbarossa/Lately Encountered on the Coast of Africa/ by George Augustus Sala
From Tent to Palace
Day-Dreams [illustrated poem] Julia Goddard

A Reminiscence of Zanzibar/by Gordon Stables, R.N.
Our Criminals
The Strange Story of the Duchess of Kingston
At the Stile/Form Lucy's Point of View [illustrated poem] Arthur Locker
In the New Forest. T.H.S. Escott
The Midland Railway and its Hotels. Henry Lake
Per Contra [poem] John C. Hutcheson
Relations of a Critic
How I Shot My First Snipe/A Legend Of the County Down/by Percy Boyd
Closing Days [poem] Astley H. Baldwin
His Second Inheritance/by Frederick Talbot, author of "Lottie's Fortune," "The Winning Hazard," etc.
The End of a Holiday [poem]

November 1875

Under Life's Key/by Mary Cecil Hay, author of "Old Myddelton's Money," "The Squire's Legacy," etc.
People Whom We Miss/by Percy Boyd
Lilies [illustrated poem] Mary Cecil Hay
English Journalism in 1832 and 1874. A Criticism and a Contrast. T.H.S. Escott
Mr. Skifter's Pilgrim's Progress. Compton Reade
Rubies and Red-Herrings. F.T.
Macbeth at the Lyceum Theatre
My Uncle. Edward Sala
The Dying Wrecker [illustrated poem] S.K. Phillips
Hostages to Fortune/by the author of "Lady Audley's Secret," etc.
Peeps at Domestic Life in India. W.A.C.
His Second Inheritance/by Frederick Talbot, author of "Lottie's Fortune," "The Winning Hazard," etc.

December 1875

Joshua Haggard's Daughter/by the author of "Lady Audley's Secret," etc.
A Mid-Summer Night/Or Two Starlight Vigils [illustrated poem] Iza Hardy
The Patent Woman/As Described in the Papers of the Late Mr. Prometheus C.C./by George Augustus Sala

London Amusements. A. Marshall, M.A.
Brighton Reminiscences. J.H. Eyre
Nunc Dimittis [poem] James Mew
Under Life's Key/by Mary Cecil Hay, author of "Old Myddelton's Money," "The Squire's Legacy"
Concerning Tusculums
His Second Inheritance/by Frederick Talbot, author of "Lottie's Fortune," "The Winning Hazard," etc.

January 1876

Joshua Haggard's Daughter/by the author of "Lady Audley's Secret," etc.
Not in the Programme/A Stroller's Story [illustrated poem] Edwin Coller
"The Rajah"
Thorleigh Moat/A Grandmother's Tale/by A.E. Barker
Tardy Locomotion
Die Nixe/A Legend of Baden [illustrated poem] Charles Hervey
How I Wrote a Novel/by Mary Cecil Hay/author of "Old Myddelton's Money," etc.
Chantry Manor-House/A Ghost Story/by Mrs Hartley, author of "Hilda and I," etc.
Charles Dickens on Bells. George Delamere Cowan
A Joint in the Harness/by Marian Northcott, author of "Tim Twinkleton's Twins," etc.
Waking Moments. T.W. Littleton Hay
J'Aime Les Militaires [illustrated poem] H. Savile Clarke
The Haunted Light-House by C.S. Cornfield
Buddha. Edward Marwick
A Drawing-Room Performance/by Beata Francis, author of "Fables and Fancies"

February 1876

Joshua Haggard's Daughter/by the author of "Lady Audley's Secret," etc.
The Art of Luxury. Horace St. John
The Theatre in Germany. Albert Stutzer
A Domestic Castle in the Air. Compton Reade
The First in After Dinner [illustrated poem] T.H.S. Escott
Monsieur de Talleyrand. William Stigand

Dum Vivimus Vivamus [poem] Charles J. Dunphie
Swells, Past and Present. C.S.
The Dwindling Length of Life's Summer Days/by the Rev. Francis Jacox, B.A., author of "Shakespeare Diversions"
The Spectre Ship. A Tale of the Polar Regions/by Percy St. John, author of "The Arctic Crusoe," etc.
Peeps at Domestic Life in India W.A. Capon
'Twixt Green and Red
How I Came to Be a Manager. Frederick Talbot
My Heart is Thine/A New Musical Valentine/written by the author of "Lady Audley's Secret"; the music composed by Miss Elizabeth Philp; published by E. Rimmel, Strand, London

Notes

Introduction

1. In the play *Her Naked Skin* (National Theatre of London, Olivier Theatre, summer 2008), which Rebecca Lenkiewicz dedicated to the public and private lives of some suffragettes, the word "sensational" appears again to refer to the activists: they are referred to as "sensational women" during an all-male conversation on the topic.
2. "On the Concept of History," in *Walter Benjamin. Selected Works.* Volume 4, pp. 394–395. While Benjamin's image of the "fleeting flashes" of history serves the purpose of undermining the implicit progress of historicism, I do not mean to use it to refer to an understanding of history as made of fragmented units left out by the historical process and scattered around randomly. I rather believe that each one of them may resemble more the "monad" to which Benjamin refers to elsewhere or become part of the "paradigm" of sensationalism.
3. See the works by Barbara Onslow, Solveig C. Robinson, Jennifer Phegley, and Deborah Wynne quoted in the bibliography.
4. See Laurel Brake, Aled Jones, and Lionel Madden in their introduction to *Investigating Victorian Journalism* and also the introduction to *The Victorian Serial* by Linda Hughes and Michael Lund. See also Virginia Berridge, "Content Analysis and Historical Research on Newspapers," in *The Press in English Society from the Seventeenth to the Nineteenth Centuries*, edited by Michael Harris and Alan Lee.
5. Deborah Wynne's *The Sensation Novel and the Victorian Family Magazine* takes several examples of sensation novels and traces their fortunes in the editorial life of the Victorian magazines they appeared in. Only one of the titles she analyzes is a novel by Mary Elizabeth Braddon, *Eleanor's Victory*, which Braddon published before she became the editor of *Belgravia*, a magazine that is not discussed at length in the book. Deborah Wynne's premise is that the family magazine provided a respectable forum for the publication of books often considered disreputable. While her reconstruction of how each editor dealt with the question of sensation novels offers an excellent insight into the workings of the literary industry, her scope at times privileges the extent to which each novel considered may have seemed to be palatable or not to an assumed middle-class readership,

disregarding the broader questions of cultural history I am interested in. I certainly agree with her call for an inclusion of other novels by Mary Elizabeth Braddon, besides *Lady Audley's Secret* and by Mrs. Henry Wood, besides *East Lynne*. On the widespread formula of sensation fiction see chapter two where I read this popular genre of industrial literature through the interchangeable presence of recurrent narrative functions. See also chapter four for the treatment of *Bound to John Company*, a novel set during the British war against France of the 1750s to obtain monopoly over the Indian market, and chapter five where I indicate the relation sensationalism had to pre-cinematic entertainment.

6. See his *Critique of Everyday Life—Foundations for a Sociology of the Everyday*.
7. See chapter five.
8. See chapter one.
9. For the industrial aspect of serial publications, see Bell Bill, "Fiction in the Marketplace: Towards a Study of the Victorian Serial," in *Serials and Their Readers 1620–1914*, edited by Robin Myers and Michael Harris.
10. *Charles Baudelaire. Un poète lyrique a l'apogée du capitalisme*, traduit de l'allemand et préfacé par J. Lacoste d'après l'édition originale étabilie par Rolf Tiedmann.
11. For an example of the popular literary genre of *flâneurie* in *Belgravia*, see G.A. Sala, "From Russel Square to Kensal-Green," in *Belgravia*'s October 1871 issue. While the author expressly wishes to leave behind the confines of the city, the presence of "posting-bills, placards, handbills, stencilled advertisements" pushes the boundaries of the city further out.
12. See chapter one.
13. Barbara Onslow in her article "Sensationalising Science: Braddon's Marketing of Science in *Belgravia*," pp. 109–122, rightly argues that sensation novels destabilized the "hegemonic domestic ideal of the feminine" (p. 161) and that the mix of genres, common to *Belgravia* and other magazines, anticipated practices later adopted by the popular press (p.164). I would like to reconsider her description of the tables of content of the July 1868 issue of *Belgravia* as a "wonderful, eclectic mix" (p. 165) by pointing out to the intertextual nature of the perusal of the magazine and to the hidden structures of meaning that appear in the seeming chaotic nature of the visual and intellectual stimuli contained in the magazine.
14. *Belgravia* had a layout that capitalized on its visual aspects connected to sensation fiction more than other periodicals, including Dickens'. The opening of each issue of *Belgravia* had an illustrated plate, like the earlier magazine *Once a Week* where Braddon published her novel *Eleanor's Victory* in 1863. The illustration helped anticipate a climactic moment in the narrative to follow. Braddon's editorship included

also poetic compositions, sometimes belonging to a thematic series, which were likewise illustrated. See chapter one.

15. See Gilbert Cross, *Next Week-East Lynne: Domestic Drama in Performance, 1820–1874,* as well as Loesberg Jonathan, "The Ideology of Narrative Form in Sensation Fiction," chapter five in Ann Cvetkovich's *Mixed Feelings* (1992), and Jennifer Carnell's biography of Mary Elizabeth Braddon, *The Literary Lives of Mary Elizabeth Braddon*, which explored her early years as a theater actress.
16. Benjamin uses this image while presenting his view on history and historiography subtracted from the "empty, homogenous time" of bourgeois historiography. The historical specificity of material history exemplified by advertisements suggests more the image of the monad, to which Benjamin resorts to in another passage, than that of fleeting flashes that may be unrelated or guided by chance, which is not the case here.
17. Martin Kayman in *From Bow Street to Baker Street* and Peter Knight in *The Cambridge Companion to Crime Fiction* similarly lament the simplistic narrative of literary histories that are detective fiction. Martin Kayman questions the narrow focus on canonical figures such as Conan Doyle at the expense of those who are unjustly referred to as his "imperfect predecessors" (p. 92, quoted by Maurzio Ascari in *A Counter-History of Crime Fiction,* p. 105). Peter Knight states that the history of the genre is a "multi layered history" (p. 7, quoted by Ascari, op. cit., 9).

1 THE CASE OF MARY ELIZABETH BRADDON'S *BELGRAVIA*

1. I also viewed the whole run of the magazine at the University of London Library and at the National Library of Scotland in Edinburgh. The volumes at the British Library, being assembled from libraries all over the British Empire, provide important evidence that allows to document the global distribution of the magazine.
2. I follow Laurel Brake's as well as Linda Hughes' and Michael Lund's view of the periodical as a macrotext mixing journalism and fiction, advertising and illustrations. In their introduction to *The Victorian Serial*, Linda Hughes and Michael Lund highlight the act of reading as an act of "linking together in their minds not just specific continuing stories but overlapping ongoing presentations tied together by editorial principles" (p. 9). I call this psychological process dialectical because the stimuli the reader was subject to in *Belgravia* were by no means homogenous and the trope of sensationalism, particularly in a monthly issue, can suggest, however paradoxically, a critique of the dominant values of the Victorian ruling class. I prefer elsewhere to use the word *montage* to describe this process in order to point to a prehistory of twentieth-century modernism, which has most notably

applied the notion of *montage* to several fields, from film to poetry and the figurative arts. As I shall indicate in chapter five, cinema studies have often overlooked the importance of print-culture in a history of the emergence of the technological and narrative innovations of the cinematograph.

3. See the history of the relationship between Charles Dickens and the contributors to his magazines traced by Deborah Wynne in *The Sensation Novel and the Victorian Family Magazine.*
4. Other popular authors turned editors, such as Thackeray who inaugurated his appointment at the *Cornhill Magazine* in 1860, did not "sign" their editorship in the front page by associating their name, or the titles of their novels, with the magazines they directed. The format of the *Cornhill Magazine*, like the *Fortnightly Review*, however, much resembled what later became Braddon's magazine in its graphic layout. Each contribution—journalistic or literary—opened the page and was not amassed in a confusing continuum like the layout of Dickens' magazines and *Once a Week* where Mary Elizabeth Braddon published her *Eleanor's Victory* in 1863. Both adopted a multicolumn partition of each page, reminiscent of the newspaper layout that gave equal relevance to articles and novelistic chapters.
5. The hybridity of the genre is a staple of periodical fiction in general, as I will further articulate in chapter six, and not solely of the sensation novel.
6. See Laurel Brake, *Subjugated Knowledges* for her view of the annual issue in book form having a higher cultural status. She also claims that the practice of bounding volumes removes the urgency of history originally associated with the periodical press, a claim that I want to implement by considering, as I do in this chapter on *Belgravia*, the similar move toward abstraction contained *in* the articles of the magazine and not only in the final product of the annual volume.
7. Laurel Brake in *Subjugated Knowledges* argues that the annual issue "purveyed the illusion of timelessness and immateriality; the appearance of bound volumes fostered their association with books and with the status of 'literature' and denied their journalistic origins" (p. 40).
8. Diana Cooper-Richet and Emily Borgeaud, *Galignani.*
9. "Familiar in their Mouths as Household Words"—Shakespeare/ HOUSEHOLD WORDS/A Weekly Journal/Conducted by/ Charles Dickens/Volume I/From March 30, 1850 to September 21, 1850/ Being from No. 1 to No. 26/London/Office, 16 Wellington Street North/ 1850.
10. One shilling was the cost of admission to Cremorne pleasure gardens (Linda Nead, *Victorian Babylon*, p. 109) and also the rate per diem of a private serving in India in 1863.
11. See the ledger books of Chatto and Windus in the archive of the publishing house. The Wesleyan Index estimates a circulation of eighteen

thousand copies, which is what Graham Law in *Serializing Fiction in the Victorian Press* confirms for 1868 only, the average of the first decade being fifteen thousand copies.

12. A summer holiday number existed, but its circulation did not surpass the average monthly issue, being actually of twelve thousand copies in July 1876.
13. See letter of March 10, [187]6, for having access to which I wish to thank Michael Bott, keeper of Archives and Manuscripts. The total cost of production of each issue was about 70 L; the sum was divided among the rubrics of copyright (10 L in May 1876, but 76 for the Annual), composition (17 in May, 15 for the Annual), illustrations (2,2 against the 19 of the Annual), printing (5 versus 15,14), small type (10,13 versus 3,4), working (23,17 versus 30,12), and advertising (1,14 versus 15,1 of the Annual that required an additional cost for corrections of 5,10). Even though the cost of the magazine was 1 shilling, like, for instance *Macmillan's Magazine* that kept the price same till the 1890s, the transaction was settled for an amount of 120 gs, as the letter of April 12, [187]6, states.
14. Collins' *The Lady and the Law* was paid L 2,000 in bimonthly installments of 333 L each.
15. A total of 12,000 copies was printed in May 1876, 10,000 in August of the same year, and 8,000 in the time span from June 1879 to July 1884, according to the numbers underwritten in the ledger book of the publishing house. The entry on November 1884 lists 4,250 copies; the total of issued numbers until the closing date of September 1889 was 3,000.
16. See Carnell Jennifer, *The Literary Lives of Mary Elizabeth Braddon*, Appendix. According to the author, Mary Elizabeth Braddon wrote part of it, then abandoned it when she suffered a nervous breakdown, mentioned also in Robert Lee Wolff's biography, and later resumed the novel to publish it in 1872 with Ward, Lock and Taylor. It is true that from its inception in November 1866 *Belgravia* had serialized up to three novels by Braddon and that was not the case after the fall of 1868 when her output had considerably diminished. The serial version, however, is interesting, whichever might have been the author, in light of the changes and revisions of the parlor (3 s. 6d) and cheap (2s. 2 or 6 if cloth gilt) editions of 1872. The edition "by the author of 'Lady Audley's Secret,'" in fact, removed the reference to John Company in the title by changing it to *Robert Ainsleigh*. In a de-historicizing mode, "the author of 'Lady Audley's Secret'" removed the most historical parts from the main text and completely changed the ending to fit a presumably more standardized narrative of eighteenth-century honor and aristocratic ethos. See chapter four in this volume.
17. See the February 1875 issue.
18. See, respectively, the April and October 1873 issues.

19. See the August 1867 issue on salamanders and gorillas.
20. In the February 1867 and February 1868 issues.
21. See the May 1869 issue.
22. In the December 1872 issue.
23. A few articles—and a poem—covered the Prussian Siege of Paris and the long period of unrest leading to the feared experiment of the commune. One of them, belonging to the journalistic genre of a war correspondent's reportage from the front, according to a successful formula of historical sensationalism that inspired also Professor Pepper's lecture-show at the Royal Polytechnic Institution on November 16, 1870: *On the War and Destructive Implements Used Thereat*. The lecture-show featured the trustworthy account of the French correspondent for *Le Gauloise* M. Paul de Katow who wrote the text accompanying the images. See Lester Smith, "Entertainment and Amusement, Education and Instruction. Lectures at the Royal Polytechnic Institution" in *Realms of Light*, p. 143.
24. See the June 1869 issue.
25. See the March 1873 issue.
26. See the April 1873 issue.
27. See the September 1870 issue.
28. See the May 1874 issue.
29. See the September 1872 issue.
30. See the April 1875 issue.
31. See the May 1875 issue.
32. See the November 1875 issue.
33. Ibid.
34. An anonymous article on fiction, published in the July issue of 1867, already makes that claim by defining and defending popular fiction both as "a picture of manners and customs" and for its delineation of "dramatic characters." The traditional opposition between the pictorial and the dramatic here does not stand. The pictorial element is in fact firmly anchored in perception and the dramatic in *Belgravia* is not stigmatized but acknowledged, studied, and even memorialized, as in the January 1867 article that chronicles the ephemeral art of mask-making for the Drury Lane Christmas pantomimes with a careful inventory of costs and fortunes of the enterprise. Theater is an important element in the magazine because it belongs to the aesthetics of sensation: the startling surprises that characterize dramatic composition do not seem different from the thrilling narratives of sensational fiction. By insisting on the dramatic and the sensational as starting point of a reading of reality and an inspiration for mimetic representation these articles introduce an often overlooked element of disruption to the idealized notions of artistic creation, and constitute a well-argued antithesis to the theories propounded by elitist criticism.

2 ABSTRACT ORDER AND FLEETING SENSATIONS

1. I follow Lauren Brake's as well as Linda Hughes and Michael Lund's view of the periodical as a macrotext mixing journalism and fiction, advertising and illustrations. See note 2 in chapter one.
2. Vladimir Propp, *Morphology of the Fairy Tale.*
3. On the tautological stress on the "excesses" of "sensation" fiction, see Sally Mitchell, *The Fallen Angel*, quoted in Jonathan Loesberg, "The Ideology of Narrative Form in Sensation Fiction." Both authors are indebted to the work of Peter Brooks, *The Melodramatic Imagination.* For a more extensive view of the melodramatic mode in nineteenth-century popular culture, see John Fell, *Film and the Narrative Tradition* (1974) and Ann Cvetkovich's *Mixed Feelings.* With my research I try to highlight an important example of the melodramatic mode in everyday practices such as pre-cinematic entertainment (see chapter five).
4. Richard Altick, *The English Common Reader.*
5. On the presence of manufactured objects in the sensational novel, I shall return in chapter four, where I discuss the system of signification of advertisement and its relevance in the periodical press.
6. See Henry James's reviews quoted in Robert Lee Wolff, *Sensational Victorian: The Life and Fiction of Mary Elizabeth Braddon* (1979), p. 153, and also in P.D. Edwards' introduction to the 1996 Oxford University Press edition of *Aurora Floyd.*
7. The sense of unity assumed in nineteenth-century fiction for Jonathan Loesberg in his article 'The Ideology of Narrative Form in Sensation Fiction' op. cit. goes as far as identifying in the narratives a structure of "inevitable," almost providential, "sequence" (p. 130). I propose instead to read the shocking revelations as narrative features that reverberate in the perusal of the whole magazine and suspend any judgment or explanation to the next month. The contradiction he sees between "narrative structure" and "thematic explanation" (p. 133), therefore, is not present in my approach, nor is the sense of "willed nonseriousness" (p. 133) that he sees as a consequence of it.
8. Chapter VI in Robert Lee Wolff, op. cit., pp. 188–221.
9. Alberto Gabriele, "Visions of the City of London: Mechanical Eye and Poetic Transcendence in Wordsworth's *Prelude*-book VII," in *The European Romantic Review.*
10. Jonathan Crary, *Techniques of the Observer*, and his further discussion in *Vision and Visuality*, the collection of lectures edited by Hal Foster. In chapter five I implement the model of the single observer by pointing to the social history of some of these forms of entertainment.

11. E.S. Dallas, *The Gay Science* (1866), p. 59. Walter Begehot in the *National Review* speaks of the casual character of modern literature in which "everything about it is temporary and fragmentary" [I, pp. 310–312; quoted in *Gender and the Victorian Periodical* (eds, Hilary Fraser, Stephanie Green, and Judith Johnston), p. 51].
12. Op. cit, p. 308. E.S. Dallas is not the only critic opposing the assumed corruption of an older and atemporal standard that nineteenth-century mass culture challenges. See also E. Pelletan in *La Nouvelle Babylone* (1863) that speaks of a "décadence de l'esprit francçaise" (the decadence of the French spirit) in relation to the overstimulation of the eye caused by modern literature (pp. 201–202).
13. E. Pelletan, *La Nouvelle Babylon*, for a similar recognition of the changes that the industrial production of books and magazines brought to the access to cultural artifacts: "Avant l'invasion de la gravure sur bois dans la librairie, la femme n'avait guère de bibliothèque [. . .]" ("before the invasion of the xilographic illustrations, women did not have much of a library," p. 200). See also Henry Brougham, *Addresses on Popular Literature*, for similar views of the transformations brought about by the industrial production of books.
14. Henry James, *The Art of Fiction* in *Selected Literary Criticism*.
15. Quoted from Wolff , *Sensational Victorian* (1979), pp. 152–154.
16. The quote is from Percy Lubbock, *The Craft of Fiction* (1929), p. 14.
17. Ibid., p. 3.
18. Ibid., p. 119.
19. The theater, not surprisingly, constitutes an interesting art form and a training ground or background for some of the contributors to *Belgravia*. George Augustus Sala and Edmund Yates, e.g., came from families of performers; Mary Elizabeth Braddon, too, as indicated by both Robert Lee Wolff's and Jennifer Carnell's biographies had started as an actress in the 1850s when pressed by the economic need to support her mother and sister. On the presence of the theater in the article published in *Belgravia*, see note 34 in chapter one.
20. *Belgravia. A London Magazine conducted by ME Braddon, author of "Lady Audley's Secret," "Aurora Floyd" etc. etc.* February 1868, p. 457.
21. Richard Altick, *Victorian Studies in Scarlet*, p. 79, quoted by Patrick Brantlinger in *The Reading Lesson*, p. 148. Dallas Liddle quotes both in "Anatomy of 'Nine Days' Wonder': Sensational Journalism in the Decade of the Sensation Novel," in *Victorian Crime, Madness and Sensation*, p. 89. In the monologue closing Balzac's *Le Colonel Chabert*, Derville, an attorney, states that the cases narrated by contemporary novelists as works of "invention" cannot compete with the reality of the true cases debated in court.
22. *Belgravia*, October 1868, p. 530.
23. "Sensationalising Science: Braddon's Marketing of Science in *Belgravia*," p. 161. Barbara Onslow rightly argues that sensation novels

destabilized the "hegemonic domestic ideal of the feminine" (p. 161) and that the mix of genres, common to *Belgravia* and other magazines, anticipated practices later adopted by the popular press (p. 164). I would like to take another perspective, however, on the seeming chaotic structure of the magazine by suggesting that an intertextual perusal of the whole magazine reveals hidden but nonetheless binding structures of meaning. Jennifer Phegley in *Educating the Proper Woman Reader* places *Belgravia* in the tradition of the "family literary magazine" and traces the discourses on women readers to argue that *Belgravia*, by presenting a positive view of female readers, allowed women to refine their taste and judge literary works by themselves. Braddon's magazine, she argues, "discouraged the blind acceptance of 'authorities,' whether they happened to be scientists or literary critics" (p. 150). The articles on sensationalism in science, e.g., would "convince them to think through the theories and reach their own conclusions about whether to place their faith in modern science to divert such catastrophic events or to dismiss the wild speculations on the grounds of faulty reasoning." In distinguishing domestic magazines aimed at consumers and the "family literary magazine" for which she imagines a public that would recognize the "proper woman as symbol of national health and vitality" (p. 16), she seems to overlook the commercial interests behind periodicals such as *Belgravia*. In insisting on the category of the "proper woman" the author reintroduces an essential notion of femininity associated to such a term that in my view was being questioned and reshaped by the culture of sensationalism.

24. See chapter three.

3 The Redefinition of the Public Sphere in the Nineteenth-Century Periodical Press

1. "Reform Bill of 1866: Gladstone's speech on the second reading (12 April)," in *English Historical Documents*, volume XII, p. 165.
2. Ibid., pp. 165–166.
3. See also Beetham Margaret, *A Magazine of Her Own?* Lovis James, quoted by Virginia Berridge in "Content Analysis and Historical Research on Periodicals," speaks of the periodical press as a "useful finger-print" of the "cultural outlook of an age" (p. 206).
4. For the industrial aspect of serial publications, see Bell Bill, "Fiction in the Marketplace: Towards a Study of the Victorian Serial," in *Serials and Their Readers 1620–1914* (1993).
5. See Jürgen Habermas, *The Structural Transformation of the Public Sphere* (1989) [1962].
6. The estimate from *The Waterloo Directory of English Newspapers and Periodicals. 1800–1900*, p. 438, is eighteen thousand. See the ledger

books of Chatto and Windus that record a circulation of about twelve thousand copies per issue the year when the magazine was bought, with the exception of the Christmas edition that reached thirty thousand. The Wesleyan Index estimates a circulation of eighteen thousand copies, which is what Graham Law in *Serializing Fiction in the Victorian Press* confirms for 1868 only, with fifteen thousand copies being the average of the first decade.

7. See Alan Lee, *The Origins of the Popular Press in England*. Alan Lee overlooks the relevance of the sensational genre in the shaping of a public of readers accustomed to strong, addictive impressions. Nineteenth-century sources on the history of journalism such as T.H. Escott, H.R. Fox Bourne, or James Grant avoid mentioning Braddon's and her husband Maxwell's enterprise altogether.
8. For the link between the professionalization of journalists and the growing importance of market economy in this cultural shift, see Liddle Dallas, "Salesmen, Sportsmen, Mentors: Anonymity and Mid-Victorian Theories of Journalism," pp. 31–68.
9. See the November 1, 1832, issue, pp. 385–389.
10. The January 1837 issue (pp. 100–136) contains the proceedings from the trial against "the Hon. George Charles Grantley Fitzhardinge Berkeley" and his brother Craven for their premeditated assault of James Fraser in his shop in Regent's street due to an unfavorable review of George Berkeley's novel published anonymously in the magazine.
11. See the Boston's *Writer. A Monthly Magazine to Interest and Help All Literary Workers* of February 1888 (pp. 21–24) and November 1888 (pp. 271–274).
12. This was written before and not in favor of the legislation that made ballot secret in 1872.
13. See Dallas' aforementioned article for *Blackwood Magazine*, p. 186, and also *The Nation* of August 8, 1867, p. 112, and *The Spectator* of September 30, 1893, p. 427: "Our people, it is true, are not so dominated by the desire for distinction as the French."
14. The letter is sine data, the date 1879 appears in the catalogue of the manuscript collection of the British Library in London that I thank for the permission to quote it.
15. This is reflected by the numerous articles on French fiction that appear in *Belgravia*. See "French Novels" by M. (July 1867), "Glimpses at Foreign Literature. George Sand" by M. (April 1868), "The Mountain of Michelet" (May 1868) or the poem "Remember Me/Suggested by Alfred de Musset" (February 1875).
16. See Robert Lee Wolf, *Sensational Victorian*, chapter 6.
17. Ibid.
18. This analysis implements the view expressed by Joanne Shattock in her entry for *Storia della Civilta' Letteraria Ingese*, vol. II, pp. 678–696, by showing how the discourse of anonymity was intertwined

with other social pressures. Referring to the signature debate, Joanne Shattock presents the argument in favor of anonymity according to which anonymity allowed for the circulation of controversial opinions. In some cases, however, anonymity did not grant a license to express controversial views. Authorship was a more nuanced category that changed considerably in relation to different audiences. The general public would perceive authorship differently from the specialized public of journalists, as the testimony of John Morley in the 1867 *Fortnightly Review* article quoted by Laurel Brake in *Subjugated Knowledges*, p. 22, attests. An anonymous article for the general public was not so for the contributors to the periodical. This different understanding of the more or less public stance of the author affected the tone of the article, according to Morley: the actual non-anonymous status that some contributors maintained in the eye of their peers who could easily identify them imposed a more "respectable" tone. Mary Elizabeth Braddon seemed to be clearly concerned more with her public persona than with the unpublished opinion of her peers.

4 The Cultural Trope of Sensationalism

1. See Wolff Robert Lee, *Sensational Victorian*, p. 229, and Carnell Jennifer, *The Literary Lives of Mary Elizabeth Braddon,* Appendix. According to Wolff, Mary Elizabeth Braddon wrote part of the novel, then abandoned it when she suffered a nervous breakdown in October 1868, and later resumed the novel to publish it in 1872 with Ward, Lock and Taylor. From its inception in November 1866 *Belgravia* had serialized up to three novels by Braddon, which was not the case after the fall of 1868 when the serialization of Braddon's works had diminished considerably. The serial version, however, is interesting, whoever might have been the author, in light of the changes and revisions of the parlor (which cost 3s. 6d) and cheap (2s. 2 or 6 if cloth gilt) editions of 1872 that Braddon published.
2. The brand name and logo of the East India Company have been in disuse since then. Only recently has Tim Warrillow of London obtained the property of the name for his business of selling "East India Company" tea and coffee. The modern product becomes, thus, a reminder of the colonial origin of the Western consumption of tea and coffee. The next launch, as I was told in an interview, will be a soft drink, the reissue of the formula sold in nineteenth-century India. The new product will circulate in the contemporary global market while suggesting the old territorial entity of the first transnational commercial empire of the East India Company.
3. The complete bound series of *The Idler* edited by J. Kerome, *The Dublin University Magazine* edited by S. Le Fanu, *Cornhill Magazine* edited by Thackeray, *Household Words* and *All the Year Round* edited

by Dickens, and the *Fortnightly Review* edited by G.H. Lewis do not include advertising sheets, and that is the case of the *Spectator* too. Only some volumes of the whole run of *Macmillan's Magazine* and *Victoria Magazine* preserved the advertising sheets. The presence of advertising sheets in the bound volumes of *Macmillan's Magazine* is not regular.

4. See R. Williams and T. Richards. For a full-page illustration advertising Cadburt's Cocoa, see the back of John Heywood's *Visitor's Illustrated Guide to the Ship Canal* (Manchester: Deansgate and Ridgefield, 1890). In other publications from the same decade the illustrations present a more detailed rendition of the uses of, for instance, Ilkley Invalid Chair (*Weddington's Guide to Movecombe and Lancaster*) or Portable Poultry Houses (TC Woodman, *The South Downs: A Literary Sketch*, 1894).
5. See the illustrations in Henry Sampson's *A History of Advertising from the Earliest Times*, specifically the one meant for the frontispiece with a rendition of "A Railway Station in 1874." The advertisements promote not only brand names such as Keatings Cough Lozanges or Dr. J Collis Brown's Chlorodyne, but common objects such as safes, diamonds and pearls, watches and clocks with the name and address of a dealer in London. In all these cases, no image is used in the advertisements, nor any elaborate picture drawn to associate the commodity with its use. See also the advertisements for Mrs. Skidder's remedy for cholera from *The Boston Daily Telegraph* of August 16› 1850, in which the name of the producer is hardly noticeable, prevailing as they do the bigger case letters of repeated words such as CORDIAL, CHOLERA, DIARRHOEA [*sic*]. An illustration of placards and sandwich boards dating back to 1834–40 and following the same mode of advertising appears in Asa Briggs, *A Social History of England*, p. 233.
6. *The Belgravia Annual*, 1872, cover, #1 verso.
7. See the *Belgravia Annual* 1872.
8. See the illustration "A Railway Station in 1874" from H. Sampson and also *Macmillan's Magazine* of November 1892.
9. See Henry Sampson, *A History of Advertising from the Earliest Times*, p. 110.
10. *Macmillan's Magazine*, November 1892.
11. *Colburn's United Service Magazine*, March 1890. While the originality of Dr. Browne's formula was defended in court as the ad specifies, referring to the *Times* of July 1864, a different sort of addictive consumption of chloroform in the form of hydrate of chloral was spreading. See Gordon Stables, "The Confessions of an English Chloral-Eater," in *Belgravia*, April 1875.
12. *Macmillan's Magazine*, November 1892.

13. *Macmillan's Magazine*, November 1892, but see also the advertisement for Gillingwater's Hair Dye in *Victoria Magazine* of August 1876 for an earlier example. M.me Valery's advertisement from *The English Woman's Journal* of August 1859 recommends, next to the picture of a woman's face both "Neolin Hair Wash," a hair dye, and Magnet Brushes to cure "Neuralgia, Nervous Head-ache [*sic*], Rheumatism and Stiff Joints."
14. *Macmillan's Magazine*, November 1867.
15. *Belgravia Annual*, 1872.
16. *Belgravia*, January 1871.
17. *Belgravia*, July 1869.
18. *Belgravia*, September 1872. See also his "Concerning Sport" from the July 1872 issue for his insistence that guns are a comparatively low priced commodity in the contemporary market. "The common cry, 'that prices *have* risen, *are* rising, and *ought* to be diminished,' with regard to useful articles, cannot be said to apply to guns" (p. 51).
19. M.R.S. Ross, "The True Story of the Sewing-Machine," June 1874.
20. "Breech-Loaders and Their Inventors," May 1872 issue, 336.
21. An advertisement from the August 1876 issue of the *Victoria Magazine*, edited by Emily Faithfull, launches OROIDE Gold jewelry, trumpeting it as a substitute for 18-Carat Gold, "one of the most *unique* discoveries of our age."
22. *Belgravia*, August 1868, p. 302. A reference to Egyptian hieroglyphs, which became a visual ancient precedent to the lure of contemporary commodities, is frequent. See also Pollington, "The Natural History of Bicycles" in the February 1870 issue.
23. "The Sporting Gun," December 1871, p. 163. A similarly chauvinistic interest in a comparative study of European guns manufacturers is behind the widely successful launch on November 16, 1870, of a new lecture-show at the Royal Polytechnic Institution by Professor Pepper called *On War and Destructive Implements Used Thereat*. The "war correspondent for the Polytechnic," M. Paul de Katow, who wrote for the French newspaper *Le Gaulois* while embedded with the French Army, validates the truthfulness of the images employed in the show. The photographic views were projected only after having been shown first to Queen Victoria and were later put on sale. See Lester Smith, "Entertainment and Amusement, Education and Instruction. Lectures at the Royal Polytechnic Institution," in *Realms of Light*, p. 143.
24. "The True Story of the Sewing Machine," June 1874.
25. "The Internal Economy of a Regiment," p. 469.
26. "Gold and Glitter," *Belgravia*, February 1870, p. 461.
27. See "Bracelets" from the July 1868 issue of *Belgravia*.
28. *Belgravia*, May 1868.

29. The advertisement for Gillingwater Hair Dye, appearing in *Victoria Magazine* of August 1876, testifies to the nonthreatening quality of the chemicals in it by quoting from the report of a Chemistry Professor, A.H. Church.
30. Horace St. John deconstructs this myth by remarking that in the colonies "money, like love, is easier to gain than to keep" in "The Art of Luxury," February 1876. See also the 1811 *Calcutta: A Poem* by an anonymous poet whose opening lines go: "Alas! The service is not what it was! How much degen'rate from those golden days, / When money steamed a thousand different ways, / When hands and pockets wisely understood/ No rule of guidance but their master's good."
31. John Harwood, "Debit and Credit," June 1873, p. 513.
32. "A Drop of Good Beer," November 1872, p. 70.
33. World's Classics edition, pp. 84, 230, 360, 33.
34. Katherine Montwieler in "Marketing Sensation" from the collection of essays *Beyond Sensation* sees Braddon's novel as a "subversive domestic manual" because of this association between commodities and the constructed nature of distinction (44). Lillian Nayder in "Rebellious Sepoys and Bigamous Wives" lists the many colonial commodities present in the plot (p. 37) that suggest in her view the recent events of the Sepoy rebellion.
35. Balzac often mentions contemporary manufacturers, like Herbaut the hat-maker, Leroy the dress-maker, for instance, in the 1830 novel *La Vendetta*. The manufacturers help define a credible realistic tone of the narrative; these commodities are not crucial to the development of the narrative.
36. Cf. *English Woman's Journal*, August 1859.
37. Cf. Oxford English Dictionary, Volume X, p. 988.
38. The military appears to be a recurrent concern in *Belgravia*, especially in the 1870s after the Parisian insurrection, at a time in which the government was also discussing a reform in the organization of the military. Many high-ranking officials, moreover, chose the Belgravia neighborhood as their place of residence. Among the articles dealing with the army, see C.J. Stone, "The Interior Economy of a Regiment" in the October 1871 issue of *Belgravia*, deploring the low pay of privates in the army and the "mechanization" of its structure in which soldiers were no longer romantic heroes but levers in a machine, and thus worthy, according to the author, of the same sympathy as "ragged street-boys, convicts, hospital matrons" that was so prominent in the public discourses. The poem "J'aime les militaries" by H. Savile Clarke was published in the January 1876 issue ("The joyous dance is ended/and lovely ladies stray/By cavaliers attended/ to where the fountains play [. . .]") and reports had appeared on the seasonal presence of the military in town, particularly in spring and autumn. See T.H.S. Escott's "Warriors in Town" in September 1875

issue. G. Forbes Crawford's "The Army and the War-Office," published in January 1870, after reviewing the disasters of the Crimean campaign, indicates the reason of its crisis in the lack of communication and of strong leadership in coordinating the many military departments.

39. *Charters/Granted to the/East-India/Company,/from 1601;/ also the/ Treaties and Grants,/Made with, or obtained from, the Princes and/ Powers in India.* The trading territory included Arabia, Persia, the Mogul's country, and other parts of India.
40. R.W. Frazer, *British India.*
41. Ibid.
42. In 1694, 744,000 pounds were asked to be added to the old stock by the new charter; see folio 72 of Royal Charters and Petitions.
43. Frazer, *British India*, p. 33. In 1656 Cromwell established a Joynt Stock Company, while Charles II confirmed the exclusive charter and the law permitting the export of bullion to the colonies. See *A True Relation of the Rise and Progress of the East-India Company* [s.d.]
44. The Consolidated Debt in 1777 amounted to 2,800,000 pounds, according to the report of the Committee of Secrecy established by the Parliament to inquire into the affairs of the Company. See *The Real Situation of the East India Company.* The report denounced that the transactions of the company were secret and that the details of the loans were "wrapped in *total darkness.*" "What must become of the authority of the company over their servants abroad under such a system? It cannot surely be expected that much obedience will be paid to the Directors, when it is known, that their powers are limited to the mere routine of office, and that all the most material dispatches are transmitted without their knowledge" (p. 32).
45. See folio 85, *An Extract of the Act of Raising Two Millions.*
46. S.d., folio 81.
47. See infra and extended quote in note 57.
48. The Nabob of Arcot, after having been vanquished by the British in 1761 and forced to repay the costs of war, was indebted to European creditors. The debts of the Carnatic region amounted to 45,32,500 Pagodas in 1781 at a time in which the area had greatly suffered from the war and the related depopulation that had reduced the revenues significantly. See the report of the Committee of Secrecy, Appendix 1 n. 1–5.
49. "The unaccountable war made with the Mogul was undertaken for private ends and purposes, giving out that the Co. should be enrich'd by taking many Millions from the Mogul and his Subjects, upon return of their Fleets from Mecha [sic] and other places, without ever so much as sending up the Mogul's court, with any Complaint or Demand of Justice, but falling upon and destroying those poor innocent Bainans and other Merchants that had but even then lent the

Co. at Suratt several Hundreds of thousand pounds, to load home their ships for England...robbing and spoiling all without the least notice or regard of their Innocency; so that for those wicked actions, with our burning, wasting and killing on Shoar in Bengale, we may justly fear God's Judgment will overtake us (without speedy satisfaction be rendered). Thus has the English Nation been made to stink in the nostrils of that People; when before, from the time we first set footing on that Golden Shoar we were the most beloved and esteemed of all Europeans." *An account of the East India Companies War with the Great Mogul*, folio 79.

50. *The Head of a Scheme whereby to Establish the Present East India Company*, folio 75.
51. Ibid. See also *Reasons Humbly Offered against the Establishment of the Present East India Co.* affirming that "All Subjects of England have an Equal Right to Trade," folio 75 verso.
52. This discontent resulted in the Charter Acts of 1813, 1833, and 1853 that challenged the monopoly of the Company by introducing the principles of free trade. See D.A. Washbrook, "India 1818–1860: The Two Faces of Colonialism," in the *Oxford History of the British Empire*, Volume III, pp. 395–421.
53. *Reasons Humbly Offered for the Passing of a Bill for the Hindering of the Home Consumption of East-India Silks, Bengals*, 1697 pp. 8–9.
54. Folio 81.
55. *A True Relation of the Rise and Progress of the East India Company*, folio 73. The British exploitation involved also placing high duties on the cultivation of land. In *The Most Deplorable Case of the Poor Distressed Planters in the Island of St. Hellen*, folio 87, one can read that the East India Company initially promised each family twenty acres and two cows free of duty. After 1683, when Sir Josia Child sent Robert Holden as deputy governor new tributes were required: 10s 6d for every black slave and 6d for every head in the family.
56. *The Advantages of the East-India Trade to England Considered* (London: J Roberts, 1720), p. 6.
57. *A Regulated Company more National than a Joint Stock in the East India Trade*, folio 71.
58. See P.J. Marshall, "The English in Asia to 1700," in *The Oxford History of the British Empire* Vol. I.
59. Robert Lee Wolff, *Sensational Victorian*, p. 229.
60. See ibid. and Jennifer Carnell, *The Literary Lives of Mary Elizabeth Braddon*, Appendix.
61. See Captain Holwell's harrowing tale, written in the form of a letter, dated February 28 from "on board of the Syren-Sloop" in *India Tracts* (1764). This might have been a source for Braddon's account, but identifying a source is not the purpose of my study. I find more remarkable, however, to point out that Holwell's account blames the cruelty of the Hindus, even though, upon realizing that some

prisoners had died in the night spent in the Black Hole, the Suba promptly releases all (p. 266). At the time of *Bound to John Company* the author identifies both the Hindus and the Muslim as the enemies. In one case, the author of *Bound to John Company* expressly identifies the evil of the latter and opposes it to the superior values of Christianity. See later in the chapter.

62. See "'The Fearful Name of the Black Hole': Fashioning an Imperial Myth" (*Writing India 1757–1990*, pp. 30–51).
63. See October 1868, p. 487 and 484.
64. See Wolff's definition of the sensational.
65. See P.J. Marshall, "The British in Asia: Trade to Domination, 1700–1765" for an outline of traditional historiography that depicted the British as peaceful traders until "Indian disorder and French aggression forced them into action" (p. 493). See also the lecture read in November 1923 and written by Douglas Dewar and Prof. H.L. Garrett: "[T]he Honourable East India Company was a body of merchants who wanted dividends and not glory nor even sovereignty. They had repeatedly shown displeasure at the way in which their servants had been compelled by force of circumstance to meddle in local politics, take part in the quarrels of others and even assume territorial sovereignty and the government of provinces" (p. 4). In this sense, the periodical edition of *Bound to John Company* can serve as "evidence" of a critique of colonialism in a sensational novel, and thus correct the claim by Kimberly Harrison and Richard Fantina in their introduction to the collection of essays *Victorian Sensations* (2006) (p. xxi) that there is no evidence of such a view.
66. Chapter XVIII, 94 (November 1868 issue).
67. October 1868, p. 491 There is therefore an acute understanding of the specific historical implications of the suffering caused by being deprived of one's will and freedom of action, as well as a critique of it, which may not fully dovetail with the notion of "masochistic fantasy" introduced by John Kuchik in *Imperial Masochism* (2007).
68. Ann Cvetkovich, *Mixed Feelings: Feminism, Mass Culture, and Victorian Sensationalism.*
69. Chapter XVIII (October 1868), p. 90.
70. Braddon dedicated her *Robert Ainsleigh* to Captain Willis who is referred to as her neighbor in Richmond. The bound edition of *Joshus Haggard's Daughter* (1876) was dedicated to Captain John Carnegie, "in acknowledgment of his kindly interest in the author's work and of his hearty cooperation in the opening scene." I cannot prove that Captain Willis or anyone else is the inspiration to her reworking, or that he is the anonymous author of the book published at the time of the author's nervous breakdown. The dedication to Captain Willis, which does not spell out his full name or any additional titles, could simply signify, besides the reference to a cherished

neighbor, a homage to the military that became the new ruler after the Indian Sepoy Mutiny war of 1857–58 and featured prominently in the post-1870 issues of the *Belgravia* magazine. On other occasions, however, Mary Elizaebth Braddon had changed controversial aspects of her novels when they displeased important readers such as Gladstone.

5 Sensationalism and the Early History of Film

1. Richard Crangle has made the point in several publications that the history of the magic lantern should not teleologically be absorbed into the linear history of the birth of the cinematograph. In many historical narratives the cinematograph has, in fact, been presented as the more "advanced" solution to earlier imperfect visual devices. He is right in charting the survival of the magic lantern image past the invention of cinema (one should think of the academic lecture-slide genre). It is clear, however—and it has been argued—that the elliptical narrative progress of the magic lantern show, particularly the photographic one of the second half of the nineteenth-century, has influenced early film narrative.
2. See Jonathan Crary's *Techniques of the Observer,* his further discussion in *Vision and Visuality*, the collection of lectures edited by Hal Foster, as well as some of the luminous fragments of Walter Benjamin's approach to the question of history. The paradigm shift Crary describes, i.e., a change from a cartesian model of vision centered on the subject placed inside a camera obscura to a nineteenth-century observer perceiving a spectacle independently of its existence is a compelling hypothesis. The reference to Descartes' use of the image of camera obscura of the mind, however, appears to be more a metaphor of metaphysical implications than a symbolic synthesis of the actual visual practices of a whole "classical" age. In other words, the insistence on the subject perceiving reality should be implemented by a more historical attention to the social history of these devices. Illustrations of scientific treatises can explain why the discourse of visuality insists on the presence of *a* subject of vision in the singular, and thus may offer a fitting image for a philosophical text. The actual practice of vision associated to the same camera obscura, however, reveals a social dimension to it that has not yet been investigated thoroughly. A historical study of the social history of the camera obscura enables a less monolithic approach; it would allow to speak of subject*s* of vision in the plural, at least in the early nineteenth century. See the *Life in London* sketches by Pierce Egan (London, 1821) where the spectacle of the camera obscura is presented as the result of multiple points of views of several spectators.

3. In *The London Illustrated News* illustrations stand out from the layout of the paper thus complicating a perusal of the newspaper that may be based on verbal signs only. Sensational illustrations offer to the eye of the reader an unmediated burst of traumatic communication. The use of sensational techniques to attract the attention of readers was common in nineteenth-century periodicals and newspaper, particularly in the mid-1860s even before the commercial priorities of the New Journalism of the 1880s. To make an example, I consulted the issues of the theatrical journal *The Play* in the 1860s. Its coverage of stage productions would make it the obvious site for a depiction of sensational scenes culled from popular plays. What emerges, however, is that up to the mid-1860s the editorial choices would assign a dominant place in the layout of the magazine to illustrations of historical dramas of little sensational resonance. The issues from the second half of the decade, by contrast, privilege sensational news, such as the frequent fires that destroyed theaters, and sensational plays inspired by authors associated to this genre. *East Lynne* opened at the New Surrey Theatre on February 22, 1866, *The Last Days of Pompeii* opened in 1872, and the Charles Reade's dramas *Workmen of Paris* and *Free Labour*, respectively, in 1864 and in 1869. All these plays opened the journal with an illustration depicting a climactic scene from the production. The popularity of sensation novels was also sanctioned by theatrical parodies, like the 1869 playbill of the *Theatre Truly Rural* at Cleaton indicates: the farce *The Secret! Or, the Devil in the House* followed each evening's performance of the "Romantic Drama" *The Jew's Daughter.*
4. Peter W. Sinnema's *Dynamics of the Pictured Page* focuses on the representation of the nation in the *London Illustrated News.*
5. See Laurent Mannoni, *The Great Art of Light and Shadow*, p. 34. Huygens, far from considering himself an inventor, in his own private writings refers to the magic lantern as "a bagatelle... already quite old." Cf. also *Light and Movement.*
6. See the inventions by Edweard Muybridge that can be seen at the museum of Kingston-upon-Thames. His research went both in the direction of improving the effects of a slide projection and of capturing movement through new versions of the classical vision of the magic lantern.
7. See David Robinson, "Henri Furniss-Lantern Showman," in *The New Magic Lantern Journal* 6 (1992). Furniss was a magic lantern showman and illustrator for several titles, including *The Illustrated London News* and *Punch*, which he joined, respectively, in 1876 and 1880.
8. See Richard Altick, *The Shows of London.*
9. See *The Lantern Image*, the whole run of the *New Magic Lantern Journal*, as well as the collection of prints in the Museo Nazionale del Cinema of Torino and in the Laura Minici Zotti collection.

10. See Dana Arnold, *Re-presenting the Metropolis.*
11. See also W.F. Ryan, "Limelight on Eastern Europe: the Great Dissolving Views of the Royal Polytechnic Institution," in *The Ten Year Book*, pp. 48–55.
12. The catalogue of the Magic Lantern Society, being mostly made of slides from the nineteenth century, is an important inventory of magic lantern iconography in the age of sensationalism, even though many slides are not dated and there are no matching records detailing how they were used in magic lantern lectures. There are many slides focusing on specific locations such as *The Alhambra*, *The Bay of Naples*, *City and Cathedral of Winchester*, *City of Florence.* Many, dating from the 1870s onwards, show an additional ethnographic interest toward the inhabitants of a specific place: *China and the Chinese* was produced in 1876, *Cuba and Cubans* in 1898. All the existing slides with an Indian topic date from a period after the Indian Sepoy rebellion and the consequent rule by the British: *India* (1875), *Literature on India* (1875), *Tale of the Great Mutiny.*
13. See Mannoni, *The Great Art of Light and Shadow*, for the history of enlightened performers such as the magician who performed in Paris under the pseudonym of Paul Philidor in Rue de Richelieu on December 23, 1792. His phantasmagoria had a satirical angle that named powerful politicians; according to the review that appeared in *La Feuille Villageoise*, his speech would dispel the supernatural aura of the phantasmagoria by revealing that the images were not ghosts but "images imagined to be ghosts in the dreams of the imagination or in the falsehoods of charlatans" (p. 144).
14. See *Vedute del "Mondo Nuovo"* and also Sergeant Bell's *Raree-Show* (1845).
15. I am thinking of Halloween celebrations in Europe and America when the dead are expected to return and receive gifts from the living to grant their protection based on the generosity of the living. Another example to keep in mind is the system of rituals honoring the christianized goddess of light, Saint Lucy, in Scandinavia and parts of Northern Italy around the same time of the year.
16. The Magic Lantern Society catalogue lists several slides—and a poem—dealing with the work of firemen.
17. A small crowd gathering around a pre-cinematic form of entertainment can also be seen in an early French film *Toto Exploite la Curiosité* (1909), in which Toto's kaleidoscope makes the happiness of a group of children he meets on the street, who are eager to take turns—at a charge—to see through the magical instrument. The film does depict a form of public, commercialized entertainment but it exemplifies the later, commercial turn that spectacles like the magic lantern took when they targeted specific niches in the market. Wordsworth's proto-cinematic depiction of the city of London in book 7 of *The Prelude*, on the other hand, is close to a very early

example of the genre "a film in the life of a big city" like Charles Urban's *Living London* (1908) whose fragmentary surviving copy (11' out of the original 40') makes the parallels between the two works even more striking.

18. Recent scholarship has taken a new look at the relation between music and literature in Victorian fiction. The collection of essays *The Idea of Music in Victorian Fiction*, edited by Sophie Fuller and Nicky Losseff (2004) investigates the metaphorical ramifications that the presence of music in novels may suggest. Phyllis Weliver's *The Musical Crowd in English Fiction, 1840–1910* (2006) reads music through the lens of cultural history, particularly by discussing the notion of the changing configuration of the public. She creates a historiographical narrative centered on the notion of public musical performance as a civic, albeit still "surveilled" experience and at times as a politically charged experience calling for political action. The genre of the novel does register a shift toward a more individualized and less communal notion of musical appreciation, which she places at the end of the century and at the beginning of the twentieth century. The examples she quotes of a communal experience of music as represented by fiction date back as far as mid-century, whereas I think they might be inscribed in a longer history of public spectacles, which are not necessarily musical, but nonetheless constantly redefined public participation.
19. see Frederik Soulié, *Oeuvres*: "Nous étions au mois de février 1822, j'abitais la province, et je passais la soirée avec mon père chez un négociant de notre petite ville, ancien lieutenant de hussards... C'était une soirée de carnaval, un cri se fait entendre dans la rue: nous nous apprêtions a voir monsieur le soleil et madame la lune... ("It was February 1822, I was spending the evening with my father at a merchant's home, a lieutenant who lived in our small town... It was Carnival, a cry was heard in the street: we got ready to see Mr. Sun and Lady Moon...").
20. See the Royal Polytechnic Institution's popular shows organized by Doctor Pepper referred to in chapter four.
21. See *The Lantern Image*. While eighteenth- and early-nineteenth-century prints still depict the savoyards with their lanterns on their back in several landscapes, rural and alpine, by the end of the century that figure disappears, to be preserved only as a linguistic relic in a series of "Proverbs and Images."
22. Cf. *Gamages Bargain Clearance* catalogue (London: 1913) or nineteenth-century publications targeting the market of young readers, like *The Boy's Journal* of 1860 offered instructions on how to make a magic lantern cheaply; cf. Mike Simkin, "The Magic Lantern and the Child" in *Realms of Light*, 25.
23. In the *Belgravia Annual*, however, Bentley novels are marketed to the general public without any indication of a gendered

audience: they are recommended for the "alleviation of hours of languor, anxiety, age, solitary celibacy, pain even and poverty."

24. There is no echo in *Belgravia* of the (indeed sensational) riots of Hyde Park of 1867 demanding the extension of voting rights. I am not aware that magic lantern producers were interested in telling this history, either, even though later the magic lantern was also used to promote an alternative to dominant political and economic practices. See Alan Burton on the cooperative movement in his "'To Gain the Whole World and Loose Our Souls': Visual Practices and the Politics of Working-Class Consumption Before 1914," in *Visual Delights.*
25. A large number of Griffith's early films are melodramas and scholars have insisted on the link between theatrical melodrama and film without giving adequate consideration to the lasting influence of the intense melodramatic emotions made popular by sensation novels or by print culture at large. See John Fell, *Film and the Narrative Tradition* (1974) and Tom Gunning, *D.W. Griffith and the Origin of American Narrative Film* (1991).
26. See Michael Lee Wolff's biography.
27. Is there a date, I wonder, that marks the end of the experimental and de-familiarizing language of Sterne, Fielding; a date past which the presence of dialects, common in the novels of Scott and Edgeworth, is increasingly reduced as the British novel progressively standardized its linguistic imitation of life?
28. This is reflected by the numerous articles on French fiction that appear in *Belgravia.* See "French Novels" by M. (July 1867), "Glimpses at Foreign Literature. George Sand" by M. (April 1868), "The Mountain of Michelet" (May 1868) or the poem "Remember Me/Suggested by Alfred de Musset" (February 1875).
29. Richard Nemesvari in his "'Judged by a Purely Literary Standard': Sensation Fiction, Horizons of Expectations, and the Generic Construction of Victorian Realism," in *Victorian Sensations* (2006) reconstructs the history of the early reception of the genre of sensation fiction to prove how a judgment of value cast sensation fiction as something "other" than traditional fiction. The "horizon of expectations" that may have defined contemporary critical reception of sensation fiction is what provided the narrow categories that critics used. I think that in dealing with popular fiction, especially periodical fiction, genre theory is not always helpful unless genre definitions be hyphenated to reflect the incorporations of many different narrative sources into the fabric of the novel. Criticism was in a sense twice removed from the multidirectional development of novelistic representation in popular novels. Publisher's catalogues and periodical fiction offer first-hand material that may better help to access the actual history of the novel.
30. See chapter six on sensational French novels from the 1860s to the 1880s.

31. Francis Lacassin, *Louis Feulliade*, p. 204.
32. At least in the narratological sense, Feuillade's film does seem to have, in my view, a consistency; its narrative structure, therefore, contradicts the claim made by Vicki Callahan in *Zones of Anxiety* that "the serial, with its repetitive structure, is a crucial factor in the mode of uncertainty" (p. 4). I prefer here to speak of demystification than of uncertainty as the recurrent mysteries in the episodes are resolved in ways that become increasingly predictable as the series continues.
33. Ibid., p. 206.
34. For the presence in popular French periodical fiction of secret criminal societies, see also the series centering on Rocambole by Ponson du Terrail, or *Les Habits Noirs* by Paul Féval. Secret societies were common in popular fiction throughout the nineteenth century, from societies of political rebels like the *carbonari*, often in hiding in Switzerland and France, to the secret plotting of the political élite behind the *coup d'etat* by the future Napoleon III or the Jesuits in Sue's *The Wandering Jew*. See Jean Tortel, "Le Roman Populaire," in *Entretiens sur la paralittérature*, pp. 53–75.

6 Mary Elizabeth Braddon in Paris

1. Stephen Knight in *Crime Fiction, 1800–2000* (2004) mentions the American edition of 1874, published in Boston by Estes and Lauriat. The French edition appears as n.d.
2. Roger Benniot in his *Émile Gaboriau* states that *L'Argent des Autres* "surclasse facilmet *L' argent* de Zola" (easily surpasses *Money* by Zola) (p. 291); Gaboriau's latest novels, published after 1870, are usually glissed over in histories of detective fiction. The investigations in *Other People's Money* do not allow the novel to be registered as "detective" novel, but rather as "roman de mœurs" or as a simple "feuilleton." Régis Messac, whose work *Le Detective Novel* (1929) offers an exhaustive and influential survey of the presence of mysteries and detection in literature since antiquity, calls Gaboriau's opus a "compromise" between the opposite aesthetic demands of the short-story à la Poe and the feuilleton novel. Only four works in his view qualify as good examples of a successful mixture of these two genres. The novels published after 1870 do not, as Messac believes that we find in them the feuilleton formula instead of "the strong hand" of Lecoq holding the narrative thread (p. 520). He does acknowledge that some characters conduct investigations, but, in his view, these quests are similar to the types we find in Rocambole's novels. He supports his claim with only one example out of the many that appear in many titles by Gaboriau: Madame Férailleure's investigation from *La Degringolade*. The terms he uses are too broad and not enough critical attention is given to the historical evolution of the narrative

codes of popular fiction in the second half of the nineteenth century, which will be my focus later in the chapter. Thierry Chevrier, in the *Dictionnaire du roman populaire francophone* (2007), reverses the terms of Messac's critique, which had become a common place of literary histories: he calls Gaboriau's later novels "romans d'enquête plus achevés... plus balzaciens et moins feuilletonesques" ("the detection novels are more accomplished, closer to the model of Balzac than to that of the feuilleton") (p. 182).

3. Bouvier, Grison, and Mary do not feature in the *Grand Dictionnaire Universel du XIX Siècle* while Féval, Ponson du Terrail, and Gaboriau do (the latter, like Busnach, only in the Supplement). Of Ponson du Terrail we read that "[his] literary works are far too many and not enough literary to sustain an analysis." The *Dictionnaire du roman populaire francophone* (2007) does not include an entry for either Bouvier or Grison. Bouvier appears in a list of authors of feuilletons whose reprints François Fosca, the author of *Histoire et technique du roman policier* (1937), still remembers seeing in Parisian second-hand book stores.
4. Yves Olivier-Martin in *Entretiens sur la paralittérature*, p. 184, reminds us that Paul Féval was threatened to be taken to court in 1856 for his novel *Madame Gil-Blas*, set at the time of the July monarchy.
5. Michel Lebrun in his article *Les Alchimistes du roman policier* (1974), after stigmatizing the unchecked narrative sprawl of Gaboriau's novels, quotes the words of Régis Messac, who, writing in 1929, said that "Gaboriau launched the detective novel without understanding it." Gaboriau does not appear in John Cawelti's *Adventure, Mystery and Romance* (1980) dedicated to formulaic writing in popular fiction, nor does he in Peter Thoms' *Detection and Its Design* (1998). Dennis Porter, on the other hand, while discussing Gaboriau's novels in his *The Pursuit of Crime* (1981), notes (p. 28) that Gaboriau's stories are not as "well-written" as Doyle's, being too close to the feuilleton formula, which is also what Boileau-Narcejac suggests in *Le Roman Policier* (1964). John Priestman in *Detective Fiction and Literature* (1990) rightly laments that the flaws associated with Gaboriau's novels presuppose a "pure" standard of crime novel that Poe, and later Doyle, would represent. John Priestman recognizes an innovator in Gaboriau, whose first success as a crime novelist dates back to the reissue in 1865 of his novel *L'Affaire Lerouge* (first published in 1863): according to John Priestman Gaboriau's tendency to employ multiple narrative voices would anticipate the style of Collins. Peter Knight in *The Cambridge Companion to Crime Fiction* similarly laments the simplistic narrative of literary histories focusing in detective fiction. Martin Kayman questions the narrow focus in canonical figures such as Conan Doyle at the expense of what are unjustly referred to as his 'imperfect predecessors' (p. 92, quoted by

Maurzio Ascari in *A Counter-history of Crime Fiction,* 105). Peter Knight states that the history of the genre is a 'multi layered history' (p. 7, quoted by Ascari, op. cit., 9).

6. In many literary histories Gaboriau features as the French author who had a pioneering role in France similar to the one Collins had in England. Régis Messac lists only Collins' *The Moonstone* in his *Le Roman policier* (1929). François Fosca in *Histoire et technique du roman policier* (1937) briefly discusses the British "sensation novel," but concludes that those works "do not merit the title of detective novel" (p. 82). Robet Deleuse dedicates an entry to Collins, but not to Braddon, in his chronological encyclopedia *Les Maîtres du roman policier* (1991), where, among the precursors of the genre, he quotes also Charles Barbara. Jean Bourdier in *Histoire du roman policier* (1996), after remembering the friendship of Charles Dickens with Robert Walker and remarking that the unfinished *Edwin Drood* had a "caractère policier" ("seemed more like a detective novel") (p. 40), mentions Wilkie Collins's *The Woman in White* and *The Moonstone*, the latter "plus nettement policier encore" ("even more so") (p. 41). Yves Reuter after defining a genre only in conjunction with the intertextual presence of a perceived category of such type of fiction in a given culture, notes that the press did recognize in *The Woman in White* a new genre (the word sensational is not used), thus complying with his definition of a genre. See *Le Roman Policier* (1997), p. 10.
7. See D.A. Miller, *The Novel and the Police* and Ann Cvetkovich's *Mixed Feelings.* A Braddon entry appears in Jean Tulard's *Dictionnaire du roman policier.* In *Le Roman Criminel* by S. Benvenuti, G. Rizzoni, and M. Lebrun, Mary Elizabeth Braddon features in the paragraph on Wilkie Collins as an imitator (p. 26) but not in the "Who's Who of Crime Fiction" in the appendix. Maurizio Ascari's *A Counter-history of Crime Fiction* builds on the broader understanding of the genre that Martin Kayman, Martin Priestman, and others have in recent times offered.
8. Kimberly Harrison and Richard Fantina, *Victorian Sensations*, p. xxii.
9. Maurizio Ascari in his *A Counter-History of Crime Fiction* does discuss the wide popularity of the pirated, abridged American versions of the novels of Gaboriau, pointing to a common destiny that many European popular authors had experienced across the ocean. He also mentions in passing the series of Gaboriau's novels that Vizetelly launched as "sensational" (p. 107), a marketing strategy that applied also to other authors in the publisher's catalogue of books in print.
10. *Sensational Victorian*, appendix, 492. No mention is made of the other feuilleton *La Chanteuse de Rue.*
11. "Rhétorique et idéologie dans *Les Mystères de Paris' Revue Internationale des Sciences Sociales,*" quoted by Ann-Marie Thiesse in "Écrivain/Public(s): Les mystères de la communication littéraire," *Europe. Revue Litteraire Mensuelle*, 46.

12. Anne-Marie Thiesse calls Raymond an "upper-class guide into the universe of depravation," op. cit.
13. A foreigner named lady Brandon appears also in Balzac's *Comedie Humaine*, in *Memoires de deux jeunes mariées*, which was published in feuilleton edition in *La Presse* in 1841. She is only mentioned as the mother of the poet whom Louise marries, and had the baby from a relationship she had outside of her marriage.
14. Part of the "foreignness" associated with the evil schemers at the time of the rise to power of Napoleon III may be due to the fact that he himself had lived abroad in exile, surrounded by his cohorts. The touch of xenophobia may also relate to the long period of paranoia regarding the supposedly foreign—particularly British—support to the opponents of the French Revolution of 1789. Exile was both a forced destination for many in order to save their lives and a place from where a reentry, which may have meant resorting to a military or terroristic action of some sort, could be organized more strategically. See the survival of these narratives drawn from the French historical memory in Balzac's *Une Ténébreuse Affaire* (1841).
15. In this sense, Eco's observation that the novels have "no critical angle" might be reexamined.
16. Another example of a noble banker, already perceived through the cynicism of one of his employees, is the Alsatian D'Aldrigger in *La Maison Nucingen* (1837), about whom Nucingen remarks: "Honest man but dumb!"
17. See the description of him made by M.L. Chabot in *Rocambole*, pp. 22–23.
18. *Histoire Littéraire de la France.* Eds, Pierre Abraham and Roland Desné, 1848–1873.
19. Roger Bellet, *Presse et Journalisme sous le Second Empire*, p. 183. The satirical journal *Charivari* would lampoon such an enterprise: "Ce journal paraître à chaque incarcération de journaliste, c'est-à-dire tous les jours ou à peu près" ("the journal is issued whenever a journalist is incarcerated, which is practically everyday").
20. See chapter one.
21. Roger Bellet, *Presse et Journalisme sous le Second Empire*, op. cit.
22. "le roman-feuilleton sera surtout populaire par sa médiocricrité" ("the feuilleton novel became popular particularly due to its mediocrity"), *Histoire Littéraire de la France*, op. cit., p. 289. François Fosca in *Histoire et technique du roman policier*, p. 76, singles out Gaboriau for the mediocrity of his literary style. He does acknowledge that Lecoq is a more vivid and real character than Poe's Dupin, but Fosca does not seem to recognize the same realist inspiration in Gaboriau's depiction of the city of Paris and of its recent history, as he willingly omits the novels that "have nothing to do with the detective novel."

Bibliography

Adorno, Theodor W. *The Culture Industry: Selected Essays on Mass Culture.* London: Routledge, 1991.

———. *Aesthetic Theory.* Minneapolis: University of Minnesota Press, 1997 [1970].

Adorno, Theodore and Max Horkheimer. *Dialectic of Enlightment.* New York: A Continuum Book, The Seabury Press, 1982.

Advantages of the East India Trade. London: J. Roberts, 1720.

Agamben, Giorgio. *Infanzia e Storia. Distruzione dell'Esperienza e Origine della Storia.* Torino: Einaudi, 1978.

———. *Signatura Rerum. Sul Metodo.* Torino: Bollati Boringhieri, 2008.

Allen, Robert. *Vaudeville and Film 1895–1915: A Study in Media Interaction.* New York: Arno Press, 1980.

Altick, Richard D. *The English Common Reader.* Chicago: Chicago University Press, 1957.

———. *Victorian Studies in Scarlet.* New York: W.W. Norton, 1970.

———. *The Shows of London.* Cambridge: Belknap Press, 1978.

———. *The Presence of the Presence. Topics of the Day in the Victorian Novel.* Columbus: Ohio State, 1991.

Anderson, Benedict. *Imagined Communities.* London and New York: Verso, second edition, 1991.

Andrews, Alexander. *The History of British Journalism.* London: Bentley, 1859.

Anonymous. *India in 1883.* Calcutta: Thacker, Spink and Co, 1888.

Armstrong, Nancy. *Desire and Domestic Fiction: A Political History of the Novel.* New York: Oxford University Press, 1987.

Arnheim, Rudolph. *Art and Visual Perception: A Psychology of the Creative Eye.* Berkeley: California University Press, 1974.

Arnold, Dana. *Re-presenting the Metropolis. Architecture, Urban Experience and Social Life in London, 1800–1840.* Aldershot and Burlington: Ashgate, 2000.

Ascari, Maurizio. *A Counter-History of Crime Fiction. Supernatural, Gothic, Sensational.* Houndsmill, Hampshire and New York: Palgrave Macmillan, 2007.

Augustus, Frederick. *The Emperor Akbar: A Contribution Towards a History of India in the Sixteenth Century.* Calcutta: Thacker, Spink and Co.; London: Trubner and Co., 1890.

Balzac, Honoré de. *Le Colonel Chabert*. Paris: Éditions Gallimard, 1976.

———. *Memoires de deux jeunes mariées*. Paris: Éditions Gallimard, 1976.

———. *Modeste Mignon*. Paris: Éditions Gallimard, 1976.

———. *Ursule Mirouët*. Paris: Éditions Gallimard, 1976.

———. *La Vendetta*. Paris: Éditions Gallimard, 1976.

———. *Les Chouans*. Paris: Éditions Gallimard, 1977.

———. *Histoire de la Grandeur et de la Décadence de César Birotteau*. Paris: Éditions Gallimard, 1977.

———. *La Maison Nucingen*. Paris: Éditions Gallimard, 1977.

———. *Une Ténébreuse Affaire*. Paris: Éditions Gallimard, 1977.

Bandish, Cynthia Louise. "Mary Elizabeth Braddon and the Bohemian Circle of *Belgravia*." *Dissertation Abstracts International* Section A (59:9) March 1999: 3463.

Barthes, Roland. *Image, Music, Text*. New York: Hill and Wang, 1977.

Baudrillard, Jean *Le Système des Objects*. Paris: Gallimard, 1968.

———. *The Consumer Society. Myths and Structures*. London: SAGE Publications; New Delhi: Thousand Oaks, 1998 [1970].

Bayly, C.A., ed. *The Raj. India and the British. 1600–1947*. London: National Gallery Publications, 1990.

Beetham, Margaret. *A Magazine of Her Own? Domesticity and Desire in the Woman's Magazine 1800–1914*. London and New York: Routledge, 1996.

Bell, Bill. "Fiction in the Marketplace: Towards a Study of the Victorian Serial," in *Serials and Their Readers 1620–1914*.

Bell, Sergeant. *Raree Show*. Philadelphia: Crissy, 1845.

Bellet, Roger. *Presse et Journalisme sous le Second Empire*. Paris: Librairie Armand Colin, 1967.

Benjamin, Walter. *Charles Baudelaire. Un poète lyrique a l'apogée du capitalisme*, traduit de l'allemand et préfacé par J. Lacoste d'après l'édition originale étabilie par Rolf Tiedmann. Paris: Editions Payot, 1979.

———. *The Arcade Project*. Cambridge and London: Harvard University Press, 1999.

———. *Selected Writings*. Volume 2, 1927–1934. Trans. Rodney Livingstone and others. Eds. Michael W. Jennings, Howard Eiland, and Gary Smith. London, England, and Cambridge, Mass.: Belknap Press of Harvard University Press, 1999.

———. *Selected Writings*. Volume 3, 1935–1938. Trans. Elmund Jephcott Howard Eiland and Others. Eds. Howard Eiland and Michael WJennings. London, England, and Cambridge, Mass.: Belknap Press of Harvard University Press, 2002.

———. *Selected Writings*. Volume 4, 1938–1940. Trans. Elmund Jephcott and others. Eds. Howard Eiland and Michael W. Jennings. London, England, and Cambridge, Mass.: Belknap Press of Harvard University Press, 2003.

Bergson, Henry. *Matter and Memory*. London: G. Allen & Co., 1929.

Berridge, Virginia. "Content Analysis and Historical Research on Newspapers," in *The Press in English Society*, 201–218.

Bessy, Maurice. *Le Mystère de la Chambre Noire. Histoire de la Projection Animée.* Paris: Pygmalion Gerard Watelet, 1990.

Biles, Susan Rebecca. "Can the Sensational Be Elevated by Art? The Fiction of Mary Elizabeth Braddon, 1863–1865." *Dissertation Abstract International* Section A (958:3) September 1997: 881.

Boileau-Narcejac, *Le Roman Policier. Paris: Payot, 1964.*

Bottomore, Stephen. *I Want to See This Annie Mattygraph: A Cartoon History of the Coming of the Movies.* Gemona: Le Giornate del Cinema Muto, 1995.

Bourdier, John. *Histoire du Roman Policier.* Paris: Fallois, 1996.

"Bound to John Company, or, the Adventures and Misadventures of Robert Ainsleigh," *Belgravia. A London Magazine*, July 1868–May 1869.

Bouvier, Aléxis. *Bewitching Iza.* London: Vizetelly, 1888.

———. *A Convict's Marriage.* London: Vizetelly & Co, 1888.

———. *The Wily Widow.* London: Vizetelly, 1888.

Bowbly, Rachel. *Just Looking: Consumer Culture in Dreiser, Gissing and Zola.* New York and London: Metheum, 1985.

Braddon, Mary Elizabeth. *Aurora Floyd.* Edited with an introduction by P.D. Edwards. Oxford and New York: Oxford University Press, 1996.

———. *Lady Audley's Secret.* Edited with notes by Jenny Bourne Taylor, and with an introduction by Jenny Bourne Taylor with Russell Crofts. London: Penguin Group, 1998.

Braddon, Mary Elizabeth, ed. *Belgravia. A London Magazine.* London: Warwick House, 1867–1876.

Brake, Laurel. *Subjugated Knowledges: Journalism, Gender and Literature in the Nineteenth-Century.* New York: New York University Press, 1994.

———. *Print in Transition, 1859–1910. Studies in Media and Book History.* Houndmills and New York: Palgrave, 2001.

Brake, Laurel, and Julie Codell (eds.). *Encounters in the Victorian Press.* Houndmills and New York: Palgrave Macmillan, 2005.

Brake, Laurel, Aled Jones, and Lionel Madden (eds.). *Investigating Victorian Journalism.* New York: St. Martin's Press, 1990.

Brake, Laurel, Bill Bell, and David Finkelstein, eds. *Nineteenth-Century Media and the Construction of Identities.* Houndsmills and New York: Palgrave, 2000.

Brantlinger, Patrick. "What is 'Sensational' About the 'Sensation Novel'?" *Nineteenth-Century Fiction* 37 1 (June 1982): 1–28.

———. *Rule of Darkness: British Literature and Imperialism 1830–1914.* Ithaca: Cornell University Press, 1988.

———. *The Reading Lesson. The Threat of Mass Literacy in Nineteenth-Century British Fiction.* Bloomington and Indianapolis: Indiana University Press, 1998.

Braun, Marta. *Picturing Time: The Work of Etienne-Jules Marey (1830–1904).* Chicago: Chicago University Press, 1992.

Briganti, Chiara. "Gothic Maidens and Sensational Women: Lady Audley's Journey from the Ruined Mansion to the Madhouse." *Victorian Literature and Culture* 101 (1992): 180–211.

Briggs, Asa. *A Social History of England.* London: Weidenfeld and Nicolson, 1983.

Brooks, Peter. *The Melodramatic Imagination. Balzac, Henry James, Melodrama and the Mode of Excess.* New Haven and London: Yale University Press, 1976.

Brougham, Henri. *Addresses on Popular Literature.* London: Edward Law, Essex, 1858.

Brown, Lucy. *Victorian News and Newspapers.* Oxford: Oxford University Press, 1985.

Brunetta, Gian Piero. *Il Viagio dell'Icononauta: dalla camera oscura di Leonardo alla luce dei Lumière.* Venezia: Marsilio, 1997.

Burch, W. Noel. *Life to Those Shadows.* Berkeley: University of California Press, 1990.

Burney Fanny. *Evelina.* Ed. Edward A. Bloom. Oxford and New York: Oxford University Press, 1968.

Busnach, W., and Chabrillat H. *Lecoq, the Detective's Daughter.* London: Vizetelly, 1888.

Byerly, Alison. *Realism, Representation, and the Arts in Nineteenth-Century Literature.* Cambridge: Cambridge University Press, 1997.

Callahan, Vicki. *Zones of Anxiety: Musidora, Movement, and the Crime Serials of Louis Feuilliade.* Detroit: Wayne State University Press, 2005.

Carens, L. Timothy. *Outlandish English Subjects in the Domestic Victorian Novel.* Houndsmills and New York: Palgrave, 2005.

Carnell, Jennifer. *The Literary Lives of Mary Elizabeth Braddon.* Hastings: The Sensation Press, 2000.

Carter, John, ed. *New Paths in Book Collecting.* Edited by John Carter. Freeport, NY: Constable, 1967 [1934].

Castle, Terry. *The Female Thermometer: Eighteenth-Century Culture and the Invention of the Uncanny.* Oxford and New York: Oxford University Press, 1995.

Castoriadis, Cornelius. *World in Fragments. Writing on Politics, Society, Psychoanalisis and the Imagination.* Stanford: Stanford University Press, 1997.

Cawelti, John G. *Adventure, Mystery, and Romance. Formula Stories as art and Popular Culture.* Chicago and London: University of Chicago Press, 1976.

Cervantes, Miguel de. *Don Chisciotte della Mancia.* Con un saggio di Eric Auerbach. Torino: Einaudi, 1957–1994.

Chabot, M.L. *Rocambole un roman feuilleton sous le second empire.* Printed, published, and distributed by the author, 1995.

Chabrillat, Henri. *La Petite Belette.* Paris, E. Dentu. Librairie de la Societé des Gens de Lettres, 1884.

Chartier, Roger. *Cultural History. Between Practices and Representations.* Cambridge: Polity Press, 1988.

Charters/Granted to the/East-India/Company,/from 1601;/also the/ Treaties and Grants,/Made with, or obtained from, the Princes and/ Powers in India.

Charters Macpherson, Samuel. *Memorials of Service in India.* London: John Murray, 1865.

Chaudhuri, K.N. "Markets and Traders in India during the Seventeenth and Eighteenth Centuries," in *Money and The Market in India*, 219–255.

Chevalier, Louis. *Classes Laborieuses et Classes Dangereuses a Paris pendant la première moitié du XIXe siècle.* Paris: Librairie Plon et éditions Perrin, 2002.

Christ, Carol T., and John Jordan, eds. *Victorian Literature and the Victorian Visual Imagination.* Berkeley: University of California Press, 1995.

Christie, Ian. *The Last Machine: Early Cinema and the Birth of the Modern World.* London: BBC Educational Development, 1994.

Codell, Julie, ed. *Imperial Co-Histories, National Identities and the British and Colonial Press.* Farleigh Dickinson University Press and London: Associated University Presses, 2003.

Cohn, Bernard. *Colonialism and its Forms of Knowledge. The British in India.* Princeton: University Press, 1996.

———. "Representing Authority in Victorian England," in *The Invention of Tradition.* Eds. Eric J. Hobsbawm and Terence O. Ranger. Cambridge and New York: Cambridge University Press, 1984, pp. 165–209.

Coissai, G. Michel. *La téorie e la pratique des projections.* Paris: Maison de la Bonne Preesse, s.d.

Collins, Wilkie, *The Moonstone.* Mineola, NY: Dover, 2002.

———. *The Woman in White.* Ware, Hertfordshire: Wordsworth Classics, 1993.

A Compendium of the History of India. Madras: Gantz Brothers, 1870.

Compère, Daniel, ed. *Dictionnaire du roman populaire francophone.* Paris: Nouveau Monde, 2007.

Cook, Olive. *Movement in Two Dimensions: A Study of the Animated and Projected Pictures which Preceded the Invention of Cinematography.* London: Hutchingson & Co, Ltd., 1963.

Cooper-Richet Diana and Borgeaud, Emily. *Galignani.* Paris: Galignani, 1999.

Crangle, Richard, Mervyn Heard, and Ine van Dooren, eds. *Realms of Light. Uses and Perceptions of the Magic Lantern from the 17th to the 21st Century.* London: The Magic Lantern Society, 2005.

Crary, Jonathan. *Techniques of the Observer.* Cambridge and London: MIT, 1990.

Crary, Jonathan. *Suspensions of Perception: Attention, Spectacle and Modern Culture.* Cambridge and London, MIT, 1999.

Crompton, Dennis, Richad Franklin, and Stephen Herbert, eds. *Servants of Light. The Book of the Lantern.* Ripon: The Magic Lantern Society, 1997.

Cross, Gilbert. *Next Week-East Lynne: Domestic Drama in Performance, 1820–1874.* Lewisburg: Bucknell University Press, 1977.

Curtis, Gerard. *Visual Words: Art and the Material Book in Victorian England.* Aldershot: Ashgate, 2002.

Cvetkovich, Ann. *Mixed Feelings: Feminism, Mass Culture and Victorian Sensationalism.* New Brunswick and London: Rutgers University Press, 1992.

Dallas, E.S. *The Gay Science.* London: Chapman and Hall, 193 Piccadilly, 1866.

——— [attributed to]. "Periodical Literature—The Periodical Press." *Blackwood's Edinburgh Magazine* (January 1859): 96–112 and (February 1859): 180–195.

Daly, Nicholas, "Railway Novels: Sensation Fiction and the Modernization of the Senses." *English Literary History* 66 (1999): 461–487.

Darmon, Jean Jaques. *Le Colportage de librairie en France sous le Second Empire.* Paris: Librairie Plon, 1972.

Davidoff, Leonore, and Hall Catherine. *Family Fortunes. Men and Women of the English Middle-Class, 1780–1850.* Chicago: Chicago University Press, 1987.

De Ereida, Godinho. *Malaca, L'Inde Meridionale et le Cathay.* Manuscrit Original Autograph Reproduit in Fac-Simile et Traduit par M. Leon Janssen. Bruxelles: Libraire Européenne C. Muquardt, 1882.

Debord, Guy. *The Society of the Spectacle.* New York: Zone, 1995 [1967].

Deleuse, Robert. *Les Maîtres du roman policier.* Paris: Bordas, 1991.

Deleuze, Gilles. *Difference and Repetition.* London: Athlore Press, 1994 [1968].

Deleuze, Gilles and Guattari Felix. *Rhizome-Introduction.* Paris: Les Editions de Minuit, 1976.

Dewar, Douglas, and Garrett H.L. *A Reply to Mr. F.W. Buckley's The Political Theory of the Indian Mutiny.* Read: November 8, 1923.

Diamond, Michael. *Victorian Sensation. Or, the Spectacular, the Shocking and the Scandalous in Nineteenth-Century Britain.* London: Anthem Press, 2003.

Dickens, Charles, "Familiar in their Mouths as Household Words"—Shakespeare/ HOUSEHOLD WORDS/ A Weekly Journal/ Conducted by/Charles Dickens/1850.

Don Vann, J., and Rosemary T. Van Arsdel, eds. *Periodicals of Queen Victoria's Empire: An Exploration.* Toronto and Buffalo: University of Toronto Press, 1996.

Douglas, David C., ed. *English Historical Documents.* New York: Oxford University Press, 1950.

Dutt, Romesch. *India in the Victorian Age. An Economic History of the People.* London: Kegan Paul, Trench, Treubner and Co, 1904.

Eagleton, Terry. *The Idea of Culture*. Malden, Massachusetts: Blackwell Publishers, 2000.

Eco, Umberto. "Rhétorique et idéologie dans 'Les Mystères de Paris' d'Eugène Sue." *Revue internationale des sciences sociales* 19:4 (1967): 588–609.

Escott, Tomas Hay Sweet. *Social Transformations of the Victorian Age. A Survey of Court and Country*. London: Seeley and Co. Ltd., 1897.

———. *Masters of English Journalism. A Study of Personal Forces*. London-Leipsic: T. Fisher Unwin, 1911.

Fayette, Mademe de La. *La Princesse de Clèves*. Ed. Bernard Pingaud. Éditions Gallimard, 1972.

———. *Great Victorians. Memories and Personalities*. London: T. Fisher Unwin, 1916.

Fell, John. *Film and the Narrative Tradition*. Berkeley: Berkeley University Press, 1986.

Feltes Norman. *Modes of Production of Victorian Novels*. Chicago and London: University of Chicago Press, 1986.

———. "Realism, Consensus and 'Exclusion Itself': Interpellating the Victorian Bourgeoisie." *Textual Practice* 1 (Winter 1987) 3: 297–308.

———. *Literary Capital and the Late Victorian Novel*. Madison: University of Wisconsin Press, 1993.

Feuillade, Louis. *Les Vampires*. Paris: Gaumont, 1915–16.

Fielding, Henry. *Tom Jones*. Ed. R.P.C. Mutter. New York and London: Penguin Books, 1966.

Finkelstein, David. *The House of Blackwood. Author-Publisher Relations in the Victorian Era*. University Park, Penn.: Pennsylvania State University, 2002.

Fleming, Gordon H. *George Alfred Lawrence and the Victorian Sensation Novel*. Tucson, Arizona: University of Arizona Bulletin no. 16. 23 (1952), 4.

Flint, Kate. *The Woman Reader 1837–1914*. Oxford: Clarendon Press, 1993.

Fondanèche, Daniel. *Le Roman policier*. Paris: Ellipses, 2000.

Fontana, Biancamaria. *Rethinking the Politics of the Commercial Society. The* Edinburgh Review *1802–1832*. Cambridge: Cambridge University Press, 1985.

Fosca, François. *Histoire et technique du roman policier*. Paris: Nouvelle Revue Critique, 1937.

Foster, Hal, ed. *Vision and Visuality*. Seattle: Bay Press, 1998.

Foucault, Michel. *Madness and Civilization. A History of Insanity in the Age of Reason*. New York: Vintage, 1988 [1961].

Foucault, Michel. *The Birth of the Clinic. An Archeology of Medical Perception*. New York: Vintage, 1994 [1963].

———. *The Order of Things. An Archeology of the Human Sciences*. New York: Vintage, 1994 [1966].

———. *Discipline and Punish. The Birth of the Prison*. New York: Vintage, 1995 [1975].

Foucault, Michel. *The History of Sexuality. An Introduction.* New York: Vintage, 1990 [*La Volenté de Savoir* 1976].

———. *The Use of Pleasure.* New York: Vintage, 1990 [1984].

———.*The Care of the Self.* New York: Vintage, 1988 [1986].

———. "Of Other Spaces," in *Other Spaces: the Affair of the Heterotopia.* Graz: Haus der Architekture, 1998, pp. 22–37.

Fox Bourne, H.R. "English Newspapers." *Chapters in the History of Journalism.* London: Chatto and Windus, 1887.

Fraser, Hilary, Stephanie Green, and Judith Johnston, eds. *Gender and the Victorian Periodical.* Cambridge: Cambridge University Press, 2003.

Frazer, R.W. *British India.* London: Fisher Unwin; New York: Putnam, 1898.

Furber, Holden. *John Company at Work. A Study of European Expansion in India in the Late Eighteenth Century.* Cambridge and London: Harvard University Press, 1951.

Fuller, Sophie and Nicky Losseff, eds. *The Idea of Music in Victorian Fiction.* Aldershot and Burlington: Ashgate, 2004.

Gaboriau, Émile. *The Lerouge Case.* London: Vizetelly, 1881.

———. *The Mystery of Orcival.* London: Vizetelly, 1884.

———. *Other People's Money.* London: Vizetelly, 1885.

———. *The Gilded Clique.* London: Vizetelly 1885.

———. *Lecoq, the Detective.* London: Vizetelly, 1885.

———. *The Catastrophe.* London: Vizetelly, 1885.

———. *The Little Old Man of Batignolles.* London: Vizetelly, 1886.

———. *The Slaves of Paris.* London, Vizetelly, 1886.

Gabriele, Alberto. "Visions of the City of London: Mechanical Eye and Poetic Transcendence in Wordsworth's *Prelude*-book 7." *The European Romantic Review* 19:4 (2008): 265–285.

Gaillard, Élie-Marcel. *Ponson du Terrail. Biographie de l'auteur de Rocambole.* Avignon: Éditions Barthélemy, 2001.

Gallagher, Catherine. *The Industrial Reformation of English Fiction: Social Discourse and Narrative Form 1832–1867.* Chicago and London: University of Chicago Press, 1985.

Galvan, Jean-Pierre. *Paul Féval. Parcours d'une œuvre.* Paris: Les Belles Lettres, 2000.

Gamages Bargain Clearance catalogue. London, 1913.

Garlick, Barbara, and Margaret Harris. *Victorian Journalism: Exotic and Domestic: Essays in Honour of P.D. Edwards.* St Lucia, Queensland, Australia: Queensland University Press, 1998.

Gay, Peter. *The Bourgeois Experience: Victoria to Freud.* New York and Oxford: Oxford University Press, 1986.

Gombrich, Ernest Hans. *Art and Illusion: A Study in the Psychology of Pictorial Representation.* Princeton: Princeton University Press, 1972.

Gordon, Colin. *"By Gaslight in Winter." A Victorian Family History through the Magic Lantern.* London: Elm Tree Books, 1980.

Graham, Walter. *English Literary Periodicals.* New York: Thomas Nelson and Sons, 1930.

Grant, James. *The Newspaper Press: Its Origin, Progress and Present Position.* London: Tinsley Brothers, 1871.

———. *History of the Newspaper Press.* London: Routledge, 1872.

Grison, Georges. *Dispatch and Secrecy.* London: Vizetelly, 1888.

Grover, B.R. "An Integrated Pattern of Commercial Life in Rural Society of North India during the Seventeenth and Eighteenth Centuries," in *Money and the Market in India,* 219–255.

Gunning, Tom. *D.W. Griffith and the Origin of American Narrative Film. The Early Years at Biograph.* Urbana and Chicago: University of Illinois Press 1991.

———. *Urban Spaces in Early Silent Film. From Kaleidoscope to X-Ray.* Copenhagen: Center for Urbanity and Aesthetics, 1995.

Habermas, Jürgen. *The Structural Transformation of the Public Sphere. An Inquiry into a Category of Bourgeois Society.* Cambridge, Mass: MIT Press, 1989 [1962].

———. "The Public Sphere." *Communication and Class Struggle.* Eds. A. Mattelart and S. Siegelaub. New York: International General; and France: IMMRC, 1979, pp. 198–202.

Hamon, Philippe. *Expositions: Literature and Architecture in Nineteenth-Century France.* Berkeley: University of California Press, 1992.

———. *Imageries: Litterature et Image au XIX Siècle.* Paris: Libraririe Jose Corti, 2001.

Hansen, Miriam. *Babel and Babylon. Spectatorship in American Silent Film.* Cambridge and London: Harvard University Press, 1991.

Hardt, Michael, and Negri Antonio. *Empire.* Cambridge, Massachusetts, and London, England: Harvard University Press, 2000.

Harris, Michael, and Alan Lee, eds. *The Press in English Society from the Eighteenth to the Nineteenth Centuries.* London and Toronto: Associated United Press, 1986.

Harrison, Kimberly, and Richard Fantina, eds. *Victorian Sensations. Essays on a Scandalous Genre.* Columbus: Ohio University Press, 2006.

Hedley, Elaine. *Melodramatic Tactics; Theatrical dissent in the English Marketplace, 1800–1885.* Stanford: Stanford University Press, 1995.

Hobsbawm, Eric and Terence Ranger, eds. *The Invention of Tradition.* Cambridge: Cambridge University Press, 1983.

Hoffmann, Detter, and Almut Junker, eds. *Lanterna Magica. Lichbilder aus Menschenwelt und Goelterwelt.* Berlin: Froelich 7 Kaufmann, 1982.

Holwell, J.Z. *India Tracts.* London: Becket and Hondt, 1764.

Houghton, Walter, ed. *The Wellesley Index to Victorian Periodicals, 1824–1900. Tables of Content and Identification of Contributors, with Bibliographies of Their Articles and Stories.* Toronto and London: University of Toronto Press, and Routledge and Kegan Paul, 1966–1990.

Hughes, Linda and Michael Lund, eds. *The Victorian Serial*. Charlottesville: University Press of Virginia, 1991.

Hughes, Winifred. *The Manic in the Cellar: Sensation Novels of the 1860s*. Princeton: Princeton University Press, 1980.

Humphries, Steve. *Victorian Britain through the Magic Lantern*. London: Sidgwick & Jackson, 1989.

Ideas and Beliefs of the Victorians: An Historic Revaluation of the Victorian Age. Foreword by H. Grisewood. London: Sylvan Press, 1949.

Inden, Ronald. *Imagining India*. London: Hurst & Co., 1990.

"The Indian Punch," January 1859–. Dehli: Dehli Press.

Jacobson, Mary, Evelyn Fox Keller, and Sally Shuttleworth, eds. *Body/Politics. Women and the Discourses on Science*. New York and London: Routledge, 1990.

James, Henry. *Selected Literary Criticism*. Ed. Morris Shapira, prefaced with a note on "James as Critic" by F.R. Leavis. New York: Horizon Press, 1964.

Jameson, Frederick. *The Political Unconscious. Narrative as a Socially Symbolic Act*. Ithaca, New York: Cornell University Press, 1981.

Jay, Martin. *The Dialectical Imagination. A History of the Frankfurt School and the Institute of Social Research 1923–1950*. Boston and Toronto: Little, Brown and Co., 1973.

———. *Downcast Eyes: The Denigration of Vision in Twentieth-Century French Thought*. Berkeley: University of California Press, 1993.

Jordan, John O. and Robert L. Patten, eds. *Literature in the Marketplace: Nineteenth-Century British Publishing and Reading Practices*. Cambridge and New York: Cambridge University Press, 1995.

Kalifa, Dominuque. *L'Encre et le Sang. Recits de Crimes et Societé a la Belle Epoque*. Paris: Fayard, 1995.

———. *La Culture de Masse en France. 1: 1860–1930*. Paris: Editions L a Decouverte & Syros, 2001.

Kaye, John, Volume I in *Kaye's and Malleson's History of the Indian Mutiny of 1857–8*. New York, Bombay, and Calcutta: Longmans, Green and Co, 1909.

Kent, Christopher. "The Angry Young Gentlemen of Tomahank." *Victorian Journalism: Exotic and Domestic: Essays in Honour of P.D. Edwards*. Eds. Barbara Garlick and Margaret Harris. St Lucia, Queensland, Australia: Queensland University Press, 1998, pp. 75–94.

Kiernan, V.C. *The Lords of Humakind. European Attitudes to the Outside World in the Imperial Age*. Middlesex, England, and Victoria, Australia: Penguin Books, 1972.

King, Andrew, and John Plunkett, eds. *Victorian Print Media. A Reader*. Oxford: Oxford University Press, 2005.

Klancher, Jon P. *The Making of English Reading Audiences, 1790–1832*. Madison, Wisocnsin: University of Wisconsin Press, 1987.

Klein, Naomi. *The Shock Doctrine: The Rise of Disaster Capitalism*. New York: Metropolitan and Holt, 2007.

Knight, Stephen. *Form and Ideology in Crime Fiction.* Houndsmills and London: Macmillan, 1980.

———. *Crime Fiction, 1800–2000. Detection, Death, Diversity.* Houndsmills and New York: Palgrave, 2004.

Koss, Stephen. *The Rise and Fall of the Political Press in Britain.* London: Hamish Hamilton, 1981.

Kucich, John. *Imperial Masochism. British Fiction, Fantasy, and Social Class.* Princeton and Oxford: Princeton University Press, 2007.

Lacassin, Francis. *Louis Feuillade.* Paris: Editions Seghers, 1964.

———. *Louis Feuillade. Maître des Lions et des Vampires.* Pierre Bordas et fils, 1995.

Law, Graham. *Serializing Fiction in the Victorian Press.* Houndsmills and 175 8th Avenue: Palgrave, 2000.

Lebrun, Michel. "Les Alchimistes du roman policier." *Revue Litteraire Mensuelle* 542 (1974): 138–143.

Leckie, Barbara. *Culture and Adultery: The Novel, the Newspaper and the Law, 1857–1914.* Philadelphia: University of Pennsylvania Press, 1999.

Lee, Alan. *The Origins of the Popular Press in England, 1855–1914.* London: Croom Helm, 1976.

Lefebvre, Henri. *Critique of Everyday Life—Foundations for a Sociology of the Everyday.* London and New York: Verso, 2002 [1961].

———. *The Production of Space.* Oxford, UK, and Cambridge, USA: Blackwell, 1991 [1974].

Lestock, Reid C. *Commerce and Conquest: The Story of the Honourable East India Company.* London: C&J Temple, 1947.

Levine, George. *The Realistic Imagination. English Fiction from Frankenstein to Lady Chatterly.* Chicago and London: Chicago University Press, 1981.

Liddle, Dallas. "Salesmen, Sportsmen, Mentors: Anonimity and Mid-Victorian Theories of Journalism." *Victorian Studies* 41 (1997): 31–68.

———. "Anatomy of 'Nine Days' Wonder': Sensational Journalism in the Decade of the Sensation Novel," in *Victorian Crime, Madness and Sensation*, pp. 89–103.

Lightman, Bernard, ed. *Victorian Science in Context.* Chicago and London: Chicago University Press, 1997.

Lindeman, Ruth Burridge. "Dramatic Disappearances: Mary Elizabeth Braddon and the Staging of Theatrical Character." *Victorian Literature and Culture* 25 (1997) 2: 279–291.

Loesberg, Jonathan. "The Ideology of Narrative Form in Sensation Fiction." *Representations* (Winter 1986) 13: 115–138.

Louis Feuillade. 1895 (2000). Numero hors-série.

Louis, Roger, ed. *Oxford History of the British Empire.* Oxford and New York: Oxford University Press, 1998.

Lubbock, Percy. *The Craft of Fiction.* New York: Jonathan and Harrison Smith, 1929.

Lukacs, Georg. *The Theory of the Novel. A Historico-Philosophical Essay on the Forms of the Great Epic Literature.* Cambridge, Mass.: MIT Press 1968 [1920].

Mac Kenzie, John. *Propaganda and Empire. The Manipulation of the British Public Opinion, 1880–1960.* Manchester: Manchester University Press, 1984.

Majeed, Javed. "Meadows Taylor's *Confessions of a Thug*: The Anglo-Indian Novel as a Genre in the Making," in *Writing India*, pp. 86–110.

Mangham, Andrew. *Violent Women and Sensation Fiction. Crime, Medicine and Victorian Popular Culture.* Houndmills and New York: Palgrave Macmillan, 2007.

Mannoni Laurent, *The Great Art of Light and Shadow. Archeology of the Cinema.* Exeter: University of Exeter Press, 2000 [1995].

———. *Trois Sièles de cinéma. De la Lanterne Magique au Cinematographe.* Paris: Espace Electra, 1995–96.

Mannoni, Laurent, Donata Pesenti Campagnoni, and David Robinson, eds. *Light and Movement: Incunabola of the Modern Picture 1420–1896.* Gemona: Giornate del Cinema Muto; Paris: Cinémathèque Française; Torino: Museo Nazionale del Cinema, 1995.

Marshall, P.J. "The English in Asia to 1700," in *The Oxford History of the British Empire.* Volume I, pp. 264–285.

———. "The British in Asia: Trade to Domination, 1700–1765," in *The Oxford History of the British Empire.* Volume II, pp. 487–507.

Martin, Henri-Jean, and Roger Chartier eds. *Histoire de l'édition française. Les temps des éditeurs: du romantisme à la Belle époque.* Paris: Promodis, 1985.

Marx, Karl. "The British Rule in India." *New York Daily Tribune*, June 25, 1853.

———. "The East India Company: Its History and Results." *New York Daily Tribune*, July 11, 1853.

———. "Indian Affairs." *New York Daily Tribune*, August 5, 1853.

———. "The Future Results of the British Rule in India." *New York Daily Tribune*, July 22, 1853.

Mary, Jules. *The Meudon Mystery.* London: Vizetelly, 1888.

Mattelart, Armand. *Advertising International. The Privatization of Public Space.* London and New York: Routledge, 1991.

Maunder, Andrew, and Grace Moore, eds. *Victorian Crime, Madness and Sensation.* Aldershot and Burlington: Ashgate, 2004.

McClintock, Anne. *Imperial Leather: Race, Gender and Sex in the Colonial Contest.* New York: Routledge, 1995.

Merleau-Ponty, Maurice. *Phenomenology of Perception.* New York: Routledge, 1962.

———. *The Visible and the Invisible.* Evanston: Northwestern University Press, 1973.

Messac, Regis. *Le "Detective Novel" et l'Influence de la Pensée Scientifique.* Paris: Librairie Ancienne Honoré Champion, 1929.

Metcalf, Thomas R. *Ideologies of the Raj.* Cambridge and New York: Cambridge University Press, 1994.

Mill, James. *The History of British India.* London: James Madden, 1858.

Miller, Angela. "The Panorama, the Cinema and the Invention of the Spectacular." *Wide Angle* 18 (1996): 34–69.

Miller, D.A. *The Novel and the Police.* Berkeley: University of California Press, 1988.

Mitch, David. *The Rise of Popular Literacy in Victorian England.* Philadelphia: University of Pennsylvania Press, 1992.

Mitchell, Sally. *The Fallen Angel: Chastity, Class and Women's Readings, 1835–1880.* Bowling Green, Ohio: Bowling Green Popular University Press, 1981.

Mitchell, W.J. Thomas. *Iconology: Image, Text, Ideology.* Chicago: Chicago University Press, 1986.

Moore-Gilbert, Bart, ed. *Writing India 1757–1990. The Literature of British India.* Manchester and New York: Manchester University Press, 1996.

Moretti, Franco. *Signs Taken for Wonders.* London: Verso, 1983.

Morison, Stanley. *The English Newspapers. Some Accounts of the Physical Development of Journals Printed between 1622 and the Present Day.* Cambridge: University Press, 1932.

Musser, Charles. *The Emergence of Cinema. The American Screen to 1907.* Toronto: Collier Macmillan Canada; New York: Maxwell Macmillan International, 1990.

Myers, Robin, and Michael Harris, eds. *Serials and Their Readers 1620–1914.* Winchester: St. Pauls' Bibliographies. New Castle, Delaware: Oak Knoll Press, 1993.

Nead, Linda. *Victorian Babylon. People, Streets and Images in Nineteenth-Century London.* New Haven and London: Yale University Press, 2000.

The New Magic Lantern Journal. The Ten Year Book. 4 (1986): 1–3.

North, John S., ed. *The Waterloo Dictionary of English Newspapers and Periodicals. 1800–1900.* Waterloo, Ontario: North Waterloo Academic Press, 1997.

Norton, Graham. *Victorian London.* London: Macdonald & Co., 1969.

Nunokawa, Jeffrey. *The Afterlife of Property: Domestic Security and the Victorian Novel.* Princeton: Princeton University Press, 1994.

Nutley, David Robinson, ed. Supplement no. 1, compiled by David Robinson. Ripon: The Magic Lantern Society, 1997.

Office of the Madras Artillery. *Notes on Pondicherry, or, the French in India.* Calcutta: Thacker and Co., 1845.

Ogborn, Miles. *Indian Ink. Script and the Making of the East India Company.* Chicago and London: University of Chicago Press, 2007.

Onslow, Barbara. "Sensationalising Science: Braddon's Marketing of Science in *Belgravia.*" *Victorian Periodicals Review* 28 (1995) 2: 109–122.

Oppenheim, Janet. *"Shattered Nerves." Doctors, Patients and Depression in Victorian England.* New York and Oxford: Oxford University Press, 1991.

Overton, Bil. *Fictions of Female Adultery, 1684–1890. Theories and Contexts.* Houndsmils and New York: Palgrave, 2002.

Owen, David. *The Government of Victorian London 1855–1889: The Metropolitan Board of Works, the Vestries and the City Corporation.* Cambridge and London: The Belknap Press of Harvard University Press, 1982.

Parry, Benita. *Delusions and Discoveries: India in the British Imagination 1880–1993.* London and New York: Verso, 1998.

Payne, David. *The Reenchantment of Nineteenth-Century Fiction. Dickens, Thackeray, George Eliot, and Serialization.* Houndsmills and New York: Palgrave Macmillan, 2005.

Pelletan, Eugène. *La Nouvelle Babylone.* Paris: Pagnerre, Libraire-Éditeur, 1863.

Pepper, John. *Scientific Amusements for Young People.* London: s.d.

Perkin, Harold. *The Rise of Professional Society. England since 1880.* London and New York: Routledge, 1989.

Perlin, Frank. "Changes in Production and Circulation of Money in Sixteenth and Eighteenth Century India: An Essay on Monetization Before Colonial Occupation," in *Money and the Market in India*, pp. 276–307.

Pesenti Campagnoni, Donata, ed. *Verso il cinema. Macchine, spettacoli e mirabili visioni.* Torino: UTET, 1995.

———. *Vedute del "mondo nuovo". Vues d'optique settecentesche nella collezione del Museo Nazionale del Cinema di Torino.* Torino and London: Allemandi Umberto and Museo Nazionale del Cinema, 2000.

Phegley, Jennifer. *Educating the Proper Woman Reader: Victorian Family Literary Magazines and the Cultural Health of the Nation.* Columbus: Ohio State University Press, 2004.

Phyllips, Walter C. *Dickens, Reade and Collins Sensation Novelists. A Study of the Conditions and Theories of Novel Writing in Victorian England.* New York: Columbia University Press, 1919.

Plunkett, John. *Queen Victoria. First Media Monarch.* Oxford and New York: Oxford University Press, 2003.

Poe, Edgar Allan. *Selected Tales.* Oxford and New York: Oxford UP, 1998.

Poovey, Mary. *Uneven Developments: The Ideological Work of Gender in Mid-Victorian England.* Chicago: Chicago University Press, 1988.

———. *Making a Social Body: British Cultural Formation 1830–1864.* Chicago: University of Chicago Press, 1995.

———. "The Liberal Civil Subject and the Social in Eighteenth-Century British Moral Philosophy." *Public Culture: Society for Transnational Cultural Studies.* Dilip Parameshwar Gaonkar and Benjamin Lee, guest editors, 14 I (Winter 2002), pp. 125–145.

Popple, Simon, and Vanessa Toulmin, eds. *Visual Delights. Essays on the Popular and Projected Image in the 19th Century.* Trowbridge: Flicks Books, 2000.

Porter, Dennis. *The Pursuit of Crime: Art and Ideology in Detective Fiction.* New Haven and London: Yale University Press, 1981.

Prendergast, Christopher. *Paris and the Nineteenth Century.* Oxford and Cambridge: Blackwell, 1992.

———. *For the People by the People? Eugène Sue's 'Les Mystères de Paris'. A Hypothesis in the Sociology of Literature.* Oxford: European Humanities Research Center, 2003.

Price, Leah. *The Anthology and the Rise of the Novel.* Cambridge and New York: Cambridge University Press, 2000.

Prieur, Jérôme. *Séance de lanterne magique.* Paris: Gallimar, 1985.

Propp, Vladimir. *Morphology of the Fairytale.* Austin: Texas University Press, 1968.

Pykett, Lyn. *The "Improper" Feminine: the Women's Sensation Novel and the New Woman Writing.* London and New York: Routledge, 1992.

———. *The Sensation Novel: From* The Woman in White *to* The Moonstone. Plymouth, England: Northcote House, 1994.

Rance, Nicholas. *Wilkie Collins and Other Sensation Novelists: Walking the Moral Hospital.* Rutherford, NJ: Fairleigh Dickinson University, 1991.

Reader, W.J. *Professional Men. The Rise of the Professional Classes in Nineteenth-Century England.* New York: Basic Books, 1966.

Regester, Seeley. *The Dead Letter. An American Romance.* New York: Beadle, 1867.

Remise, Jac, Pascale Remise, and Reegis Van de Walle, eds. *Magie Lumineuse. Du théatre d'ombres á la lanterne magique.* Paris: Balland: 1979.

Reuter, Yves, ed. *Le Roman Policier et ses personnages.* Saint-Denis: Presses universitaires de Vincennes, 1989.

Richards, Thomas. *The Commodity Culture of Victorian England 1851–1914.* Stanford: Stanford University Press, 1990.

Ritter, Roland, ed. *Other Spaces. The Affair of Heterotopia.* Graz: HAD, 1998.

Robinson David, ed. *The Lantern Image. Iconography of the Magic Lantern 1420–1880.* Nutley: The Magic Lantern Society, 1993.

Robinson, Solveig C. "Editing *Belgravia*: M.E. Braddon's Defense of 'Light Literature.'" *Victorian Periodicals Review* 28 (1995) 2: 109–122.

———. "'Amazed at Our Success': The Langham Place Editors and the Emergence of a Feminist Critical Tradition." *Victorian Periodicals Review* 29 (1996) 2: 159–172.

Rodger, Richard. *Housing in Urban Britain 1780–1914.* Houndsmill and London: Macmillam 1989.

Rojek, Chris. *Capitalism and Leisure Theory.* London and New York: Tavistock Publications, 1985.

Le Roman Populaire en Question(s): Actes du Colloque International de Mai 1995 a' Limoges. Limoges: Presses Universitaires, 1997.

Rowell, George. *The Victorian Theatre: A Survey.* London and New York: Oxford University Press, 1956.

Said, Edward W. *Orientalism.* New York: Pantheon Books, 1978

———. *Culture and Imperialism.* New York: Knopf, 1993.

Sala, Goerge Augustus. *The Life and Adventures of George Augustus Sala Written by Himself.* London, Paris, and Melbourne: Cassell, 1895.

Sampson, Henry. *A History of Advertising from the Earliest Times, Illustrated with Anecdotes, Curious Specimens, and Biographical Notes.* London: Chatto and Windus, 1874.

Sarfatti, Larson. *The Rise of Professionalism. A Sociological Analysis.* Berkeley, Los Angeles, and London: California University Press, 1977.

Schivelbusch, Wolfgang. *The Railway Journey: The Industrialization of Time and Space in the Nineteenth-Century.* Berkeley: California University Press, 1986.

———. *Disenchanted Night: the Industrialization of Light in the Nineteenth Century.* Berkeley: California University Press, 1988.

Schwartz, Vanessa, and Leo Charney, eds. *Cinema and the Invention of Modern Life.* Berkeley: University of California Press, 1995.

Second, Albéric. *The Wheel of Fortune.* London: Vizetelly, 1888.

Sedgwick, Eve Kosofsky. *Between Men: English Fiction and Male Homosocial Desire.* New York: Columbia University Press, 1985.

Sen, Sudipta. *Empire of Free Trade. The East India Company and the Making of the Colonial Marketplace.* Philadelphia: Philadelphia University Press, 1998.

Shattock, Joanne. "Gusto Letterario e Stampa Periodica nell'800 Inglese." *Storia della Civiltà' Letteraria Inglese.* Edited by Franco Merenco. Volume II. Torino: UTET, 1996, pp. 678–696.

Shattock, Joanne, and Michael Wolff, eds. *The Victorian Periodical Press: Samplings and Soundings.* Leicester University Press and University of Toronto Press, 1982.

Shomes, Mehendronath. *The Spirit of Anglo-Bengali Magazines.* Calcutta: Thacker, Spink and Co., Berigny and Co., 1873.

Showalter, Elaine. *A Literature of Their Own: British Women Novelists from Bronte to Lessing.* Princeton: Princeton University Press, 1977.

———. *The Female Malady: Women, Madness and English Culture 1830–1980.* New York: Pantheon Books, 1985.

Shuttleworth, Sally. "Female Circulation: Medical Discourse and Popular Advertising in the Mid-Victorian Era," in *Body/Politics*, pp. 47–68.

Simmel, Georg. *The Conflict in Modern Culture and Other Essays.* New York: Teachers College, Columbia University: 1968.

———. *On Individuality and Social Forms. Selected Writings.* Chicago and London: Chicago University Press, 1971.

Simon, Eliot. *Some Patterns and Trends in British Publishing. 1800–1919.* London: The Bibliographical Society, 1994.

Singer, Ben. "Modernity, Hyperstimulus and the Rise of Popular Sensationalism," in *Cinema and the Invention of Modern Life*, pp. 72–92.

Sinnema, W. Peter. *Dynamics of the Printed Page. Representing the Nation in the London Illustrated News.* Aldershot and Brookfield: Ashgate, 1998.

Smith, Neil. *Uneven Development: Nature, Capital and Production of Space.* Oxford and New York: Basil Blackwell, 1984.

Spivak, Gayatri Chakravorty. "The Rani of Sirmur." *Europe and its Others. Proceedings of the Essex Conference on the Sociology of Literature July 1984.* Ed. Francis Barker et al. Colchester: Essex University Press, 1985, pp. 128–151.

Stern, J.P. *On Realism.* London and Boston: Routledge and Kagan, 1973.

Stewart, Garrett. *Between Film and Screen: Modernism's Photo Synthesis.* Chicago: Chicago University Press, 1999.

Stoler, Ann Laura. *Race and the Education of Desire. Foucault's History of Sexuality and the Colonial Order of Things.* Durham and London: Duke University Press, 1995.

Subrahmanyam, Sanjay, ed. *Money and the Market in India 1100–1700.* Delhi: Oxford University Press, 1994.

Suleiman, Susan, and Inge Crosman, eds. *Reader in the Text: Essays on Audience and Interpretation.* Princeton: Princeton University Press, 1980.

Suleri, Sara. *The Rhetoric of English India.* Chicago and London: Chicago University Press, 1992.

Taleyarkhan, Dinshah Ardeshir. *Riots of 1874: Their True History and Philosophy Tracing the Origin of Moslem Fanaticism Throughout Asia and Ascertaining its Real and Thorough Remedies as Applicable to the Continent in General.* Bombay: Thacker Vining and Co., Atmaram Sagoon and Co., 1874.

Taylor, George. *Players and Performances in the Victorian Theatre.* Manchester: Manchester University Press, 1989.

Teltscher, Kate. "'The Fearful Name of the Black Hole': Fashioning an Imperial Myth," in *Writing India*, pp. 30–51.

———. *India Inscribed: European and British Writing on India 1600–1800.* Delhi: Oxford University Press, 1995.

Thackeray, William Makepeace. *Vanity Fair.* Ed. Peter Shillingsburg: New York and London: Norton, 1994.

Thapar, Romila. *The Past and Prejudice.* New Delhi: National Book Trust, 1975.

Thérenty, Marie-Ève. *La Littérature au quotidien. Poétiques journalistiques au XIX siècle.* Paris: Seuil, 2007.

Thiesse, Anne-Marie. "Écrivain/Public(s): Les mystères de la communication littéraire." *Europe Revue Litteraire Mesuelle* 643–644 (1982): 36–46.

Thoms, Peter. *Detection & Its Designs. Narrative & Power in 19th-Century Detective Fiction.* Athens, Ohio: Ohio University Press, 1998.

Tierney, George. *The Real Situation of the East India Company Considered, with Respect to Their Rights and Privileges Under the Operation of the late Acts of Parliament establishing a Board of Control and a Committee of Secrecy.* London: Debrett, 1787.

To Catch a Sunbeam. Victorian Reality through the Magic Lantern, designed and edited by G.A. Household from the collection of LMH Smith. London: Michael Joseph, 1979.

Trodd, Anthea, *Domestic Crime in the Victorian Novel.* New York: St. Martin's Press, 1989.

Tromp, Marlene. *The Private Rod: Marital Violence, Sensation and the Law in Victorian Britain.* Charlottesville: Virginia University Press, 2000.

Tromp, Marlene, Pamela Gilbert, and Aaron Haynie, eds. *Beyond Sensation: Mary Elizabeth Braddon in Context.* Albany: State University of New York Press, 2000.

Trotter, Lionel. *History of India Under Queen Victoria from 1836 to 1880.* London: W.H. Allen & Co., 1886.

A True Relation of the Rise and Progress of the East-India Company [s.d.].

Tsivian, Yuri, ed. with an introduction. *Lines of Resistance. Dziga Vertov and the Twenties.* Gemona: Le Giornate del Cinema Muto, 2004.

Tulard, Jean. *Dictionnaire du roman policier. 1841–2005.* Librairie Arthème Feyard, 2005.

Turner, Mark. "Saint Paul's Magazine and the Project of Masculinity," in *Nineteenth-Century Media and the Construction of Identities*, pp. 232–252. See under Blake, Laurel.

Vaillant, Alain, and Marie-Ève Thérenty, eds. *1836: l'an 1 de l'ère mediatique. Etude litteraire et historique du journal 'La Presse' d'Emile de Girardin.* Paris: Nouveau Monde Éditions, 2001.

Vann, J. Don. *Victorian Novels in Serial.* New York: MLA of America, 1985.

Vlock, Deborah. *Dickens, Novel Reading, and the Victorian Popular Theatre.* Cambridge: Cambridge University Press, 1998.

Walker, David. *Outrage and Insight: Modern French Writers and the "Fait Divers."* Oxford UK, and Washington DC: Berg, 1995.

Walkowitz, Judith. *City of Dreadful Delight: Narratives of Sexual Danger in Late-Victorian London.* Chicago: Chicago University Press, 1992.

Washbrook, D.A. "India, 1818–1860: the Two Faces of Colonialism," in *The Oxford History of the British Empire.* Volume III, pp. 395–421.

Weliver, Phyllis. *Women Musicians in Victorian Fiction, 1860–1900. Representations of Music, Science and Gender in the Leisured Home.* Aldershot and Burlington: Ashgate, 2000.

———. *The Musical Crowd in English Fiction, 1840–1910. Class, Culture and Nation.* Houndsmills and New York: Palgrave Macmillan, 2006.

Wheeler, J. Talboys. *India Under British Rule from the Foundation of the East India Company.* London: Macmillan and Co., 1886.

White, Hayden. *The Historical Imagination in Nineteenth-Century Europe.* Baltimore and London: Johns Hopkins University Press, 1973.

Wicke, Jennifer. *Advertising Fictions: Literature, Advertisement and Social Reading.* New York: Columbia University Press, 1988.

Williams, Raymond. *Culture.* Glasgow: William Collins & Sons, 1981.

Williams, Rosalind. *Dream Worlds: Mass Consumption in Late Nineteenth-Century France.* Berkeley: Berkeley University Press, 1982.

Willis, John Walpole. *On the Government of the British Colonies.* London: Trelawney Saunders, 1850.

Witkovsky, Matthew S. *Foto. Modernity in Central Europe, 1918–1945.* New York: Thames and Hudson, 2007.

Wolff, Robert Lee. "Devoted Disciple: The Letters of Mary Elizabeth Braddon to Sir Edward Bulwer-Lytton 1862–1873." *Harvard Literary Bulletin* 22:1 (January 1974): 1–35, and 2 (April 1974): 129–161.

———. *Sensational Victorian: The Life and Fiction of Mary Elizabeth Braddon.* New York and London: Garland, 1979.

Wood, Henry Mrs. *East Lynne.* Edited by Margaret Cole. London: Collins, 1954.

Wordsworth, William. *The Prelude 1799, 1805, 1850.* Ed. Jonathan Wordsworth, M. H. Abrams, and Stephen Gill. New York and London: Norton, 1979.

Wynne, Deborah. *The Sensation Novel and the Victorian Family Magazine.* Houndmills and New York: Palgrave, 2001.

Zotti, Laura Minicci, ed. Le Lanterne Magiche. Prima del Cinema. La Collezione Minici Zotti. Venezia: Marsilio, 1988.

Index